D0962235

Out of Left Field

How the Mariners Made Baseball Fly in Seattle

ART THIEL

SASQUATCH BOOKS
SEATTLE

For Julia.
Muse and chanteuse.

Printed in the United States of America
Published by Sasquatch Books
Distributed by Publishers Group West
10 09 08 07 06 05 04 03   6 5 4 3 2

Cover design: Bill Quinby
Cover photographs: Ben Van Houten
Author photograph: Dan DeLong
Interior design and composition: Stewart A. Williams
Production editor: Cassandra Mitchell
Copy editor: Don Graydon
Proofreader: Miriam Bulmer
Indexer: Miriam Bulmer
All interior photographs reprinted with permission by the *Seattle Post-Intelligencer* unless otherwise noted.

Library of Congress Cataloging in Publication Data

Thiel, Art.
    Out of left field: how the Mariners made baseball fly in Seattle / Art Thiel.
       p. cm.
    Includes bibliographical references and index.
    ISBN 1-57061-390-7
    1. Seattle Mariners (Baseball team)–History. I. Title.

GV875.S42T55 2003
796.357'64'09797772–dc21

                                                                                    2003054219

Sasquatch Books
119 South Main Street, Suite 400
Seattle, Washington 98104
(206) 467-4300
www.sasquatchbooks.com
books@sasquatchbooks.com

Contents

Acknowledgments

G etting a large, reluctant person through the keyhole of book authorship requires many helpers. Some pushed, some pulled. Most laughed, which might have been the most important grease in the enterprise. Because the project had to be fast, the helping hands were many, so shaking all of them will take a little while here.

For research into matters sporting, there is no one better than Steve Rudman, assistant sports editor at the *Seattle Post-Intelligencer*. He has a remarkable facility for looking at the obvious and producing a fresh way to see it. If ever there were a black belt for abstract reasoning, he is Mr. Seventh Degree. Any fact in this book that makes the reader say, "I didn't know that," Rudman did it. The stuff he came up with that didn't make the book is a book in itself. And if somebody doesn't redirect us, that might happen too.

He also supplied the flashlight for my literary footfalls and said "Stop!" whenever the cliff found its way under my sneaks. He also is a friend who knew the emotional support was more important than the analytical.

Many others at the *P-I* were also instrumental, chief among them the chief, publisher Roger Oglesby. He made the connection between Sasquatch Books and me, and gave it his blessing, knowing that the project would sometimes take me away from my day job in his sports department. He sensed a good idea and said go for it, making available *P-I* resources, when he could have recalled the times we disagreed and said, "Are you kidding me?" His predecessor at the *P-I*, J. D. Alexander, is one to whom I remain indebted for having the courage to ignore his best instincts when he gave me the job as sports columnist in 1987.

The *P-I*'s managing editor, David McCumber, is a much-published author who knows the book drill so well that he held my trembling hand without me even knowing it. The ability to tolerate whining is a little-appreciated art among newspaper MEs, and McCumber is absolutely snivel-proof. Along with executive editor Ken Bunting, the honchos displayed an enlightened approach to moonlighting, understanding that knowledge and experience gained in authorship benefit the newspaper as well as the newspaperman. Well, at least they didn't laugh when they heard me say that to them.

One of the great achievements in human civilization is the *P-I* sports staff, a group that could be given six bricks and a bucket of mud with orders to re-create the pyramids at Giza—and, after finishing, ask what was needed the rest of the afternoon. No metro-daily sports department in America lifts more, faster, and better than these people. They were so busy that they probably didn't notice how many little things they offered, whether tangible or personal, that meant a great deal to me during the book struggle. All are worthy of mention here, but I offer a special salute to the longest-tenured-staffers: Scott Anderson, Angelo Bruscas, Clare Farnsworth, Jim Moore, Keith Olson, and Dan Raley. Their wear and tear seems invisible, except for those of us who know where to look. And a shout goes to John Levesque, a latecomer to sports who provided cool, professional column cover by having my back in the final stages of manuscript horrors.

Sports editor Ron Matthews, along with assistants Rudman, Bill Hayes, and Nick Rousso, indulged my absences and distractedness with aplomb. Time means everything to a daily newspaper person, and no one gives more of it to the *P-I* than Matthews, who turned around and offered the precious commodity to me when I needed it most. Matthews's predecessors at the paper, Pete Wevurski, Glenn Drosendahl, Bill Knight, and John Owen, allowed my column-writing career to survive by taking numerous shots from bosses and readers while telling me to keep firing.

Mariners coverage at the *P-I* has been blessed with a splendid line of beat writers who shined in the database research. J Michael Kenyon, Tracy Ringolsby, and Bill Plaschke blasted light on the early darkness, while Jim Street, Tyler Kepner, and John Hickey were around to see the confetti and sort the lingering confusions. The recent works of Hickey and fellow baseball scribe Dave Andriesen, plus former *P-I* national baseball writer Jim Caple, were a particular bounty.

Adding to the collective wisdom from which I and Mariners fans benefited greatly were numerous stalwarts from other publications in the Puget Sound market: Bob Finnigan, Ron C. Judd, Steve Kelley, Rod Mar, Blaine Newnham, Bob Sherwin, and Larry Stone at *The Seattle Times;* Dave Boling, Larry LaRue, and John McGrath of *The News Tribune;* and Greg Johns at the *King*

County Journal. Rivals, yes, and honorable press box companions as well.

When I required a single needle in a field of ten haystacks, Lytton Smith and his research staff at the *P-I* library would produce the needle, along with its serial number and parental ancestry. And smile after having done it. Also contributing heavily was the *P-I* photography staff, whose work captures well in these pages what I failed to in words.

When I approached the Mariners about this book, I asked for their cooperation, knowing well that many executives, managers, coaches, and players at one time or another hoped a stadium foul ball might catch me unaware in the press box, and do the damage they could then avoid having to deliver on their own. The job of a newspaper sports columnist is to offer honest opinion, and many of those opinions over sixteen years have been barb-hooked when it came to Mariners' failures, shortcomings, and misjudgments.

But apparently a few folks remembered the occasional praises, too, because there was little hesitation in saying yes to my book request. That may prove to have been another misjudgment, but it also is testimony to the surefootedness of a once-wobbly franchise that it can handle whatever arises from discovery. The Mariners accepted the premise that I would attempt to draw a line between column opinion and the book, which was proposed as an attempt to do an honest narrative of the successes, failures, and controversies in a remarkable sports story that screamed for telling in long form.

Thanks to Howard Lincoln, John Ellis, Chuck Armstrong, and several members of the ownership group and senior baseball executives, current and former, who offered stories, opinions, and time they had previously not shared with outsiders. Tim Hevly, who might be the best in the business of baseball media relations, and his staff were unfailingly cooperative in uncovering answers to the most moronic and repetitive of questions. Photographer Ben Van Houten was wonderful in meeting my hasty needs for images. Special thanks to Paul Isaki, the club's former vice president for business, who remembered my criticism of the club during the stadium turmoil. He put aside his resentment and offered six hours of honesty and insight that was a book unto itself.

Current and former players, coaches, members of the baseball and training staff and broadcast crew, and player agents were almost universally accommodating in providing memories and re-creations of vivid times. To all quoted herein, thank you. Two are worthy of special mention: Lou Piniella and Jay Buhner, who besides being central figures in the book understood fully the unlikeliness of the story. They provided hours of honesty, humor, and poignance. Buhner's candor, earthiness, and wise-guy wisdom, spanning nearly the entirety of the franchise's turnaround, became a delightful literary muse not often found in a major league clubhouse.

Special props to Randy Adamack, the club's vice president for communications, who brokered many an interview request, sat in on some, and stayed awake through nearly all. He also endured numerous annoying requests for niggling details, lost files, and missing phone numbers. A club employee since 1978, Adamack has ridden out many a cockeyed enterprise around the Mariners, so he came properly equipped with the humor and counsel for yet another.

Politics were always a part of the Mariners story, so the book could not have been done properly without cooperation from Slade Gorton, Mike Lowry, Ron Sims, and Pete von Reichbauer, and their staffs, as well as from King County employees who wrestled with the problems of baseball and the Mariners for nearly a quarter century. The Public Facilities District, including Shelly Yapp and Terrence Carroll, was crucial in understanding the stadium controversy.

My new friends at Sasquatch Books were wonderfully tolerant of rookie authorship. Given my abuse of deadline, they could have kicked dirt and thrown bases. Instead they indulged my excuses and made the book better. Editorial director Gary Luke admitted right away he was no baseball expert. But he did know storytelling, character development, and the English language, for which I am grateful. Anybody can learn the infield fly rule. Cassandra Mitchell and Don Graydon were marvelous in sifting through the overdone parts to help bring out whatever was worthy. Stewart Williams provided a deft eye for presentation.

Help in the business end of authorship was big. Attorneys Glenn Schroeder and Kenyon Luce and researcher Karen Brewer provided handrails for the dark corners, and Fred Moody was astute counsel.

Help on the personal side came from niece Alena Waite and a splendid in-law cast of Alex, Tom, and Tiffany Akoury, along with friends Mike and Jennifer Marceau, Jack Smith, Brian and Cindy Vance, John Maynard and Robin Erickson, and the Lake Chelan morale-building group that included Tim Egan, Joni Balter, Casey Corr, Sally Tonkin, and Dave and Nole Ann Horsey. As they occasionally watched, under the pressure of deadline, bits of my brain trickle out of my ears, nobody made fun of me. In fact, they often provided free beer or Scotch. And to those friends and associates whom I abandoned in favor of the book, the condition was temporary. Please have me back.

Then there is the Bridal Unit. Whether it is physiologically and/or cosmically possible to be both backbone and soul of a book project, I cannot prove. I just know what I know. Julia Akoury Thiel volunteered to lose her husband for most of a year, except for the occasion of a meal handoff at the writing desk or a stumbling arrival to bed at 3 A.M.

She also chipped in on the dreary detail of interview transcription. After the one featuring Bob Gogerty and his bad cold, all she suggested was that he blow his nose, passing on the temptation to blow my brains out. Her discerning literary eye spotted manuscript disaster while it was a speck on the horizon instead of at the front door. Her discerning heart spotted author collapse before it happened, and made that all better, too.

The truncated holidays, forgone trips, and unattended performances with her Orchestra Seattle/Seattle Chamber Singers classical-music group cannot be made up. Nor can lonely nights be regained. But rather than regrets, I choose to remember how the love of a great woman makes worthy all endeavors, and look ahead to the joy I will have in the rally to get back over .500 again with her.

Introduction

If I had been asked ten years ago to write a book about the Seattle Mariners, I would have responded with three questions. "What? A diet book? How to Lose Your Appetite for Baseball, and Sports in General?"

But ten years ago, no one would have asked me, or anyone, to write a book about the Mariners. Nor would I have suggested it. As a native Northwesterner, I knew the beleaguered condition of our forests, which need not make another pointless sacrifice. Besides, many of the good Seattle baseball stories were already published when Jim Bouton penned his seminal sports book, *Ball Four*, which chronicled parts of his season with the Seattle Pilots.

That little baseball experiment in the Northwest lasted only the summer of 1969. The foundering club was sold to a Midwest automobile salesman named Allen H. (Bud) Selig. He renamed the team the Brewers and put them in his hometown of Milwaukee. It has yet to be determined whether Milwaukee or Seattle was more upset by the deal, but it took a quarter century before major league baseball in the Northwest would register more than a dial tone. The Pilots' successors, the Mariners, took fifteen years to break .500—the slowest meander to a winning season of any expansion team in modern American professional sports.

Up to that point, a book on the topic didn't seem likely, although a half-hour comedy show on HBO had merit.

Playing in an indoor park with the baseball ambience of a sensory deprivation tank and compromised by a succession of underfunded ownerships, the Mariners were targets of contempt from the lords of baseball. The other franchise owners were eager to be rid of Seattle, assailing its distance from the rest of the baseball world, its fitness for baseball, and its uncompliant politicians. The skepticism was not confined to outlanders. A joke in Seattle became the sum and substance of the Mariners' early local legacy: "Two Mariners tickets were left on the dashboard of an unlocked car. When the driver returned, there were four tickets."

But by 1993, change was underway, in baseball and in the Puget Sound region. Ten years later, my perspective had changed too. After a couple of well-timed conversations, the notion of a book on the Mariners was at least more plausible than a guide to fine dining in Kabul.

The first conversation came at a party, where I fell into talk of sports, a relentless social hazard for newspaper sports columnists. I'm usually the only one who wants to talk about taxes, religion, death, war–anything but sports, when it's my dime and my time. Hey, do barbers want to come home every night and cut hair?

Anyway, a giddy Mariners fan in the group was gushing about how enjoyable the 2001 season had been, what with the club winning 116 regular-season games after losing three of the best players in the game–Ken Griffey Jr., Randy Johnson, and Alex Rodriguez. Even the jaded national baseball literati were in agreement that the Mariners were the story of the regular season.

"Isn't it great," she said, "to be in a place where the baseball's always so much fun?"

Struck nearly dumb–not an unusual development, readers of my newspaper column will tell you–I searched the room for a seat. *Always so much fun?* My knees jellied.

She had no idea. Turned out the woman moved to Seattle in 1995, when the Mariners first crawled into the sporting consciousness with something other than dread. Since then, she saw the Mariners make the playoffs four times. They moved into a grand, retro-style ballpark–America's most expensive single-purpose sports palace–with a retractable instead of fixed roof, built mostly by the extraction of hundreds of millions of dollars in tax money from a public that had seen less than two months of sustained baseball success in the franchise's first eighteen years. In the Mariners' most recent three regular seasons, they averaged 100 regular-season wins. They led the majors in home runs in 1997 and in pitching in 2001. They had two batting champions, an American League Cy Young Award winner, and two AL Most Valuable Player award winners. They led the major leagues in attendance two years in a row, earned gross revenues second only to the New York Yankees, and owned some of the most lucrative broadcast-rights contracts in sports. And nearly throughout the renaissance, they were led by one of the most irascible and endearing managers in the game.

Lou Piniella first came to the distant, bemused attention of the Northwest in the mid-1960s, as a minor league outfielder for the

Portland Beavers. After hitting into a double play, the volatile Piniella was so mad at himself that, as he took his defensive position at old Multnomah Stadium, he kicked the eight-foot-high, portable outfield fence.

"As I walked away, the damn thing fell on me," Piniella said, smiling. "The grounds crew had to come get me out."

Ah. Here was a fellow worth writing about—particularly since his baseball life wrapped around the Northwest like blackberry canes. By kicking dirt, throwing bases, flinging spittle, and flapping arms until everyone's attention was purchased, Piniella helped Seattle do a decade-long baseball version of an Indiana Jones movie. Swapping out a ball cap for the leather fedora, he and the franchise dodged boulders, snakes, and blow darts while dangling from a fraying suspension bridge.

The tortured analogy breaks off here, because Piniella and the Mariners got neither the girl nor the prize. They didn't make the World Series. But that takes nothing away from the story of perils escaped. The Mariners' decade-long penchant for drama was in the back of my mind during a second conversation, this one with Chad Haight, publisher of Sasquatch Books. He asked, "Is there a worthwhile book about the Mariners?"

Oh, hell yes. This franchise has been to the edge so many times that entire cliffs are wedged beneath its fingernails. The Wallenda family would take one look at the Mariners story and turn away, knees knocking. For fifteen years, the Mariners faced a series of choices critical to the future that easily could have gone a different, and debilitating, way.

➤ They almost didn't draft Ken Griffey Jr.

➤ They almost didn't hire Lou Piniella.

➤ They nearly moved to Florida until a five-minute phone call to the other side of the world found an eccentric billionaire who knew little of baseball but didn't have much else to do with $75 million.

➤ Having to triumph to save its Seattle life in 1995, the team that never won anything won nearly everything, including $372 million in stadium funding.

➤ Not liking the terms for the $372 million, the club went up for sale again, until its political benefactor brass-knuckled the entire civic leadership into playing ball.

➤ The three superstar players who were the foundation of the

Most Combined Losses: 1980s–1990s

The Mariners lost so many games in the 1980s—they led the majors with 893 defeats—that, despite five winning seasons in the 1990s (1991, 1993, 1995, 1996, 1997), they led in combined defeats over the two decades.

Team	Losses 1980s	Losses 1990s	Total
Seattle Mariners	893	787	1,680
Minnesota Twins	833	833	1,666
Chicago Cubs	821	813	1,634
Pittsburgh Pirates	825	779	1,604
San Diego Padres	805	799	1,604
Philadelphia Phillies	780	823	1,603
Anaheim Angels	783	817	1,600
Texas Rangers	839	747	1,586
Detroit Tigers	727	852	1,579
Cleveland Indians	849	728	1,577
Milwaukee Brewers	760	811	1,571
San Francisco Giants	795	766	1,561
Kansas City Royals	734	825	1,559
Oakland Athletics	764	781	1,545
Chicago White Sox	802	735	1,537
Cincinnati Reds	783	746	1,529
Montreal Expos	752	777	1,529
New York Mets	743	786	1,529
St. Louis Cardinals	734	794	1,528
Baltimore Orioles	761	757	1,518
Toronto Blue Jays	746	754	1,500
Los Angeles Dodgers	741	757	1,498
Houston Astros	750	742	1,492
Boston Red Sox	742	741	1,483
Atlanta Braves	845	629	1,474
New York Yankees	708	702	1,410

Most losses in any decade: Phillies, 1920s, 962.
Most losses in consecutive decades: Phillies, 1920s and 1930s, 1,905.

team up and left, leaving the franchise on the shoulders of a skinny, 5-foot-9 rookie from Japan, who helped carry the Mariners to a baseball Everest.

If any one of these episodes had turned out other than the way it did, the Mariners would be gone from Seattle, or at least floundering in the American League West basement. But each pivot point turned the Mariners' way, making them a pop-culture fixture in the Northwest with the resources for perennial contention.

In retracing the hazardous, often hilarious, and occasionally heartbreaking route that brought the Mariners to permanence and baseball respectability, it became clear there were so many forehead-slapping moments that it would be a shame if they weren't written down in one place. Haight and Gary Luke, Sasquatch's editorial director, agreed, with cruel stipulations: finish in ten months, and don't rehash my columns in the *Seattle Post-Intelligencer*. They did, however, permit me to use both hands while typing.

My only retort was that the project wouldn't be a vanity book. When I approached the team's owners, executives, staff, and players for their cooperation, I told them the book would be an attempt at an honest narrative, including controversies and mistakes, not just gee-whiz-ain't-it-grand. For some reason, they said OK. Presumably they are, by now, used to life on the tightrope.

Nor would the book be a comprehensive Mariners history, although many of the highlights and lowlights of twenty-six seasons get some moment. Compared with the lengthy, baseball-rich histories of the New York Yankees, Boston Red Sox, Cincinnati Reds, and St. Louis Cardinals, as well as more recent high-profile achievers such as the Los Angeles Dodgers, San Francisco Giants, and Atlanta Braves, the Mariners came in low and late—somewhere around the twenty-first hour of a twenty-four-hour baseball day. But come in they did, barrel rolling, throwing off despair and delight into a community that has loved and hated them, alternately caring not at all and sometimes too much.

The transformation of the Mariners was more than baseball, more than sports, and more than a little preposterous. The story includes the passions, the politics, and the conflicted values of the Puget Sound market—for that matter, a five-state region as well as parts of Canada—that has in recent years embraced baseball in the swooning manner of teen love.

A lasting irony came when the club's unstable and unentertaining history was resolved in 1992 by an entertainment tycoon never entertained by baseball. Hiroshi Yamauchi had never attended a game, nor had he examined the Mariners before his $75 million purchase. He had simply said yes to a phoned request from his son-in-law Minoru Arakawa. Asked why the cantankerous Japanese business maverick would buy a team that had lost like no other in baseball, Arakawa smiled.

"He didn't know," he said.

Perfect. Anyone who *did* know the Mariners' story to that point never would have bought the team, or anything about it.

Herein lies an opportunity to know some of that story. Whether it is told well is in the judgment of the reader. If the storytelling flops, fault lies squarely with me. Error sportswriter, if you're scoring at home.

One of the small virtues of chronicling a relatively young team is that its future and its past are within reach of one another. In the Mariners' case, one of the faceless flops of their early years—a pitcher/prankster who on the last day of his baseball career sold peanuts, in uniform, for an inning in the Kingdome—would twenty years later sell the Mariners on acquiring the player who would prove to be among the world's greatest.

If your logical mind doesn't follow that, welcome to the story of major league baseball in Seattle.

CHAPTER ONE

There's Bad, and Then There's the Mariners

A one-hopper back to the mound, and it was over. Pitcher Billy Swift made the easy throw to first base for the final out in a 4-3 victory over the Texas Rangers in a game no one would remember except for the guys hopping up and down on the field in the quiet decrepitude of Arlington Stadium. In the press box, the scramble by radio broadcaster Dave Niehaus to get to down to the visitors' clubhouse was complicated a bit by the tears in his eyes. He didn't care what anyone thought. After what he witnessed for fifteen years, a celebration with his fellow brethren of the lost was in order. So he was a little sloppy. When he arrived at party central, champagne bottles were making the rounds. Alvin Davis, the slugging first baseman known as Mr. Mariner for his years of franchise service as noble as they were futile, ran over to Rick Griffin to deliver a bear hug, lifting the skinny trainer off the floor.

"We're not losers anymore!" Davis yelled to his pal, relief as much as joy in his voice. The 81st win of 1991 assured the first non-losing season in club history—the first time they would not lose more games than they won. Didn't matter that it wasn't quite yet a winning season in a 162-game schedule. The season just wouldn't be a loser. The worst expansion team in American sports history had reached an elusive milestone of mediocrity. For the long-abused, it was exhilaration times ecstasy.

"This was huge," said the manager, Jim Lefebvre. "It's a huge weight off the backs of the players, the coaches, the front office, the city, and everyone who has anything to do with baseball in Seattle."

Niehaus also could not resist the pull of oral hyperventilation.

"It was almost like we had won the World Series," said Niehaus, who began with the club from its litigious birth in 1977 to become its most familiar and beloved figure. "I was so emotional, and so was Jimmy. For all of those guys who had been there for those years—Alvin Davis, Dave Valle, Harold Reynolds—it was just a huge, huge burden off our backs.

"For some stupid reason, we could never reach .500. Year after year after year, it was unreachable. But in baseball, it's very reachable."

That's what Jay Buhner thought. A Mariners short-timer, less than three years removed from the sport's winningest franchise, the New York Yankees, Buhner watched the little celebration and shook his head. He walked away, silently, into the training room.

"A celebration for .500," he said, embarrassed over the salute to tepidness. "I couldn't believe it."

Arriving via trade halfway through the 1988 season, the outfielder lacked an appreciation for the number of upturned rakes upon which this franchise had stepped. If there was a banana peel, or an open manhole cover, anywhere in the neighborhood, the Mariners were on it and in it. From the 1977 startup through 1992, the franchise was arguably the most consistently misbegotten enterprise in American sports. For what seemed like forever to Niehaus and the small knot of fellow masochist foolhardies who followed the Mariners, it was always two outs and nobody on base.

For those who knew the M's then, the franchise's subsequent achievements are so ungraspable they must perform the daily pinch upon entry to the club's twenty-first-century home of Safeco Field and ask: Is this a dream?

⚜

The Mariners' pre-1993 legacy of shallow-pockets ownerships, inept players, bumbling managers, forehead-slapping trades, and stadium controversies created a depth of pathos that was hard to comprehend until heights were reached in later years. The little moments, however, had an unshakable stickiness, starting with the first practice at the freshly opened Kingdome in 1977.

A rare moment of joy with the 1977 Mariners: the franchise's first win, a 7-6 victory over the Angels in the Kingdome. ©1977 SEATTLE POST-INTELLIGENCER/GRANT M. HALLER

Inspecting their crisp new ballyard for the first time in its base-ball configuration, club officials discovered outfield dimensions eight to ten feet less than the distances posted on the walls. For a franchise seemingly destined to come up short unto perpetuity, the metaphor was as subtle as a freight train.

So were the first two games, losses of 7-0 and 2-0. The Mariners went on to lead the major leagues in most cumulative defeats through the 1980s—and the 1990s. In the stands was a corollary to the performance: After the big opening-night crowd in 1977, the Mariners attracted 22,000 combined for the next two home con-tests, when that number was about the major league average for a single game. For the decade of the '80s, the Mariners drew the majors' fewest fans.

If there was a single episode that damned the franchise to national sports ridicule, helping persuade rival American League owners that baseball didn't belong in Seattle, it happened in April 1982 when Mariners pitcher Gaylord Perry won his 300th game of a praiseworthy career. The achievement was a rare baseball milestone—only fourteen others had done it—that elsewhere would have been greeted with fanfare and hosannas in a sport drunk on its history. Only 27,369 showed up at the Kingdome that night to hail the aged spitballer, the Mariners' only real star. Two nights later, club promoters gave away a funny-nose-and-glasses trinket to ticket holders, and 36,716 appeared for an otherwise unevent-ful game. The rest of baseball prayed that no one in the Mariners promotions department thought about whoopee cushions.

Perry didn't say much about that, but he did have something to say about another idea unique to the Mariners: a goofy mini-tugboat that brought in relief pitchers from the bullpen. He viewed the idea as a humiliation so pronounced he began a hun-dred-dollar clubhouse fine for any pitcher sitting in the thing. "I'll be damned," Perry said, "if anybody's going to come in and pitch for me riding a goddamn tugboat."

The Mariners didn't confine their original thinking to the field. In 1978, Kip Horsburgh, director of marketing, announced the team would not turn over the Kingdome dates necessary in April 1984 so Seattle could stage the NCAA Final Four men's basket-ball championship. The club, he said, might want to have a public practice. Even though the outcry shamed the club into abandon-ing its claim on the stadium, the episode began a long series of civic facial welts, mostly self-induced, that no grimy boxing gym could hope to duplicate. Fortunately, most of the foibles were at least good for a laugh.

Halfway through the inaugural season, pitcher Stan Thomas decided he would exercise a grudge against the first Minnesota batter of the game, Mike Cubbage, who years earlier in some minor league town became involved with Thomas's girlfriend. Thomas tried to hit him with a pitch. He missed—all four times. As Cubbage walked to first base, Mariners manager Darrell Johnson came flying out of the dugout, so mad that upon reaching the mound, he fined Thomas and catcher Bob Stinson on the spot.

"Don't fine me—I don't know what's going on," said Stinson, recounting the episode ten years later to the *Seattle Post-Intelligencer*'s Bill Plaschke. "I just know if he was trying to hit him, he wasn't doing a very good job."

No one was doing a good job that day—the Mariners lost, 15-0— or that year. In a game against Oakland, they had six runners thrown out on the base paths, including two at home in the same inning. The Mariners were thrown out for the cycle: Besides the usual complement at first base, Dave Collins was thrown out at second, Dan Meyer at third and home, and Skip Jutze at home twice. Somewhere in heaven, the bulbous helmets of Keystone Kops had to be adorned with little Mariners trident logos.

Such buffoonery was the price of expansion in those days. Of the original twenty-eight players (three began on the disabled list), ten were out of baseball after that season, another four were gone one year later. The roster flush was typical of newly created teams of the 1960s and 1970s, before the advent of free agency made it possible to purchase contention, in the manner of Florida (1997 champions after five seasons) and Arizona (2001 champions after four seasons).

Darrell Johnson was fired in 1980 and replaced as manager by former Los Angeles Dodgers great Maury Wills, who proved himself one of the game's most bewildered occupants of a major league manager's seat.

Asked once who his starting center fielder would be, Wills said, "I wouldn't be surprised if it was Leon Roberts." Five weeks earlier, Roberts had been traded to Texas. Wills once called for a relief pitcher, but forgot to tell any of them to warm up. Before another game during spring training, Wills forwarded the

The Worst Expansion Team

The Mariners had more losing seasons from inception than any sports franchise in modern American pro sports history, including all teams in the National Football League, National Hockey League, National Basketball Association, and Major League Baseball.

Club	First Year	Consecutive Losing Seasons
Seattle Mariners	1977	14
New Jersey Devils NHL	1974	13
New Orleans Saints NFL	1967	12*
Houston Astros MLB	1962	10
Montreal Expos MLB	1969	10
Milwaukee Brewers MLB	1969	9
New Orleans/Utah Jazz NBA	1974	9
Washington Capitals NHL	1974	8
Minnesota Timberwolves NBA	1989	8
San Jose Sharks NHL	1991	8
Memphis Grizzlies NBA	1995	8**
Houston Rockets NBA	1967	7
Pittsburgh Penguins NHL	1967	7

* The Saints had two 8-8 seasons after twelve straight losing years. They did not post their first winning season until 1987.
** Active streak as of 2003.

paperwork to release outfielder Willie Norwood. But because Wills didn't inform him until after the game, in which Norwood played the ninth inning, he used a player no longer employed by the club. Wills once made out a lineup card with two third basemen and no center fielder, and on another occasion sent up a pinch hitter who had already pinch-hit and left the game. In a Kingdome game against Oakland, Wills had the batter's box redrawn to extend a foot toward the mound to help one of his hitters, Tom Paciorek. A's manager Billy Martin spotted the rules violation. Wills was suspended for two games and fined five hundred dollars.

After the overdue firing of Wills in 1981, umpire Ken Kaiser said, "He was absolutely the worst manager I've ever seen. He didn't even know how to argue." After his departure came an explanation for at least part of Wills's problems: He entered a clinic for treatment of cocaine addiction.

His replacement, Rene Lachemann, was a good choice, but came about oddly. The *P-I*'s Mariners beat writer, Tracy Ringolsby, was a friend of Lachemann's and made the recommendation to the club's new owner, George Argyros, who didn't know better than to listen to a sportswriter.

Lachemann, on the other hand, knew better than to listen to a rookie owner. When Argyros called him once on the Mariners' dugout phone, he ripped the phone off the wall. "He was just a fan," said Lachemann, "one who didn't know the game."

But Argyros owned the team, and he decided he didn't like Lachemann, who was popular with players, fans, and media. When he was fired in the middle of the 1983 season, the uproar was so pronounced that the club declined to introduce his successor, Del Crandall, before his first game.

⁂

Mariners of the dark times made at least one contribution that seems a fixture in the lore of baseball. Naturally, it was a symbol of futility: the Mendoza Line.

Acquired by trade from Pittsburgh, Mario Mendoza was the starting shortstop in 1979. In 148 games, he batted .198, tying the major league record for worst average by a regular player. Playing that much, that poorly, is a hard thing to do. All-Star infielder George Brett of Kansas City was credited with inventing the Mendoza Line expression as the dubious distinction for any hitter's average below .200, although Mendoza himself gave "credit" to former Mariners teammate Tom Paciorek. Whoever owns the copyright, the Mariners have the legacy. Hey, you gotta start somewhere.

Throughout the 1980s, haplessness was the club's steadiest fan. In a stretch of 17 games in 1986, the Mariners struck out 180 times—including a record 20 in one game against a young Boston pitcher, Roger Clemens—for an average of almost 11 strikeouts per game. That season, they set the major league record for whiffs.

In the third game of 1988, starting pitcher Steve Trout threw 22 of his 29 pitches out of the strike zone. In two-thirds of an inning, he walked five batters in a row, made a throwing error, and delivered two run-scoring wild pitches. The most galling aspect was that Trout was not a stage-frightened rookie. He was thirty years old, in his tenth major league season, and the highest paid player ($990,000) in club history.

"My man vapor-locked," said pitching coach Billy Connors. "Wow, he went bad."

As did the Mariners. For fourteen years, never a winning season. No major league expansion team had ever been worse.

They were not helped by their home park. Hailed at its 1976 opening as "the finest stadium for the money in the land," the Kingdome turned out to be considerably less. While the 59,000-seat stadium, with its eleven-acre concrete roof, was an engineering marvel that couldn't be beat for functional utility—at different times, it was home to the Mariners, the NFL Seahawks, the NBA Sonics, and the North American Soccer League's Sounders—it was an aesthetic cringe. Too early in what turned out to be a short, twenty-four-year life, it became economically obsolete for pro sports' ravenous demands for cash.

The colorless bulge at the south end of downtown served baseball especially poorly. For many fans, playing inside during a Seattle summer bordered on the felonious. The automatic handicap of indoor baseball meant the team had to be compelling. But the Mariners had all the appeal of the first scratch on a new car.

"We knew when football started in September, we'd lose half our fans," said Rick Griffin, the trainer who joined the club in 1983. "They'd be watching the Huskies and Cougars on Saturday and the Seahawks on Sunday. In '84, when the Seahawks were 'really good, the Kansas City Royals came to town in September with George Brett in his prime and we drew 15,000 total for the three weekend games. We'd come out on the field and think the fans got stuck in the turnstiles."

Indeed, the Mariners' bleakness coincided in Seattle with great popularity for all the other big sports enterprises. The Sonics won the NBA title in 1979—still the region's only modern major pro sports championship. The University of Washington football team enjoyed a renaissance under coach Don James that sent the Huskies to the Rose Bowl in 1978, 1981, and 1982. The Seahawks, an NFL expansion team in 1976, had winning records by 1978–79 and played a recklessly entertaining style of football. Sounders soccer outdrew the Mariners in the Kingdome from 1977 through 1982.

Even the baseball comparison reflected poorly. By 1983 the Mariners' expansion brethren, the Toronto Blue Jays, had a winning season. In 1992 they won the World Series. In 1993 they won it again. The teams started at the same time, but were nations and even worlds apart. The financial capital of Canada, Toronto had a larger population and corporate base than Seattle and campaigned vigorously for an expansion team. The Blue Jays were viewed almost as a national team, sharing major league baseball in Canada only with the Montreal Expos in French-speaking Quebec.

Though the Mariners' total of 290 wins through the first five years was 20 more than Toronto's, the patience that was shown by Blue Jays ownership in youth-player development began to pay off in 1983, the first of eleven consecutive winning seasons. In 1989 the first retractable-roof baseball park, the half-billion-dollar Skydome, opened in Toronto to favorable reviews while drawing 3.3 million fans (the Mariners that year drew 1.3 million). Fifteen corporations threw in $5 million apiece for construction, just to be part of the party.

Through the World Series successes, the club was owned primarily by giant Labatt Breweries and a local family. The beer maker saw the obvious cross-promotional advantages in owning a team with national broadcast rights.

"Toronto had the benefit of wealthier ownership and more stability," said Pat Gillick, the Blue Jays' general manager from the beginning through 1995. (He later took the same post with the Mariners.) "There were four changes in ownership in Seattle by the time the Blue Jays won their first title. Our ownership then gave us chances to get support."

The wealth permitted the Blue Jays to play the rapidly changing money game within baseball. The year before the expansion teams began, the players union, an increasingly powerful force in the industry, won in federal court the right of free agency for players with six years of major league service. Before that, a player and his contract were typically bound to his original club for life, until the club chose to trade or release him. But the new rules allowed six-year players to choose the highest bidder for their services, causing a huge spike in team payrolls—and ticket prices.

In a parallel development, the advent of cable TV and its need for twenty-four-hour programming created a lucrative revenue stream for teams in the larger metropolitan areas, which typically had more cable hookups. So the Blue Jays joined a handful of bigger-market clubs that had the bankrolls to harvest the premium players. Over the last quarter of the twentieth century, the gap between the haves and the have-nots grew so large that as many as two-thirds of the teams began spring training without even a remote shot at the championship.

But that situation also became a convenient excuse to hide poor decisions by management. The "small-market blues" should have had no influence on a management's ability to select young players. But in the early years the Mariners had a propensity for taking athletes who didn't have what it took to play a tough game well—players who too easily accepted their tepid fate.

"This organization was known in its early years as very religious," Jay Buhner said. "I don't want to slap the guys in the face, but it was almost a passive scene: 'That's what the Lord wanted, so that's how it was meant to be.' I heard that endlessly in the locker room after I got here. I wouldn't say that about Alvin Davis, Harold Reynolds, and Dave Valle, because those three guys took me under their wings when I was a hothead out of control.

"I consider myself a Christian, but there's a right way and a wrong way to play the game, and I think they were playing the wrong way. With the Yankees, I had won at every level in the minors, instilling an attitude that you *will* win. Then I come here— one extreme to the other. There was a lot of uncertainty and underachievement, guys who settled for second-best. Not a real winning attitude, and it started at the top."

The top meant ownership, historically the biggest hole in Seattle's baseball lineup.

The futility that permeated the Mariners' early years was less a matter of faith, of which there was plenty, than money, of which there was little. The fundamental problem with baseball in Seattle went back as far as 1969, the single year of the Pilots: The town lacked the dilettante wealth that made up most pro sports ownerships in other parts of the country.

Mariners Attendance: From Worst To Best

After drawing 1.2 million fans in their inaugural season of 1977, the Mariners failed to reach 1 million in attendance in six of the next seven seasons. In the 1980s, the Mariners were not only the worst draw in the major leagues, but their ten-year total of 9.6 million was doubled by nine franchises. From the opening of Safeco Field in mid-1999 through the 2002 season, the Mariners drew 12 million fans—nearly 2.5 million more than watched the Mariners at the Kingdome in the entire 1980s.

Team	Attendance in the 1980s
Seattle Mariners	9,565,630
Cleveland Indians	10,144,299
Pittsburgh Pirates	11,350,932
Atlanta Braves	13,018,380
San Francisco Giants	13,292,023
Texas Rangers	13,862,069
Chicago White Sox	14,448,273
Minnesota Twins	14,914,466
Houston Astros	15,017,104
San Diego Padres	15,775,478
Oakland Athletics	15,812,728
Cincinnati Reds	16,673,118
Milwaukee Brewers	17,144,759
Chicago Cubs	17,245,805
Montreal Expos	17,722,204
Baltimore Orioles	18,659,772
Detroit Tigers	18,977,619
St. Louis Cardinals	19,367,506
Boston Red Sox	19,551,184
Philadelphia Phillies	20,573,622
New York Mets	20,712,308
Toronto Blue Jays	21,144,821
Kansas City Royals	21,230,337
New York Yankees	22,077,255
California Angels	24,412,059
Los Angeles Dodgers	30,894,722

The Mariners finished last or next to last in American League attendance nine times from 1977 through 1992 and never finished higher than eighth (out of fourteen teams) in the league in any of those seasons. From 1996 through 2002, the Mariners outdrew the Yankees four times and the Dodgers three times.

The odd economic demographic surprised Slade Gorton when he first moved to Seattle in the mid-1950s. Chicago-born, the Dartmouth- and Columbia-educated lawyer would become one of the state's most influential political leaders. He would eventually ride in on three crises over major league baseball's first twenty-six years in the Northwest before the game was firmly anchored.

"When I first arrived, Seattle was profoundly different in one major respect: This was, perhaps more than any other American city of its size, quintessentially middle class," Gorton said. "Coming from the East, my observation was there were no slums that were typical of Eastern cities. There were also no concentrations of wealth. The Boeing and Weyerhaeuser families had had several generations to spread out their wealth. There was literally no one in Seattle to buy a major league franchise and operate it as a toy, at a loss, and spend money to be competitive.

"If there were someone with that kind of money, he had no interest in sports. The Nordstroms had the Seahawks for a while (1976–88), but they were never prominently mentioned with baseball. And, in any event, baseball was a more expensive sport. Through the Pilots and early Mariners, there was never any logical person here to buy and treat them the way extremely wealthy families treated their teams in other cities."

The Seattle Pilots had local owners—brothers Dewey and Max Soriano—but they bailed out in 1970 and sold the franchise to a Milwaukee car dealer by the name of Bud Selig, who planned to spirit the team away to his city. Gorton, then the state's attorney general, filed suit against the American League, seeking to make baseball comply with its promises to field a team in Seattle. The game had long been protected by a Supreme Court decision that exempted baseball ("the national pastime," it said) from antitrust law. So Bill Dwyer, the brilliant young Seattle attorney hired by Gorton, came up with the notion of suing instead for breach of contract and fraud, charging that the AL owners violated lease and other agreements in allowing the team to move.

Most legal pundits, including Gorton, thought the premise was thin. Even with an unlikely legal victory, damages would be paid in cash, whereas the goal was a replacement team. But Dwyer's idea was to get the case in front of a jury, then put on the witness stand some of the club owners who approved the move of the Pilots.

After meeting individually and collectively with some of the American League owners during negotiations and discovery prior to trial, Gorton felt Dwyer's strategy had a shot. He figured the jury would find the owners as loathsome as he did.

"They were a terrible bunch of people," Gorton said. "My conclusion was that if any American League owner moved into your neighborhood, he would lower property values."

When the often-postponed trial finally began in Everett, north of Seattle, in January 1976, the first witness was Charles O. Finley, the cantankerous, ill-mannered owner of the Oakland A's. Finley treated the jury as he had treated Gorton and other Seattle inquisitors over the years: He arrogantly talked down to them, and he repeatedly disclosed strategies baseball didn't want revealed. As testimony from Finley and other owners and executives proceeded over eighteen days, baseball's lawyers realized their position was withering.

"I've always put it, a little facetiously, that the American League lawyers recognized quickly that the jury was going to vote for capital punishment," Gorton said, smiling.

Owners of the teams in the American League and National League have sole discretion in determining which cities and which individuals will have a major league franchise, either by expansion or relocation. But their decisions can be influenced by adverse legal action, which appeared highly likely in Seattle. So the AL lawyers decided the wiser course was to avoid millions of dollars in damages. If the suit were dropped, baseball promised to give Seattle an expansion team for the 1977 season.

Gorton and Dwyer said yes, and the settlement was hailed throughout Puget Sound. But a legal victory is not considered the premier way to begin a sports affair that needs passion, not depositions. The absence of an emotional groundswell haunted the early years. As *P-I* columnist Emmett Watson wrote at the time, the team should have been nicknamed the Litigants.

Still, the club was coming, and the Litigants needed an owner. Later on in 1976, four local businessmen—jeweler Stan Golub, furniture executive Walter Schoenfeld, department store chief Jim Walsh, and construction magnate Jim Stillwell—joined up with a Seattle broadcast and recording executive, Lester Smith, who had a moneybags friend and partner, Hollywood entertainer Danny Kaye. Only Kaye was considered wealthy by any standard. The

Danny Kaye (left), baseball commissioner Bowie Kuhn, and part-owner Lester Smith watch Senator Henry M. Jackson throw out the ceremonial first pitch for the Mariners' inaugural game at the Kingdome on April 6, 1977.

©1977 SEATTLE POST-INTELLIGENCER/BOB MILLER

rest were wealthy only by a far more modest Seattle measure. As with the Soriano brothers, the group was undercapitalized, even though the purchase price was just $6.5 million. The group also made a baseball mistake, selecting in the expansion draft more established players instead of growing with kids. The urgency was to win quickly in a market of unproven yearning for baseball.

"Everyone in baseball was so nice, and made so many promises," Smith, the broadcast executive, said in 2001. "Then they froze all the good players [the expansion draft limited the Mariners and Blue Jays to the least productive major league players]. What were we going to do? If I knew what was going to happen, I wouldn't have touched it with a ten-foot pole."

But he did, and by 1981 the pole had splintered. Two of the partners left and the remaining four squabbled. Soon the word was out nationally: club for sale. For the next eleven seasons, the Mariners were owned by two out-of-towners, George Argyros of Orange County, California, until 1989 and Jeff Smulyan of

Indianapolis until 1992. They, too, were underfunded, given the changes brought about by free agency.

For more than a decade, the owners battled periodically with King County over the lease and the conditions at the Kingdome, fought with the Seahawks over stadium conflicts, and complained to local businesses and media outlets about a lack of support. The fact that Argyros and Smulyan were not from Seattle made their direct and implied threats of franchise relocation irritatingly plausible.

The nearly universal community retort: Win some games first.

In 1985, Ron Sims, the politically ambitious son of a Baptist pastor from Spokane, Washington, was elected to the King County Council, the municipal government that ran the Kingdome on behalf of its taxpayer owners. Eleven years later, he became the boss: King County executive, the top elective post in one of America's biggest counties. He bore weary witness as a participant in baseball's seemingly endless wrangling over the Kingdome and the baseball marketplace.

"To tell you the truth, I loathed baseball meetings," he said. "Baseball meetings are always combative." Throughout their tenure in the county-owned facility, through the terms of six county executives, the Mariners always seemed more aggressive in local politics than they were on the field.

⁂

The biggest annoyance for fans was the club's refusal to hang on to its talented youngsters. In its initial amateur draft of 1977, the Mariners chose in the first round Dave Henderson, a fast, eighteen-year-old center fielder from the San Francisco Bay area with some pop in his bat and a smile for all occasions. He had a big baseball future, and as it turned out a front-row seat to watch the franchise's futility in the '80s.

"It was pretty simple," said Henderson, who spent fourteen seasons in the majors and would star with Oakland and Boston in the World Series. "We were trying to do things in halves and quarters instead of wholes. We were a half, they were trying to get us to three-quarters, then they'd make mistakes and lose it. Young guys would leave. The team was also a dumping ground for older veterans. It was a place where you ended your career, to get some stats, 300 wins or 300 home runs. If you were a good player with a rising salary, they said, 'We're going to lose anyway; let's get rid of him.' "

In 1981, Henderson graduated from the minors to reach the Mariners, where he played under five managers in his six Seattle seasons. "Every new manager wanted to create his own identity," he said. "But they didn't get to have a spring training, because the firings would be in midseason."

In the final season before his free agency and the big money, he experienced the standard treatment for young Mariners with a good baseball future.

"When you get traded from the organization that drafted you No. 1 and was going to build around you, it hits you right in the stomach," he said of his 1986 trade to Boston. "It wasn't like I was traded to a team that needed me. It was a dump, really."

Henderson was dispatched with shortstop teammate Spike Owen to the Red Sox in exchange for what was also typical of the times—four forgettables: shortstop Rey Quinones, pitchers Mike Trujillo and Mike Brown, and outfielder John Christensen, none of whom would have impact with the Mariners. If Dave Niehaus, the broadcaster, had need to look for a "stupid reason" the Mariners couldn't get to a .500 season, such trades would be the starting point.

Owner George Argyros, a real estate developer with no previous sports background, was the primary culprit in the malaise. A bruising, blustery, self-important sort who bought the club in 1981 for $13.1 million and sold it for $76 million in 1989, Argyros was perpetually agitating the public as well as local government. Early on, he built a Mariners TV ad campaign not around his players or baseball, but himself. In 1985 he threatened to file for bankruptcy, in order to obtain huge lease concessions.

In 1987, with his marriage crumbling and a need to be closer to his Orange County home, Argyros pulled his most ham-fisted stunt—infuriating Seattle and shocking baseball when he abruptly tried to buy the San Diego Padres of the National League while owning the Mariners. When a San Diego columnist asked Jim Street, the P-I's Mariners beat writer, about the Argyros personality, Street replied, "San Diego is the luckiest city since Beirut."

Baseball commissioner Peter Ueberroth, a close Argyros friend, was forced to fine him $10,000 when Argyros called the Padres manager, a violation of baseball's rules against tampering with

Mariners owner George Argyros was escorted from the Kingdome under police protection after a boisterous crowd booed him heavily on opening night in 1987. He recently had announced he was attempting to purchase the San Diego Padres while still owning the Mariners, a gambit that failed two months later.

©1987 SEATTLE POST-INTELLIGENCER/HARLAN CHINN

other teams. The Mariners were put in trust for two months until the proposed Padres deal fell through, mostly because the National League owners, as one baseball source said, felt Argyros "wasn't the kind of person that they wanted around them."

There was hardly a more disliked character in Seattle sports, or in all of baseball, for that matter. National League president Bart Giamatti called him "the James Watt of baseball," referring to the former secretary of the interior and his reputation for foolishness in public. Compounding the contempt in the Northwest, Argyros spurned any local efforts to purchase the club. He hung on to the Mariners through 1989, then surprised everyone by selling to Smulyan, a radio-broadcast mogul from Indianapolis. Argyros's original 80 percent share in the club made him more than $50 million on the sale. For all of his complaints about the lousy market conditions for baseball in Seattle, he made a $2 million operating profit in his final year.

Compared to the bellicose, distant Argyros, Smulyan was a younger, hipper, more engaging personality who understood sports marketing. But as with Argyros and his predecessors, he was more borrowed money than made money. His glib banter failed to counter the growing suspicion that Smulyan was biding his time until he found a way out of Seattle, with the team in his U-Haul. His hidden business agenda dictated another mostly inexplicable baseball move.

After the Mariners' "breakthrough" season of 1991 that finished 83-79, the first with a winning record, general manager Woody Woodward fired Jim Lefebvre, a high-energy bulldog of a manager who sometimes couldn't find the "park" gear on his motor-mouth. The dismissal wasn't a complete surprise. A few players, especially Buhner, found him intolerable, and the team's public relations staff even faxed critical stories about Lefebvre to some writers around the country. But the firing still was something of a mystery, given that the club improved from 73 to 83 wins over his three years. For the first time, the Mariners topped the 2 million mark in attendance.

What wasn't revealed at the time was that Smulyan had told Woodward in confidence that the club was going to move to Tampa, probably by 1993. Lefebvre, who had complained in the media repeatedly during the season about management's unwillingness to add payroll for needed players, could not be trusted to keep a company secret.

"I knew ahead of everyone," Woodward said of the Tampa plan. "I was told not to tell anyone. I thought, wow, this isn't going to be easy. I could not tell Lefebvre about the impending move, and that put us all in a very difficult situation. Jimmy didn't know what was happening, but he shouldn't have voiced his complaints about ownership and management in the media.

"I think if you're Jeff, you'd do the same thing."

Still, the firing of the only manager to pull off a winning season, and the subtle campaign-by-fax to discredit Lefebvre, made the point that the Mariners didn't even know how to win right.

"There is no logical reason why a manager's image should be attacked when the season still has a month to run," wrote

Post-Intelligencer columnist John Owen after the firing. "Such a public mugging is unjustifiable."

The Mariners not only couldn't win for losing, they couldn't win for winning.

⚜

Despite all the intrigue with ownership, the lagging attendance, and the low comedy on the Kingdome rug, the dark years were not deviod of light. Small successes and delights made life semibearable for die-hard fans who took their ball thrills indoors.

Tom Paciorek beat the dreadnought Yankees with ninth-inning homers in back-to-back games and finished second in the 1982 batting race—the same year that Gaylord Perry, a future Hall of Famer, won his 300th game. Second baseman Julio Cruz became one of the premier thieves in baseball, stealing more than 40 bases for six years in a row. In 1984 first baseman Alvin Davis won the club's first major award, Rookie of the Year. In April 1985, Phil Bradley hit an astonishing walk-off grand slam to win a game. Second baseman Harold Reynolds won the American League stolen-base title in 1987, the same year pitcher Mark Langston led the league in strikeouts, and each won a Gold Glove for fielding prowess.

There were glimpses of hope off the field, too. The organization's talent hunters occasionally would find something in their forays around barrel's bottom. In 1982 they signed a skinny nineteen-year-old third baseman from Puerto Rico named Edgar Martinez, who turned out to be a twenty-year keeper. In 1984 a flashy Venezuelan shortstop, Omar Vizquel, was signed as a seventeen-year-old free agent. In 1988 the Mariners acquired Buhner, a hacker with a high-caliber arm, from the Yankees, the same year they chose in the amateur draft a powerful first baseman, Tino Martinez.

In 1989 the Mariners traded away the best pitcher in club history, Langston, to Montreal, only this time they got something back: right-handed pitchers Gene Harris and Brian Holman and a virtually unknown prospect named Randy Johnson. At 6-foot-10 the tallest major league pitcher ever, Johnson would go on to replace Langston as staff ace and then become one of the most dominant pitchers in the history of the game.

None of the incremental achievements and small developments compared with June 1987, when the Mariners used the No. 1

choice in the amateur draft on Ken Griffey Jr., whose genes were etched with superstardom. As the son of a former star in the Cincinnati Reds' Big Red Machine of the mid-1970s, the high schooler was as elegant and glorious a baseball natural as there ever was. True to the Mariners' pattern, however, they almost passed on him.

Having just been embarrassed nationally by his failed purchase of the Padres, George Argyros didn't want another laughingstock moment by wasting the top pick on some seventeen-year-old who didn't grade out as well as the player Argyros wanted: a college pitcher in Argyros's Orange County neighborhood who would help more quickly. If it weren't for some subterfuge by the baseball scouts, including a former Argyros chauffeur, the Mariners would have passed on Griffey.

Even with Griffey on the major league roster two years later, progress was agonizingly slow. After the winning season in 1991, the Mariners fell back into pathos. Smulyan's plan to move the club to Tampa suddenly was thwarted in January 1992 by an utterly unexpected $100 million offer to buy the club, from a mostly local group headed by a mysterious businessman from Japan. But approval for the controversial purchase was in constant jeopardy and remained unsettled until June, too late to fix the season.

Hired as a caretaker manager for the '92 season was the ineffectual Bill Plummer, a longtimer in the organization's minor leagues who didn't have the emotional wherewithal for the bigs, but worked cheap. A disastrous off-season trade brought overweight outfielder Kevin Mitchell for three pitchers who would go on to have solid careers: Billy Swift, Mike Jackson, and Dave Burba. Closer Mike Schooler tied a major league record by giving up four grand slams in a season. Injuries cost the Mariners 747 man-games.

It didn't much matter that Edgar Martinez won the club's first individual offensive title, a batting championship, with a .343 average, or that Griffey was the Most Valuable Player at the All-Star Game. All that mattered in '92, according to Buhner, "was whatever you do, don't lose 100 games. Again, it was a negative thought process. Every year, there was a negative thought process. It's tough enough to play the game. It was not a place you wanted to come work every day."

Buhner and his mates achieved the minimalist goal by two games, finishing with a 64-98 record. The mark was particularly odious: It was identical to the inaugural season of expansion dreariness. From 1977 to 1992, the Mariners completed a circle of futility. After sixteen years, they seemed back at the beginning, 32 games out of first place, while the Blue Jays were winning the first of two World Series.

But the Mariners were not back at the beginning. Below baseball's radar, and even unappreciated in Seattle, where opinions about baseball were as dark as the ubiquitous coffee, the Mariners assembled some splendid baseball talent that hadn't yet been traded away. And the collective wealth of the new ownership dwarfed that of their Seattle predecessors. The owners were among America's—and Japan's—richest individuals.

An odd incident during the 1987 season offered a portent of these new days. Late in a game, manager Dick Williams summoned Rey Quinones, the mercurial shortstop who came in the Henderson trade, to pinch-hit. But Quinones, blessed with great physical gifts but no head for baseball, was not on the bench. When he was discovered in the Kingdome clubhouse, he refused to enter the game, but not particularly out of spite, or even laziness. The twenty-three-year-old Puerto Rican was engrossed in one of the new line of home video games that had become the rage among young people. A fast-rising company called Nintendo had put out something called Super Mario Brothers. Quinones said he couldn't break off because he was about to reach the game's seventh level—a more important achievement than a few hacks in a meaningless baseball game, even though that was what he was paid well to do for a living. Williams was furious.

The episode didn't amount to much for either man. Williams was fired early the next season; Quinones was traded in early 1989. What did matter in the episode was the Nintendo game. The power it had over Quinones's imagination represented a significant key to the Mariners' future in Seattle.

CHAPTER TWO

The Chauffeur, The Kid, and the Start

G lancing up from the back seat of his Mercedes as it sped along a freeway in Orange County, George Argyros saw the face reflected in the rear-view mirror and decided to get to know his new guy.

"What do you want to do with your life?" he said in his perpetually blunt manner. "You're not going to drive me around forever."

In his first week on the job as chauffeur, Tom Mooney glanced back nervously. The chance was upon him. He had been a front-desk clerk at the Balboa Bay Club in Newport Beach, where he watched Argyros mingle with the Hollywood crowd that added glitter to the exclusive private club. Mooney was among the few locals who knew or cared that Argyros owned the flailing Seattle Mariners. Mooney loved baseball. He played through high school and college, then coached at the high school and American Legion levels in his native Massachusetts before heading west. In his two years at the club, he befriended Argyros's executive assistant, who spent most of his days hanging out at one fancy place waiting to drive the boss to the next fancy place. It seemed like a decent gig. Mooney told him if he ever moved on, he'd like a shot at the job.

Soon enough, the fellow moved on to AirCal, a brash new airline Argyros purchased not long after he bought the Mariners in 1981. He recommended Mooney as his replacement. Argyros liked giving menial jobs to ambitious young people. He wanted to see if they had the same stuff that he had when he went from stock boy to real estate baron, baseball owner, and airline magnate by his early forties. Mooney, who was thirty-one, took the entry-level job—a thousand dollars a month, always on call, and be prepared to stand around and wait, from 6 A.M. to midnight—because he desperately wanted to follow his passion. The moment was upon him.

"I want to get into baseball," Mooney said.

Argyros laughed.

"You're crazy," he said. "There's no money in baseball. Only the players get money."

It didn't matter that Argyros was wrong—he ended up making a lot of money in baseball. Mooney wanted to get into pro baseball, and Argyros was his ticket. In that first week, Mooney drove his boss to the airport in Burbank, where they picked up San Francisco Giants owner Bob Lurie and Peter Ueberroth, chieftain for the 1984 Olympic Games in Los Angeles (and soon to become baseball commissioner). He drove them to the Los Angeles Country Club for a round of golf. A guy could catch a break, you know?

"I likened it," he said, "to those old stories of waiters and waitresses getting acting breaks on Broadway or in Hollywood."

After a year of being with Argyros for ten to twelve hours a day, washing the car, running the kids around, and acquitting himself well as go-fer, Mooney made a positive impression. He also prepared some scouting reports on major league free agents that interested the boss's baseball people. Argyros called Mariners general manager Hal Keller in Seattle and asked that his chauffeur be put on the scouting staff. No special favors, he said: Mooney had to pull his weight, or he was gone. Given Argyros's past and future moves as owner, the idea of chauffeur-as-scout was fairly far down on the list of absurdities.

In the summer of 1984, Mooney piled his stuff into an aging Volkswagen Jetta and headed to Columbus, Ohio. From there he would scout Ohio, Michigan, and Indiana for the Mariners. It wasn't long before he picked up the trail—hell, it was a turnpike—to Ken Griffey Jr., the high school–age son of a famous major leaguer whose skills were already a growing legend in baseball-steeped Cincinnati.

"The major league scouting reports all said the same thing

about this kid—tremendous tools, a man in a kid's body, the sky is the limit," Mooney said. "But you never know."

Mooney soon knew. His reports duplicated many others in superlatives and anticipation. As Griffey entered his senior year, the reports became even more significant, because the Mariners finished the 1986 season with another dreadful effort—a last-place, 67-95 mark, worst in the American League. The only virtue of the season was that it gave the Mariners the first pick in the first round of major league baseball's amateur free-agent draft the following June (the AL went first in odd-numbered years). Mooney's territory became important. Griffey's name went on a list of about twenty prospects, high school and college, who had potential to be the top choice. Scouts fanned out around the country, and cross-checkers started showing up in Cincinnati to verify Mooney's reports.

In the spring of '87, Griffey's sky-high evaluations prompted a visit from Roger Jongewaard, the Mariners' director of scouting. A respected talent hunter, Jongewaard came to the Mariners in 1985 from Detroit. Before that, he had been with the Angels, Rangers, and Mets. Among the players he signed were Cy Young Award winner Mike Scott and National League MVP Kevin Mitchell, as well as Darryl Strawberry, Tim Leary, and Lenny Dykstra. The top Mariners sleuth heard enough from Mooney that a visit was mandatory.

Jongewaard and Mooney showed up to watch Griffey's Moeller High School team in a game played at a new community park. Beyond right field was a grove of trees that began about twenty yards from the outfield fence. In his second at-bat, Griffey took a smooth, easy swing and sent a ball high toward right. The first and second basemen retreated, then slowed. The right fielder began a slow backpedal. He stopped too.

Jongewaard was looking at his notes when he heard yelps from the crowd.

"I didn't see that," Jongewaard said. "Which tree did it hit?"

"Roger," said Mooney, "it went over the trees."

The astonishing parabola of the ball was something that not many major leaguers would be capable of, much less a seventeen-year-old. Jongewaard didn't need to see much more.

"I was comparing him to Strawberry but I had to get that out of my mind—I was afraid I'd jinx it," Jongewaard said. "After I broke it down, I thought he'd be better than Strawberry, although maybe not with as much power."

The obviousness of the talent didn't necessarily make for an obvious choice. This was, after all, the Mariners. Griffey was not the guy the boss wanted.

⁂

In Seattle the franchise was in tumult because of the Argyros plan to buy the San Diego Padres of the National League from McDonald's hamburger diva Joan Kroc. But he had not bothered to sell the Mariners first, and baseball commissioner Peter Ueberroth, Argyros's golf buddy, was sensitive to the appearance of a conflict of interest. He removed Argyros from daily operations of the Mariners. Argyros was permitted only one call daily to team president Chuck Armstrong, who had to have an independent witness during the call.

Nevertheless, Argyros made his feelings known about the No. 1 draft choice. The Mariners weren't going to take another kid, not after the way Jongewaard blew the club's top pick in the 1986 draft when the Mariners used their No. 1 selection on a North Carolina high schooler, shortstop Patrick Lennon. He proved to be a problem with a history of unpaid bills and run-ins with the law. He would play only briefly with the Mariners in 1991 and 1992.

"Lennon was a mistake," Jongewaard said. "He was a high-maintenance kid who got in some trouble. George thought I was making another mistake."

Argyros had his mind set on a college pitcher, which made some sense since the Mariners finished next to last in 1986 in pitching. A good college kid could help right away. It didn't hurt that the guy he had in mind, Mike Harkey, was pitching well for Cal State–Fullerton, practically next door to Argyros's offices in Orange County.

Besides, Griffey wasn't free of baggage. A trend popular among baseball executives was emphasis on a standardized psychological test, the sort of evaluator that is supposed to help forecast behavior and character. The Mariners' general manager, Dick Balderson, was a believer.

"Dick felt the top three qualities for players were makeup, makeup, and makeup," Armstrong said. "Dick put a premium on the tests."

The emphasis threatened to put an end to the interest in Griffey. His test result was the "worst score they'd ever seen," Mooney said. Balderson was dubious. If Argyros found out, there was no way Griffey could be taken. Or, if they took him and he was a Lennon-like bust, Argyros would almost certainly find out about the test, and some baseball careers would end up buried.

The baseball people didn't want to let a bad test score deny the Mariners a potential superstar. Something had to be done; no one could have tested so poorly. The suspicion was that Griffey, a mediocre student, simply put no effort into answering the questions, or gave the test to someone else to fill out.

Jongewaard decided on a second try. He dispatched Mooney to Griffey's home to personally take him through the test again.

Griffey wanted no part of retesting. But the Mariners had some leverage. He wanted desperately to be the first pick in the first round. The Mariners told him that they wouldn't use that pick on him unless he completed the test properly.

"The thing in our favor was that he knew everyone would remember who the No. 1 pick was, and no one would remember No. 2," Mooney said. "He was very proud of that and wanted to show his dad."

So on a spring Saturday, when Ken Griffey Sr. was playing with the Atlanta Braves, Mooney showed up at Griffey's home and was greeted by Griffey's mother, Alberta, known to everyone as Birdie, and a grandmother. Junior waited at the kitchen table.

"He had a copy of the test, and I had a copy," Mooney said. "I'd read the questions to him, and he'd mark the answers. There were 175 questions on four pages. It was crazy. It would have been an annoying test for a college player."

Griffey fidgeted and squirmed, but Mooney made him stick with it. As the afternoon dragged on, Mooney couldn't help but notice something else—a house that was the neighborhood playground.

Friends of Griffey and his brother, Craig, two years younger, drifted through the house and into the basement, where an array of pinball machines and other pre-computer-era games entertained them. Someone was always passing through the kitchen for goodies and a "watcha doin'?" tossed at Griffey.

"There were all these valuable baseball mementos on the walls and shelves, but there were no airs here," Mooney said. "Nobody had to take off their shoes. This wasn't a trophy house. This is where kids came to play. Forget the test results. That afternoon was valuable time to see him interact with his mother, grandmother, brother, and friends."

Despite the distractions and difficulties, Griffey slogged through the test, grading out at middle-of-the-road. The test results and the revealing afternoon at the Griffey home allowed Mooney to declare him a normal kid. He couldn't wait to call Jongewaard.

"He could hear the excitement in my voice," Mooney said. "He got excited too."

The next morning, Mooney was on a conference call to Seattle with the senior baseball people. Jongewaard offered his endorsement. Bill Kearns, the club's Eastern scouting supervisor and a talent hunter for more than thirty years, spent three days watching Griffey and offered this: "He is easily the best-looking all-around player I've ever seen." Yet the baseball boss, Balderson, still had to be sold.

"Baldy didn't know me from the wall," Mooney said. "He hired Roger for these kinds of things. Baldy wasn't the type to emote; he always had a poker face. But I had enough confidence that I knew what I was doing. I said, 'I'm telling you, he's normal, better adapted than most. If my dad was Senior Griffey, I'd probably be a jerk, but he isn't.' "

The results of the retesting made Balderson comfortable. Strong endorsements from the scouts were persuasive. Finally, he accepted the unanimous opinion. He passed on the recommendation to Armstrong, who had to do the serious grunt work: persuading Argyros.

⁂

Chuck Armstrong was president of Argyros's Arnel Development Company in Santa Ana, California, before moving to Seattle in October 1983 to run the Mariners—into the ground, critics said. He took a lot of heat in Seattle for the decisions of his mostly absentee boss. On Armstrong's watch as Mariners president, four managers were fired and the club traded away solid young major leaguers such as Danny Tartabull, Spike Owen, and David Henderson for next to nothing. Attendance never exceeded 1.1 million in any season, well below the major league average.

On top of all that, he was suddenly on the outs with Argyros. Once the owner announced his dubious plan to purchase the

Padres, Armstrong made calls around Seattle to see if he could put a group together to buy the Mariners. Argyros saw that as borderline traitorous. "My relationship with him was never the same again," Armstrong said. Now he had to tell Argyros he was wrong once more: Griffey not only wasn't Lennon, he was better than Harkey.

Armstrong had clandestine help. During an organization meeting in Seattle three days before the draft, Bob Harrison, West Coast scouting supervisor, noticed that Harkey and Griffey scored identical 70s on the club's 80-point talent rating scale. A rating of 50 was considered an average major leaguer, an 80 a Hall of Famer. Harrison simply erased the number next to Griffey's name and wrote in 72.

"I had never rated a player that high and I haven't rated one that high since," Harrison told the P-I in 1994. "But I thought that's what I had to do to convince George."

Armstrong, who shared Argyros's initial skepticism about Griffey before being converted, went to work on the boss. He had an additional, pivotal argument: Griffey was going to come cheap, relatively. The previous year's No. 1 choice, a college player, signed for a $225,000 bonus, which Ueberroth thought was a troubling escalation of player costs. In case Griffey balked, the Mariners were negotiating with Harkey and two other players.

The notoriously cheap Mariners caught another break. Griffey was represented by Brian Goldberg, a young Cincinnati attorney who befriended Ken Sr. when they attended college classes together. Senior had recently switched agents to Goldberg, and his son was about to be Goldberg's second client.

Years later, Goldberg acknowledged that his inexperience worked to the club's advantage. "If the Mariners didn't have an agent new to this, it may not have been such a quick and friendly agreement," he said. But neither he nor the Griffeys begrudged the situation: "Senior trusted me and was willing to give me a start with him and Junior."

The Mariners' final offer was $160,000. If Griffey refused to agree ahead of the draft on the bonus, the club said it was prepared to take Harkey. The team drafting second, the Pittsburgh Pirates, was itching for Griffey, even though they already had an outfield wunderkind by the name of Barry Bonds.

Griffey asked Goldberg how much money he was leaving on

the table if he signed with the Mariners. Goldberg said $30,000 to $40,000.

"I'll make up for that later," Griffey said. "Let's be No. 1."

"I'll be damned," Argyros said delightedly when informed of the agreement. He gave the fateful OK the day before the draft, but not before letting Jongewaard know how he felt.

"One more chance, Roger," he said. "If he's not a player, it's your ass."

Griffey would indeed be a player, the kind who could lift the back bumper to get a franchise out of the mud. Obvious as the choice may have been to others, the Mariners were not a club with a long tradition in making good decisions. But this one was a no-brainer even for an outfit with no brains. If persuading Argyros would have required dressing in lingerie, the scouts would have been six deep at the Victoria's Secret counter.

On the morning of June 2, 1987, Mooney, the scout, clattering along in his beat-up diesel Jetta with duct tape on the passenger window, arrived at the Griffey home. Already there were a couple dozen cars, including a TV truck from CNN. Senior Griffey had flown home overnight from Atlanta, CNN's home base, so the cable network deemed the story national news.

The first pick in the first round beamed into the cameras and signed the contract that would begin the transformation of one of sports' most dilapidated outfits. Mooney, with his oddball career and cranky car, was a splendidly metaphorical Mariners representative for the signing.

"I went from George's driver to holding press conferences on CNN," he said. "A friend of mine at home had the TV on over breakfast and couldn't believe he was hearing me." Nor could Mooney believe his ridiculously good fortune. The chauffeur-turned-Griff-grabber was just the first of many unlikely episodes surrounding the dazzling kid with the TV-commercial-grade grin.

A week later, accompanied by his mother, Griffey arrived in his future hometown of Seattle, where he had a batting practice in the Kingdome. After teasing from a couple of players, Harold Reynolds and Alvin Davis, about his mini-Afro, Griffey stepped into the left-hand box in the batting cage. His hecklers fell silent as he clubbed numerous balls into the empty Kingdome bleachers, where he would eventually deposit 198 home runs.

"This is the first time I've been away from home," he told

reporters later, in a rare moment of bashfulness, "and the first time I've been on a [major league] field without my dad being there to tell me what to do."

He adapted quickly, because for most of his seventeen years, this was life as he imagined it to be.

"I know he's ready to get started," Birdie Griffey said that day. "He was kind of antsy on the plane and antsy waiting to get picked up at the hotel.

"He gives himself three or four years to reach the majors."

He was off by a couple of years.

A week after his Kingdome practice, Griffey was on his way as scheduled to the minor leagues, where even the best talents can require four to five seasons of tutelage from the franchise's instructors. But Griffey was a quick study. His first hit with the Mariners' rookie-league in Bellingham, Washington, was a home run. His next season in Class A San Bernardino, California, was so good they retired his jersey, despite playing in only 58 games.

In the big club's spring training of 1989 in Tempe, Arizona, the plan was to advance Griffey to the top minor league affiliate, Class AAA Calgary, then perhaps move him onto the major league roster at midseason. But the Mariners' new general manager, Woody Woodward, who took over in the middle of the previous season when Balderson was fired, saw it a little differently.

"I'd like to start him at AAA, too," Woodward told Jongewaard, "but how can I send out my best player?"

At nineteen, Griffey was beyond precocious. Through spring training, he set club records for hits and runs and batted .359. During exhibition games against Oakland, another former Mariners' No. 1 draft choice, Dave Henderson, watched his Seattle successor closely from his perch as the A's starting center fielder.

"He looked like a singles hitter with doubles power," said Henderson, traded in 1986 to Boston. "I knew he was good–he could throw, run, and hit the other way. But when the bell rang, we thought he was vulnerable" to inside pitching.

Woodward said Griffey belonged on the big club. On opening day of 1989, Griffey became the youngest player in the majors that season as he joined the starting lineup against the A's in Oakland, facing one of the game's most formidable pitchers,

Dave Stewart. As per the scouting report, Stewart went inside right away. In his first major league at-bat, Griffey sent a shot over Henderson's head for a double.

As Henderson chased the ball down and Griffey eased into second base, one word described the collective impression in the Mariners' dugout: awe.

"Some guys leave a lasting first impression," said Jay Buhner, the right fielder who would become Griffey's closest clubhouse confidant. "He was an unbelievable talent."

The first at-bat also signaled a Griffey panache that would prove irresistible to millions of baseball fans. "I don't know how players get this—I wish I did—but he had that flair for the dramatic," Woodward said. "He was so young and loved to play so much. Fans loved him. He was the perfect fit for us."

A week later, Griffey underscored Woodward's point about drama. In the home opener against the Chicago White Sox, Griffey pounded the first regular-season pitch he saw in the Kingdome for a home run.

When he batted .600 for the week of April 24–30, he was named the AL's player of the week. Before the Fourth of July, he tied a club record with eight consecutive hits, won a game with a two-run homer in his first pinch-hit appearance, hit an inside-the-park home run against the Yankees, and twice had a two-homer game. Defensively, he was all over the Kingdome's outfield walls, practicing a baseball-edition Spiderman routine that would become as vivid as his feats at the plate.

The Kid, as he was quickly if mundanely nicknamed, was electric. But behind the sparks, his manager, Jim Lefebvre, worried.

"There's a tremendous expectation from fans and media that this guy is going to tear up the league," said Lefebvre, familiar with high-stakes ball as a key player in the Los Angeles Dodgers clubs that dominated the 1960s. "The media pressure has been phenomenal. He's going to card shows already at three thousand dollars a pop. That's good money for a kid, but he's not here to sign autographs.

"He's too young for all this exposure."

Physically capable as Griffey was, Lefebvre was on to something. Thrust into an extraordinary role of baseball savior for a desperate franchise, Griffey was sometimes overwhelmed. He may well have been his father's little pal growing up in Cincinnati's

Ken Griffey Jr. made his professional baseball debut with the Mariners Class A farm club in Bellingham, Washington, in the summer of 1987.

©1987 SEATTLE POST-INTELLIGENCER/HARLAN CHINN

Riverfront Stadium, but he was raised mostly by his mother and grandmother and missed them terribly. Two years earlier Griffey was so homesick during his first month in the minors that his mom, Birdie Griffey, had to fly to Bellingham to be with him. The phone bills to Cincinnati would regularly run to more than a thousand dollars a month. In the spring of '89, when word began circulating in the clubhouse that The Kid had made the big club, teammates worked up a prank in which he was informed he was going back to the minors. Griffey broke into tears.

"He was the only player I've ever dealt with where I'd have to call his mother," Woodward said. "I'd known the family a long time, and Senior told me one day, 'You have a great relationship with Birdie. You call her if you need help.' "

Griffey's immaturity took a serious turn in late July when he showed up for a game against the White Sox at Chicago's Comiskey Park with a bone broken in the little finger of his right hand. The official explanation was that he slipped in the shower of his hotel room, but years later club sources acknowledged that the injury occurred when he slammed his hand in anger against a hotel room wall during an argument with a girlfriend.

At the time, he was hitting .287 with 13 home runs and 45 runs batted in. After his August 20 return, he had only three more homers and 16 RBIs, finishing the year at .264. The injury was of no great consequence to him or the club. Even with a healthy Griffey, the Mariners wouldn't have made up much of their 26-game deficit in the AL West, where they finished 73-89. But the incident did point up that a boy still lurked inside the man's body. His mother and his agent would make frequent trips to Seattle to keep him company.

"There was no one to share his big moments—only three hours later by phone," agent Brian Goldberg said. "He was lonely."

So the Mariners devised an answer, according to Jongewaard: "A big reason we signed his father was so he would be with him."

On August 31 of the 1990 season, one of the most endearing moments in sports history unfolded when Ken Griffey Jr. jogged out of the dugout alongside Ken Griffey Sr. as they took their places in the Kingdome outfield for a game against Kansas City.

Senior had been a part-timer with the Red's, his old club, which was in the midst of a wire-to-wire run to the National League pennant and, eventually, a World Series championship. But in mid-August, they needed pitching help from the minor leagues and had to clear a roster spot. The Reds manager, a feisty firebrand by the name of Lou Piniella, asked Griffey Sr., who had been his teammate on the Yankees clubs of the early 1980s, if he would go on the disabled list.

"I'm not hurt," Griffey told Piniella. "I don't want to be doing that."

Instead, he abruptly retired. But according to Goldberg, officials within Major League Baseball, who recognized the publicity potential of a Griffey reunion in Seattle, asked him to hold off. They maneuvered Reds owner Marge Schott into allowing the Reds to release him after he passed through waivers, during which he could have been claimed by any other club.

"I don't know what was done by baseball, but he passed through waivers without a claim, including Seattle," Goldberg said. The ploy not only allowed Seattle to sign him as a free agent, but it also forced Schott to pay the balance of his $520,000 guaranteed contract—after she was thwarted in her demand for a percentage of the gate receipts in Seattle each time the Griffeys played.

The Mariners, almost helpless over twelve years in creating baseball excitement, at least advanced to a Hallmark card moment—a father and son playing on the same major league team. When the forty-year-old Griffey and the twenty-year-old Griffey began their warm-up tosses to each other before the first pitch, millions of sports-playing American men experienced a watershed event, right out of the eyes. It didn't matter that the elder Griffey's career was on fumes, or that cynics dismissed it as a publicity stunt. There was no mistaking that day the joy of the men and the warmth in an otherwise sterile silo known as the Kingdome.

The other outfielder, Buhner, felt like a second son. Among his most cherished baseball souvenirs are a T-shirt with the words "Like Father Like Son" and one of the twenty lineup cards, in triple carbon, taken by manager Jim Lefebvre to the pregame presentation to the umpires at home plate.

"Awesome," Buhner said. "To get an opportunity to see that happen was unbelievable."

On top of delivering history, the family delivered performance. In his first at-bat since being released by the Reds two weeks earlier, Griffey the elder, batting second, singled up the middle. Griffey the younger, hitting third, singled to right.

"I wanted to cry," Junior would say afterward. "It was his day."

The hits helped produce a three-run first inning that led to a 5-2 win over the Royals, who provided a second indelible moment. In the sixth inning, Royals outfielder Bo Jackson, trying to duplicate on the baseball field his legendary football success, hit a shot into

Teammates Harold Reynolds (left), and Alvin Davis had some laughs as Ken Griffey Jr. wipes down his father, Ken Sr., after making a long, running catch in a 1991 game at the Kingdome. ©1991 SEATTLE POST-INTELLIGENCER/KURT SMITH

the left-field corner that looked like a double, but caromed cleanly to Senior. He whirled and fired a one-hopper to second base, where Harold Reynolds tagged out one of the fastest men in sports. Many acres of concrete shook with the standing ovation. In center field, Junior dropped to his knees and buried his grinning face in his glove.

Senior, who won World Series titles in 1975 and 1976 with the Reds but had been a platoon or part-time player for the previous five seasons, found his youth again. In September, he and his son again strummed the baseball heartstrings, hitting back-to-back homers in the first inning of a game in Anaheim against the Angels. In 21 games with Seattle in the 1990 season, Senior hit .377 and drove in 18 runs. Father and son helped lead the breakthrough toward the Mariners' 1991 record of 83-79, their first winning season.

"It seemed to revive Senior a little bit, feeding off Junior's energy," Buhner said. "Senior came up with some big hits and ran down some big outs. He'd come into the dugout and Junior would wave him down with a towel, laughing and giggling, getting each other in headlocks. They had a blast."

Senior's presence also helped muffle his son, who had often masked his teenage insecurity by overacting in the clubhouse. Craig Beatty, a clubhouse aide who was four years younger than Junior, saw the change.

"He was definitely a teenager, but he toned down when Senior got there," he said. "He went from a brash and outspoken kid to someone more respectful of elders. He really quieted down a lot."

The direct influence of Senior was short-lived. Before spring training began in 1991, a car accident in Phoenix left him with a herniated disk. Although he managed to play 30 games and hit .282, back surgery in September ended his career after nineteen major league seasons. He stayed with the club for three more seasons in a variety of jobs—hitting coach, broadcaster, instructional league manager, minor league coach—but never really found a niche. "I don't know why I haven't been able to find exactly what I want to do," he said in 1995.

.⸎.

For Junior, the absence of his father meant that he became, by dint of accomplishment rather than veteran savvy, a team leader. It was a bad time to be a leader. The '92 Mariners, in ownership limbo because of resistance by baseball owners to a Japanese-led group attempting to buy the club, had not invested in personnel in the off-season. A caretaker manager in Bill Plummer and a grim list of injuries created an atmosphere of complaints and bitterness over the regression to a 64-98 mark.

"He was a star and had a lot of clout, but he was very young," said third baseman Mike Blowers, who arrived in the off-season from the New York Yankees. "There was a lot of pressure on him, not just fans, but from veterans in the clubhouse. Guys weren't happy, and it was put on Junior to speak up.... I think that took a toll on him over the course of time."

Griffey, by now a three-time All-Star, understood well and early his immense value to the Mariners. He knew it brought power, although its deployment frequently became a matter of intrigue. His frustration with renewed losing boiled over on fan appreciation day late in the lost season. Having played Griffey without a day off in a while, Plummer told him he could come out of the game after a couple of at-bats. But the game was close, and Plummer decided to keep him in.

"Afterwards, Junior was livid, screaming at Plummer about how he'd lied to him all year," Blowers said. "He was really upset. He said if anyone in this clubhouse was going to be gone, it was Plummer. And he was, quickly."

Plummer's major league career was doomed anyway. But his dismissal seemed to remove any clubhouse doubt as to who would call the shots around the Mariners. Over the years, Griffey would lament about various issues, often implying that if things didn't change, he might not want to stay. A long-running sore point was younger brother Craig, whom the Mariners drafted in the 42nd round in 1991. At 5-foot-11 and 175 pounds, Craig was four inches shorter and thirty pounds lighter than his older brother, and proved to have been a better cornerback at Ohio State than he was a pro baseball outfielder. The draft was a courtesy gesture to the Griffeys. Craig never rose beyond Class AA in seven minor league seasons before being released in June 1997. Both brother and father thought he should have gotten a better break from the Mariners.

"Junior and Senior gave me a hard time about Craig," Jongewaard said. "They really wanted him up. I told them he has to put up some numbers. He's hitting .210 and he's the fastest guy in the organization, but he can't steal bases. I think they resented that I would say that."

Junior was often at odds with club management over the departures of some of his major league teammates. The churn of rosters, an inevitable part of baseball, was acute in Seattle because of undercapitalized owners and the ceaseless struggle for quick respectability. But it was also painful for the sensitive Griffey.

"In both baseball and personal relationships, Junior is loyal to a fault," Goldberg said. "It's hard for him to separate the two." But as the de facto leader, Griffey, was not shy about peddling his influence, telling managers and club executives whom he wanted kept in the club, and occasionally whispering the same to reporters. Griffey was often indulged a hearing, but usually didn't get his way. Frustrations lingered. It couldn't be said that he was always wrong, since it would not be until his seventh season in the majors that the team made the playoffs. But Griffey wore on the bosses as much as losing wore on him.

"Junior found out early in his life how star treatment worked in the Reds clubhouse," Jongewaard said. "But he never was as happy as he should have been. He seemed a confused person." Griffey found some personal happiness in October 1992 when he married Melissa Gay of nearby Gig Harbor. In January 1994 the couple had a son, Trey Kenneth, and in October 1995 a daughter, Taryn Kennedy. The advent of a stable home life dovetailed with another element of constancy–the franchise. The new ownership group, which finally was approved and took over halfway through 1992 to end years of uncertainty, made its first big splash by hiring as manager Lou Piniella, who left his job with the Reds.

The combination of personal and professional calm allowed a physically maturing Griffey to turn 1993 into a breakout year. Smashing club records for runs scored (113), total bases (359), intentional walks (25), and slugging percentage (.617), he also set an AL record for consecutive errorless games by an outfielder: 542.

For a player who disliked the stereotype label of slugger, Griffey hit 45 home runs, 18 more than his career high and second in the majors. More astonishing was a period in late July when he hit homers in eight consecutive games, tying a major league record. The streak, which included six shots measuring more than 400 feet, altered perceptions of Griffey, who to that point lacked only the dimension of consistent power to be labeled the game's most complete and formidable position player.

After Griffey hit his eighth in a row–the first two were in Yankee Stadium, the next four in Cleveland, and only the last two in the homer-friendly Kingdome–in a game against Minnesota, Twins All-Star outfielder Kirby Puckett marveled at what he saw.

"He can do anything he wants," Puckett said. "He's phenomenal. He's fun to watch and he's definitely the best in the game."

That same evening, catcher Dave Valle, who came up to the Mariners in 1984 and was in his final year in Seattle, was equally slack-jawed: "As far as I'm concerned, he's the best thing that's happened to the game in a long time. If he were in any other city, he would be the Michael Jordan of baseball."

In terms of popular appeal, Griffey was indeed on his way to rivaling the basketball megastar. The next summer, he set a record in the All-Star Game fan balloting by receiving more than 6 million votes. The biggest difference between Jordan and Griffey was not the cities but team successes. In the month prior to Griffey's streak of eight

By 1993, first base was a rare stopping point for Ken Griffey Jr. as he emerged as one of the game's great sluggers. ©1993 SEATTLE POST-INTELLIGENCER/KURT SMITH

home runs, Jordan and the Chicago Bulls won their third consecutive NBA title. Griffey's team had yet to do anything significant.

Griffey's father won two titles with the Reds, and Senior rarely missed a chance to remind Junior of that fact. Occasionally, Senior would twist one of his gaudy World Series championship rings so the diamonds faced inward, then slap his palm gently on his son's forehead. The diamonds left a physical impression, but the idea went deeper. Griffey's sense of baseball history and his desire to emulate his father's success created an urgency to win. In the next six years, the passion would drive the Mariners' success, but would also contribute to driving him away from Seattle.

Five years after they almost passed on drafting him, the Mariners were Griffey's team, in his park, in his town. Baseball was at his command. But few things in team sports endure. As swiftly as his mastery developed, changes would come that left him cold. They would lead him to the biggest mistake of his baseball life.

CHAPTER THREE

'Are You Out of Your Mind?'

The problem with being the richest man in the world—aside from insistent skepticism that one so loaded could have any problems—is that just about everyone ranked second or lower backs up a truck to your sofa, hoping to catch spare change.

That was standard drill for Bill Gates, the local kid who made good like good had never been made. Every civic project, social cause, political action committee, construction project, and charity agency looked to the chairman and co-founder of Microsoft for more gruel, even if in a post-Dickensian sort of way—via e-mail. Gates was not an easy hit, having established numerous figurative firewalls between himself and the unwashed. His foundation would take care of his philanthropy, so he did not have to personally look into any big, baleful eyes or touch trembling hands.

Nevertheless, the subject of baseball came up in his presence. Baseball, as the most high-profile street urchin in Seattle public life, often came up during the idle musings of the Northwest elite.

At a restaurant in Kirkland, east of Seattle, Gates attended a dinner gathering of Microsoft's financial managers and guests. Business talk ended and baseball insinuated itself. Gates, with an estimated net worth of more than $15 billion at the time, could have bought and sold all the sports leagues and a couple of the cities they occupied, but he could not imagine mustering a nickel to put in a pot to buy the Mariners.

"Look," he said, "if owners take money from fans and media, then hand it all over to players, there's not enough to put in their own pockets. There's no way in hell I would get involved in the business of baseball. It's insane."

One of the assembled, Craig Watjen, who had retired as Microsoft's chief treasurer in 1992, looked at his former boss.

"You know, Bill," he said, "you're damn right."

He spoke from experience. He was in the insane asylum.

Watjen was one of seven senior managers of the computer software company who two years earlier contradicted the wisdom of Chairman Bill and invested in baseball, the most chaotic of major American sports enterprises, by choosing to rescue the worst expansion franchise in modern sports history.

⚜

By transforming the work tools for businesses and individuals worldwide, Microsoft and other Puget Sound–area enterprises also created stupendous wealth that transformed the region from the way lawyer Slade Gorton had first found it: a vast middle-class area absent either profound poverty or great wealth. In a period shorter than it took the Mariners to reach a .500 season, the Puget Sound region exploded with opportunity as sudden as it was unimaginable. It brought to the Northwest what seemed the birthright of industrial titans of the East, Midwest, and South—the power to do foolish things without regard for financial consequence.

In late 1978, Bill Gates and Paul Allen, a couple of college dropouts in their early twenties, moved their three-year-old computer software company from Albuquerque, New Mexico, back to where they grew up. Graduates of Seattle's prestigious Lakeside School, the pair thought seriously of relocating Microsoft to California's Silicon Valley before deciding that family ties and rain—what better weather to encourage workaholics to stay hunkered indoors?—made better sense. They moved into rented office space in a bank building in downtown Bellevue, the growing suburb east of Seattle. They were now only blocks from the offices and studios of Lester Smith, the broadcast executive who was the Mariners' lead local owner.

Another ambitious local fellow, Craig McCaw, also set up shop in Bellevue, in March 1980. McCaw, a cable-TV entrepreneur, formed a business called Northwest Mobile Telephone to try to create a national cellular telephone network. McCaw and his brothers, John, Bruce, and Keith, also were Seattle natives, Lakeside prep grads, and aggressive businessmen.

Around the same time and twenty miles south, near the Southcenter shopping mall and Seattle-Tacoma International Airport, another young entrepreneur who was to become a key figure in the Mariners drama, Minoru Arakawa, rented one of the ubiquitous two-story business-park warehouses that were replacing the small farms of the Green River Valley. Arakawa was president of Nintendo of America, a fledging outpost of Nintendo Company Ltd. of Japan, the maker of home and coin-operated video games that were popular throughout Asia and were catching on in the West.

Arakawa knew nothing of Gates and Microsoft, nor McCaw and cellular telephones, and those outfits weren't paying much attention to video games. Nor was the world cocking an eyebrow at the goings-on in Seattle's faceless suburbs. But in about a decade, the three enterprises would be so outrageously successful that a handful of employees from each company would find themselves unexpectedly thrown together with the money, passion, and time to engage in the public folly of buying the Mariners.

In common with many international businessmen seeking a foothold in the United States, Arakawa began the business in New York. He soon realized he was on the wrong coast, given the delays associated with shipments from Japan, plus the hassle and expense of a warehouse operation in New Jersey. Besides the business advantages of the Northwest, he had already worked in the area and had grown fond of it.

Born into a wealthy family in Kyoto, Arakawa came to the United States and earned a degree in engineering from MIT. Returning to Japan, he married Yoko Yamauchi, the eldest child of Hiroshi Yamauchi, president of Nintendo Company Ltd. and one of Japan's most independent-minded, successful business leaders. In 1977, Arakawa was assigned by the Japanese construction company for whom he worked to move to Vancouver, British Columbia, where he managed the development of a large condominium project.

Yamauchi, flush with success in Japan, soon had other things in mind for his English-speaking son-in-law. Even though Arakawa had no experience in the video-game business, Yamauchi wanted him to become his point man in North America. Yoko was furiously opposed, recalling how Nintendo seemed to have stolen and hardened her father when she and her siblings, sister Fujiko and brother Katsuhito, were children.

In the 1993 book *Game Over: How Nintendo Zapped an American Industry, Captured Your Dollars, and Enslaved Your Children* (Random House), author David Sheff explored the Yamauchi family dynamic:

> Yamauchi terrified his children. They hated Nintendo, for they saw how it consumed him. The only attention he paid to his daughters and son was to exercise his strong will and issue edicts. He laid down the law at home, enforcing a strict curfew. Yoko had to be home at the dinner table at six, although Yamauchi himself was absent on many of those evenings.

Yoko feared the same kind of obsession would envelop her husband. But the chance to run Nintendo in the United States, well financed, with a substantial growth potential, intrigued Arakawa. Despite his wife's dread and his own inexperience, he left the Vancouver job to accept Yamauchi's offer. Mino, at age thirty-one, and Yoko, twenty-nine, became the first two employees of Nintendo of America.

Once the move to New York faltered, Arakawa began scouting the West Coast for relocation options. Seattle, Tacoma, and Vancouver had the best ports, all about nine shipping days from Japan. Electricity was cheap. Washington's absence of state income tax loomed large, too. "In Seattle, the quality of living and the quality of labor was quite high, with the University of Washington and Boeing," Arakawa said. "We wanted to be here."

So by November 1980, Arakawa and a handful of employees were accepting shipments at their new base of operations in the Seattle suburb of Tukwila. It was hardly the oddest name they would encounter that fall. Yamauchi shipped them two thousand copies of what was said to be Nintendo's hottest new video game. Arakawa installed a copy of the game. On the screen, up popped the name, Donkey Kong.

The group was stunned, believing that teenage Americans, primed by earlier video games full of action and violence, would have no time for something that looked and sounded so insipid. Nor did Arakawa and his staff like the game's look or characters. But Yamauchi refused to take back the order. So the group set about to translate the game into English. As they worked away in disappointment, a knock came at the warehouse door. It was the landlord, Mario Segale, who was upset that the rent hadn't been paid. Arakawa assured him the check was in the mail, and Segale departed, but not without leaving a legacy.

The Nintendo employees suddenly knew they had a name for

the prime character in Donkey Kong, a round little workman with a mustache—Mario. What they didn't know was that they had on their hands what would become the most successful product, and most popular characters, in video game history. In the next few years, Mario would rival Mickey Mouse in terms of familiarity among children and young teenagers.

The game's success was yet another improbable business triumph for Yamauchi, who in 1949 inherited the family business, which began as a maker of playing cards. A fierce competitor, Yamauchi was aggressive from the out-

Hiroshi Yamauchi surprised his native Japan as well as the U.S. sports world when he offered to purchase the Mariners in January 1992.

PHOTO COURTESY OF NINTENDO OF AMERICA

set in diversifying and expanding the business. He made a licensing agreement with Disney in 1959 to market Mickey Mouse & Co. on children's trading cards. In the 1960s he invested in a taxi company and created a "love hotel," rented hourly. Nintendo Company Ltd. went public and began making toys and games as well as cards.

By the 1970s Nintendo moved into audiovisual entertainment with the first video games played on home computers. The games proved immensely popular. Soon they were translated into coin-operated machines that spread wildly through bars, restaurants, and arcades. By 1987, thanks primarily to Donkey Kong, net sales reached more than $1 billion, Nintendo of America sales account-ing for more than half. By 1991, sales were up to $3.3 billion, and pretax profits were more than $1.1 billion. In terms of profits per employee, Nintendo was considered more successful than Toyota.

By the time Yamauchi was approached in 1992 to purchase the Mariners, Nintendo had nearly 80 percent of the $5.3 billion in annual worldwide sales of video games. The company ranked 86th on *Business Week* magazine's Global 1,000 companies, with a market value of about $14.5 billion.

As a 10 percent shareholder in the company, Yamauchi was extraordinarily wealthy even by the high standards of the time in Japan, when the country's rollicking economy sent investors and venture capitalists around the world looking for treasure.

In Seattle, Nintendo of America outgrew Segale's warehouse and bought twenty-seven acres of business park land in Redmond, a woodsy suburb east of Seattle that was on its way to becoming the region's microchip haven. About the same time, Microsoft also moved to Redmond, employing 1,200 people. By then the company had made its long-awaited public stock offering, creating a Wall Street frenzy that shortly made Gates, at thirty-one, a billionaire. In American history no one had accumulated more wealth at so young an age. And the company had barely begun work on what became its most popular software program for home and office computers: Windows.

Meanwhile, at McCaw Cellular, as it was now known, Craig McCaw, his brothers, and company executives were racing around the country buying up licenses to become the nation's largest independent cell phone company. In 1986 there were only a half-million users nationwide, but the company still had revenues of $78 million. By 1987 the idea that cellular phones were going to be the next American electronics rage had caught on among investment analysts and ordinary stock buyers.

The initial public offering of stock in McCaw Cellular resulted in a sale of $2.39 billion, largest in Northwest history. Although the family web of investment made individual values hard to calculate, the Wall Street–estimated value of the holdings of the McCaw brothers was nearly $1 billion. But as a business, McCaw Cellular, with an asset value of more than $1.3 billion, was not yet profitable. The McCaw leadership had grown comfortable with the notion of being asset-rich and profit-free. It was a characteristic they would find most useful when it came to investing in a new business with the same setup—baseball.

In less than ten years, the arrival of personal computers, cheap cellular telephones, and home video games into the national economic mainstream—items that would become almost as standard as toilets in most middle-class homes in America—unleashed a wave of enterprise unprecedented in Puget Sound business history.

≈

As Microsoft, Nintendo, and McCaw Cellular flourished, big-time baseball in the Northwest seemed to be expiring. By the fall of 1991 the Mariners left their fourteen-year doldrums by producing that winning 83-79 season, but outside of a handful of champagne drinkers in the clubhouse, the feat captured the fancy of few people—certainly not that of Jeff Smulyan, the radio entrepreneur who owned the club.

In just his third year in Seattle, Smulyan—whose Indianapolis-based Emmis Broadcasting empire included as a minority investor a former TV weatherman named David Letterman—was in trouble. Despite the winning season, record attendance of 2.1 million, and a player payroll of less than $17 million, Smulyan was losing money and feeling the hot breath of his creditors, who had advanced him most of the money for his $76 million purchase of the club from George Argyros.

The Seattle Times reported in August that Smulyan owed his New York investment bank partner, Morgan Stanley, $39.5 million for the Mariners, with little hope of repayment. The paper said Smulyan's Seattle bank, Security Pacific Bank Washington, had an internal document that said Smulyan's strategy was to put the team up for sale in November in order to move it out of Seattle after the 1992 season.

"I will dispute to the death that that is our strategy," he said. But he also passed along what he viewed was the growing belief throughout the Seattle business community: "I'll tell you this: There are people in that bank who say baseball doesn't work in Seattle.... They have concluded this isn't a viable business."

In September, Smulyan asked community leaders for a plan in forty-five days that would bring the club's revenues for 1992 to within 90 percent of the American League average, an increase of about $15.2 million more for the next season. The money would have to come from a huge increase in season ticket sales from a meager total of 5,500, more corporate sponsorships and

A teary George Argyros (left), announces the sale of the Mariners in August 1989 to Jeff Smulyan (right), and partner Michael Browning.

©1989 SEATTLE POST–INTELLIGENCER/GRANT M. HALLER

advertising, the club's first cable TV deal, and perhaps minority partners in ownership.

If the revenues fell short and specified attendance minimums were not reached, the Mariners' lease with the county-owned Kingdome contained an escape clause that would allow the team to break the deal. But Smulyan never gave the plan much chance to work.

On December 6, he announced the club was for sale. The lease obligated him to offer the club to local buyers for a period of 120 days for a mutually agreed-upon appraised value, which turned out to be $100 million—a price he figured would never be met by anyone in Seattle, particularly in view of the national economic recession well into its second year.

Chuck Armstrong, who lost his job as Mariners president in 1989 when Smulyan bought the team, said Seattle banking sources told him that Smulyan had considered and rejected plans to relocate the M's to his hometown of Indianapolis or to Washington, D.C. The sources said the owner then reached a private agreement to move the club to Tampa, Florida—a claim Smulyan denied.

But Tampa did have a domed stadium needing a baseball tenant. Some major league club owners felt they owed a debt to Tampa, since no fewer than five other franchises had used the city in civic extortion schemes for new stadiums or lease concessions in their own markets—threatening to move to Tampa unless they got what they wanted.

Smulyan denied he was part of any long-term plan to satisfy Tampa interests by moving the Mariners. But there was no doubt Florida business leaders were courting him. They publicly offered guarantees of a season ticket base of 22,000, as well as a $12 million annual cable TV package. But before he could move to Florida, he had to get out of Seattle. The 120-day local-buyers provision, quietly inserted in an earlier lease renegotiation primarily by King County deputy prosecutor Dick Holmquist, would prove to be a critical roadblock.

The campaign to find a local baseball philanthropist was going nowhere, at least at the corporate level. Microsoft spokesperson Marty Taucher said, "Owning a baseball team wouldn't make any sense for us. We're in the software business, not the sports business." Boeing made a similar statement. After reading that, spokesman Rich Long of timber giant Weyerhaeuser said, "Boeing is not in the business of buying baseball teams, and neither are we."

Local business leaders appointed one of their own, respected real estate developer Herman Sarkowsky, a former part-owner of the NFL Seahawks, to head a business/government committee to find a new owner, as well as more business support. His committee reported little progress.

Smulyan, meanwhile, attended an annual meeting of his fellow baseball owners in Miami, where he filled them in on what many longed to hear—the plan to get baseball out of Seattle. Led by a Smulyan mentor, Chicago White Sox owner Jerry Reinsdorf, the owners were looking for reasons to flee the Northwest, where baseball had been, to them, a long-distance, money-losing proposition. The managing director of the Texas Rangers, a small-time oilman with big connections, gave Smulyan his full support: "Whatever Jeff has to do," said George W. Bush, "we're behind him."

Slade Gorton stepped in at this point with another idea for saving major league baseball in Seattle. Back when he was state attorney general, Gorton's suit against the American League over the loss of the Seattle Pilots had resulted in Seattle getting the Mariners. Now a U.S. senator, Gorton wondered about the possibility of Japanese investment in the club.

It was a notion Gorton first pursued four years earlier, when George Argyros tried to buy the San Diego Padres while still owning the Mariners. Gorton responded by putting out a feeler toward Japanese interests.

"The negative reason [to pursue a Japanese buyer] was there wasn't anybody in Seattle," he said. "The positive reason was the nature of the Japanese economy, plus the huge interest in baseball. I was trying to think out of the box, and I guess I did, but it was a bit early."

At that time, Gorton went through the U.S. ambassador to Japan and found no response. This time he had a better connection locally. His secretary placed a cold call to the president of the Japanese-owned Nintendo of America in Redmond. Informed that the topic of a potential meeting was baseball, an assistant to Minoru Arakawa said, "Well, we aren't interested in baseball, but of course, if the senator would like to come see Mr. Arakawa, we would be happy to have him come."

Gorton met with Arakawa and Howard Lincoln, Nintendo's senior vice president, for ninety minutes, a surprising amount of time for a company that wasn't interested in baseball.

"There was no remote commitment," Gorton said, "but there was a great deal of interest in the history and what we had gone through, and how I felt about it."

Gorton's inquiry was for knowledge of any potential investors in Japan. At least, that is how Arakawa soon put it in a phone call to his father-in-law, Hiroshi Yamauchi, head of Nintendo Company Ltd. Yamauchi's bold push with Nintendo into the United States had, by 1991, made Nintendo the No. 1 video game maker in the world, and the most popular toy of any kind. He was predisposed to look favorably upon propositions that might further enhance Nintendo in America. Arakawa explained Gorton's search for individuals or companies that might like to invest.

"You don't have to look for other companies," Yamauchi told Arakawa. "I will do it."

"What did you say?" Arakawa said, incredulous.

"I will do it."

"It's not a good investment."

"I don't care."

The beginning of the end to a fourteen-year quest (twenty-one years, if the abortive Pilots episode is included) to solve the Mariners' ownership travail had come in a five-minute phone call to the other side of the world.

Arakawa, who attended his first Mariners game the previous summer, quickly relayed the news to his senior vice president, a baseball fan and longtime Seattle resident. Howard Lincoln was aghast.

"Are you out of your fucking mind?" Lincoln said. "Do you realize what this means?"

Surprised, Arakawa stepped back. "What?"

"Do you know what it is to own a baseball team? To own the Mariners? It's going to be great for a while, and Mr. Yamauchi will be perceived as a savior. But mark my words, the day will come when we'll be attacked by the media, and you're going to have people calling you and complaining about the Mariners' performance."

Lincoln sputtered on, but Arakawa said Yamauchi was resolute. The money would come not from Nintendo but from Yamauchi's personal wealth, estimated at more than $1 billion. The purchase would be a good public relations gesture, Arakawa said—and it is always good to have a senator as a friend.

❧

Gorton, in fact, was already in the Nintendo corner—the same corner occupied by Microsoft. As a member of the Senate commerce committee, Gorton was influential on a hot topic for both companies: intellectual property rights. Microsoft and Nintendo were losing many millions of dollars in revenues worldwide to counterfeiters who pirated games and software and sold the products without paying licensing fees or royalties.

Arakawa estimated that in 1991 about half the Nintendo games sold worldwide were counterfeit, and Microsoft had a worse ratio. Primary culprits were companies in Taiwan, Hong Kong, South Korea, and China, which would make and smuggle the products around the world.

"Slade asked the FBI and U.S. Customs to enforce the law," Arakawa said. "When the U.S. government asks Asian governments to enforce the law, it helps. It's difficult to measure what slowed the counterfeiting, but we believe the government had a big role. It has improved every year, and now it's much better."

For much of his time in the Senate, Gorton was known as the unashamed congressional voice of Microsoft, whose No. 1 business problem—until the U.S. Justice Department began an antitrust investigation in 1994—was intellectual property rights violations. Gorton attended more than two dozen Senate hearings on the subject, and spent time jawboning officials of the George H. W. Bush and Bill Clinton administrations.

"They were valuable constituents to us," Gorton said of Microsoft, second only to Boeing among the Puget Sound region's top employers. "My distinct impression is that the amount of counterfeiting that goes on in Taiwan has declined dramatically over the last two decades. I think the same is true for South Korea. Both are much more dependent on the U.S. and wanted to be part of the world's trading system, where protection of intellectual property rights is important."

Critics of Microsoft and Nintendo contended the companies hardly needed help, since both were so dominant in their fields that the federal government and various states launched investigations in the 1990s centered on anticompetitive practices that rivals called abusive.

In a landmark verdict in June 2000, a federal judge ordered Microsoft broken in two, saying the company repeatedly violated antitrust laws. He called its leadership "untrustworthy" and its compliance with previous orders that promoted competition "illusory" and "disingenuous." But in 2002 the breakup order was overturned on appeal, and Microsoft in a settlement agreed to restrictions on some of its business conduct and products. Many software industry observers called the consequences to Microsoft's position and future more or less a flesh wound.

As early as 1989, Nintendo was the subject of Congressional hearings over monopolistic business practices with similarities to the charges later brought against Microsoft, principally the bundling of software with popular hardware products in order to close out software competition and keep profits artificially high. By April 1991, Nintendo settled with the Federal Trade Commission on fifty consent decrees that forced the company to refrain from price fixing and to offer rebates to many consumers. But relative to Nintendo's wealth and power, the punishment was more an embarrassment than a derailing.

As with Microsoft, Nintendo remained in its field a ruthless defender of its considerable turf and a conqueror of silicon worlds. In the coming months, the defiant, hardball attitude of both companies would prove crucial in another world. The boardroom barons of baseball had some hard stuff waiting for the Northwest tech tycoons.

CHAPTER FOUR

McCaw Loses Money, Nintendo Makes Money, Microsoft Prints Money

S lade Gorton thought he had pneumonia. It was two days before Christmas 1991, he had just returned home from a miserable U.S. trade mission trip to Moscow, and he felt like hell. But the phone was ringing, and politicians rarely can afford the endless ring. It was Minoru Arakawa, calling from Hawaii, where he and his wife, Yoko, were vacationing with Howard and Grace Lincoln. He delivered news that almost instantly restored Gorton's health.

"Mr. Senator," Arakawa said, "my father-in-law says Seattle and the state of Washington have been very good to us. We have done extremely well here. We believe we owe something to the community. If you need $100 million to buy a baseball team, you've got $100 million."

Quicker than a TV evangelist's laying on of hands, Gorton's case of the crud vanished.

"This is the finest Christmas present I have ever received," Gorton told Arakawa, a rare exuberance washing over his patrician demeanor. Gorton could barely believe it: The long, local baseball nightmare might be over. Out of the video-screen blue, the Mariners had a sugar daddy, Hiroshi Yamauchi, even if he was unknown in Seattle and cared very little about baseball. But because he was Japanese, the nightmare would have a six-month final scene, one that would stretch to the White House as well as across America's front pages and over the Pacific Ocean.

The offer came at a time when anti-Japanese sentiment was running strong in places beyond the Northwest. The booming Japanese economy produced a cadre of offshore investors who were snapping up various icons of American pop culture: California golf courses such as Pebble Beach, La Costa, and Riviera; Columbia Pictures movie studio; Rockefeller Center in New York City. Investors from Japan bought into National Hockey League clubs, minor league baseball teams, and the 1989 winner of the Kentucky Derby, Sunday Silence. In the minds of Lincoln and others at Nintendo of America, the threat of Japanese economic dominance was at the heart of pressure the company faced in Congress, in the video-game industry, and in the courts.

Having battled the lords of baseball off and on for twenty years, Gorton knew that in this atmosphere the appearance of Japanese encroachment upon the game's self-styled sacred greensward would unleash among owners heavy public scorn and heavier private resistance. To have a chance, Yamauchi's gesture would need U.S. partners and local faces. When Arakawa and Lincoln returned from vacation, they met with Gorton at Arakawa's lakeside home, once owned by film director Stanley Kramer, in the exclusive Seattle suburb of Medina.

"He said we'd need to have a group of really local people who would participate as minority owners," Lincoln said. "We said fine. And he said we'd also need to get some community leaders."

First up on the list was John Ellis, an attorney and one of Gorton's closest friends. Ellis was CEO of Puget Power & Light Company, the region's largest electric utility. He was used to controversy and the public spotlight, having headed his company's dubious foray into nuclear power in the 1980s that turned into one of the largest economic debacles in state history. What better experience for a major league baseball team?

Ellis, sixty-one years old, was planning early retirement. A Seattle native, he was much more into sailing and boating than baseball. He and his older brother, Jim, also had a long history of involvement in civic causes and public works projects. Earlier, John Ellis had helped in the initial futile search for local investors after it became clear that Mariners owner Jeff Smulyan was attempting to bail out of Seattle.

A few days after the meeting at Arakawa's home, Arakawa and Lincoln, along with John Bauer, managing partner of the Coopers Lybrand accounting firm, walked into Ellis's office in Bellevue. They revealed that a buyer for the Mariners had been found.

"I was astounded," Ellis said. "I thought, 'It can't be!' "

They outlined the plan to Ellis: A key link in Hiroshi Yamauchi's purchase would be a group of local investors. Would Ellis join the group? He said he would love to help—except that baseball was too rich a game for him. The visitors left, but they would soon be back.

Ellis had a lunch conversation with another longtime Seattle business figure, Dave Cohn, a prominent restaurateur who was on the committee led by Herman Sarkowsky to find a local buyer for the club. Cohn said he had received a call from some kid at Microsoft named Larson, who was interested in baseball. But Cohn said he never took Larson seriously.

"It was just typical of the way those Microsoft guys were viewed at the time," Ellis said. "He wasn't part of the establishment."

⁂

Almost none of the Mariners' eventual new investors—including the "kid" from Microsoft, Chris Larson—were among the old Seattle elites. Yet Larson was one of the nation's richest people. He also was, in the words of another soon-to-be Mariners part-owner, Wayne Perry, "so deep in the plumbing" at Microsoft that few outside the insular world of code-writing programmers knew him.

Larson, thirty-two at the time, grew to love baseball via TV. He attended a Pilots game as a ten-year-old and was in the nether reaches of the Kingdome for the Mariners' inaugural opener. In seventh-grade English class, he sneaked in a transistor radio to listen to the World Series, back when the Series was a day event and children proved their dedication to baseball by conducting covert operations below the gaze of America's educational despots.

Larson was four years behind Bill Gates at Lakeside School, and he worked for Gates and Paul Allen in Albuquerque during the first summer of Microsoft's existence. He quickly became a trusted friend and colleague. Stories have Gates taking Larson with him on high-speed drives late at night into the New Mexico desert. Fixed in company folklore are episodes in which the pair would drive to highway construction sites and fire up the engines on the giant yellow-iron machinery to stage night races.

After graduating from Princeton, Larson was plied with stock options in 1981 to return to work for his buddy Bill in Bellevue as chief programmer for development of the pioneer MS-DOS software. When Microsoft made its initial public stock offering in 1986, it made instant billionaires out of Gates, co-founder Paul Allen, and president Steve Ballmer, and multimillionaires out of Larson and at least two thousand other Microsoft employees, nearly all in the Puget Sound region. By the time Larson became curious about the Mariners in 1991, Microsoft was valued at $21.9 billion, more than General Motors.

As the search for a local Mariners buyer heated up in mid- to late 1991, the heaviest hitters at Microsoft—Gates, Allen, and Ballmer—showed no interest. Allen had already spent some of his play money to buy the NBA Portland Trail Blazers in 1988. But below the top layer of Microsoft players, Larson was part of a group of relatively young senior leaders, some ready to retire with wealth that was burning holes in their imaginations. Craig Watjen, the retiring treasurer, said Larson was the most baseball-passionate in a group that included himself, chief financial officer Frank Gaudette, chief counsel Bill Neukom, and several others. But even with all their wealth, devoting $100 million to a money-losing project was too much of a stretch.

"We didn't have the money to do it on our own without someone with deeper pockets," Larson said. "Several people, including his father, approached Bill, and he had no interest. At the same time Frederick & Nelson [a popular, venerable department store in downtown Seattle] was going bankrupt. Many people in the community thought it was more important to save Frederick's than the Mariners. Bill had a lot of people pressuring him to bail out Frederick's."

Still, at the rate the Microsoft share price was soaring, more than one civic rescue seemed possible for Chairman Bill.

"There was the thought in the back of our minds that if we did due diligence and gathered enough information, that Frank would approach Bill," Watjen said. But in the fall, Frank Gaudette was diagnosed with lymphatic cancer; he died the following April at the age of fifty-seven. The illness of Gaudette, the architect of

Microsoft's dazzling financial performance, pushed aside any internal discussion of a Mariners purchase. But it didn't stop knocks at the door.

Tipped about Larson's interest, Gorton late in December called him with news about the willingness of Nintendo's boss to play Mr. Big. Larson quickly contacted a number of his colleagues—Craig Watjen, Jeff Raikes, Rob Glaser, husband and wife Carl Stork and Judith Bigelow, plus two later investors, Bill Marklyn and Buck Ferguson—who agreed with him that roles as minority owners just might work for them.

Gorton made another call, this one to a businessman he had known for years who was also a personal friend. Wayne Perry, a native of Olympia, Washington, was a straight shooter, staunch Republican, avid outdoorsman, and Little League coach. He was also the No. 2 man at McCaw Cellular, as trusted as any of the McCaw brothers and perhaps more valuable to boss Craig McCaw, who could be as oblique as Perry was direct. Perry spent a fair amount of his work time in Washington, D.C., where the ever-changing rules of the Federal Communications Commission impacted the cell-phone industry, and where Gorton would some-times take up telecom industry issues with the commerce committee. This time, Perry was in his Bellevue office when Gorton called from the capital. Perry was surprised. Normally he was the one calling the senator. But this was neither an election year for Gorton, nor was any legislative issue pressing.

"When the senior senator calls, you don't treat him as someone selling whole life insurance," Perry said. "So I sat up straight in my chair and said, 'Yes, Slade, what can I do for you?'"

Said Gorton, "Look, you've been following what's happening with the Mariners. Smulyan wants to sell it, or he's going to move it—there's no question he's going to move it. I have secured Nintendo of America as the lead investor. We need significant, material local participation.

"You've made a lot of money. It's time to give back."

Perry was taken aback, but only momentarily.

"You know, that's a great line for a senator; it also rang true," Perry said. "Like a lot of young guys [Perry was forty-one], we worked awfully hard. People didn't know what we were doing. For years in the media, there would be reports about the fifteen largest businesses in the area, and we were never on the list. We all chuckled, because if they had ever figured us out, we'd have been on the list. We were below the radar."

Perry was in, joining as representative of John McCaw, who had already been contacted by Gorton. Perry and McCaw Cellular's recently retired chief financial officer, Rufus Lumry, would later buy Mariners shares from John McCaw. The three formed the McCaw section of the budding purchase group, joining with seven Microsofties and the Arakawa-Lincoln tandem from Nintendo representing the principal purchaser, Yamauchi. A final piece would be added—a link to what suddenly had to be classified as "old" Seattle—when Frank Shrontz, chairman and CEO of the Boeing Company, was invited to join. His investment, like the eventual investments of Ellis, Lincoln, and Arakawa, was a token $10,000, but "we really needed the support of key community leaders," Lincoln said. The group would soon organize as the Baseball Club of Seattle.

❧

The first three weeks of 1992 became a whirlwind, albeit a quiet one: The public, and Major League Baseball, would know nothing of the group's existence until January 23. In meetings at Nintendo headquarters as well as at the Bellevue Athletic Club, with Gorton listening in via teleconference from Washington, D.C., the group decided it would not only pay $100 million to Smulyan, but would also commit to an extra $25 million of operating capital.

Yamauchi, willing to fund the entire $125 million, was talked into accepting partners he had never met and reducing his investment to $75 million. Larson was the next-largest investor at $27.5 million. John McCaw put up $11.25 million. No one else was in for more than $3 million. Of his huge stake in the local investment package, Larson said, "I guess I was the only one foolish enough to risk an irresponsible portion of my wealth in such a risky venture."

Because of his high community profile and CEO experience, John Ellis was approached again—but this time not for money. He was asked by Lincoln, Arakawa, and Gorton to lead the group in preparation for its bid to buy the M's. Ellis, whose last emotional interest in Seattle baseball evaporated when the minor-league Rainiers shut down prior to the arrival of the Pilots, was floored. And flattered.

"They wanted me to put it together and represent a group that had no representative of its own," Ellis said. "I have never approached anything in my life with less knowledge of how to do it." But Ellis, with retirement imminent, had the time as well as the connections with the Seattle community. He also had experience managing large projects. The business of baseball could be learned.

Since no one had immediate contacts with the game's important people, Ellis's first major decision was to bring in Chuck Armstrong, the club president from 1983–89 under former owner George Argyros. He had been interim athletic director at the University of Washington. Armstrong was hired as a consultant, advising the newbies on baseball protocol and politics.

He wasn't in the job very long before he noticed something unexpected.

"It was amazing how they got along," he said. "Nintendo and Microsoft were business rivals in some areas, so when we'd look for potential season ticket buyers, each company would give us names of customers and suppliers. But one company wouldn't ask to see the rival's list. It was all very ethical. And nobody talked about how much money they were going to make."

Or not make, as would prove to be the case. The three companies involved in ownership had such different styles that divergent expectations about losses could have thrown off the works. That was particularly true for the investors from Microsoft, who were not accustomed to losing money or deals.

"Those guys historically negotiated with a D-8 Caterpillar," said McCaw's Wayne Perry. "They'd just go over the top of people. I lived in a different world. In telecom, you cajoled people." Neither was Nintendo used to operating a losing enterprise. During an early meeting of the group, profit-and-loss statements from previous Mariners seasons were distributed. Perry saw Arakawa's eyes grow large.

"Are those brackets, like losses?" Arakawa said, looking at the forms. "Is that really true?"

The red ink didn't bother Perry. In the telecommunications industry, paper deficits were standard operating procedure. Before things started going sideways in the meeting, he cut the tension.

"I really feel good about this group," he said, smiling. "You've made the guys from McCaw feel good because you put together pro formas that make it look like us—big losses all the time. Makes us feel at home."

The McCaw comfort with high-risk deal-making was reinforced in a later meeting when it was discovered that the payment to baseball's central fund upon entry to the American League was set at $2 million more than expected. The Microsoft contingent balked: Late changes in payment wasn't how they did business.

"Look, guys, this is how it works," Perry said. "I've done more deals than anybody in this room. You don't go into a $125 million deal thinking there won't be some give and take. Did I think when we got into this that we might have to kick in more than our minimum investment? Yeah. As far as I'm concerned, this is in the ballpark."

After some grousing, the Microsoft folks went along. Soon the group had its own little joke: "McCaw loses money. Nintendo makes money. Microsoft prints money."

There was little interest in the group for any approach to ownership in which the lust for attention, power, and press conferences gets in the way of baseball, in the style of the Yankees' George Steinbrenner. Part of the explanation was that many in the group were relatively young and at peak business productivity.

"We were all busy," Perry said. "It's not like I'm going to go down to watch batting practice for four hours because I have nothing else to do and then tell the manager what the lineup should be. You had all these young guys who were still growing their businesses. They had day jobs, and that was good."

Another part of the low profile came from having a superior sports ownership model in town. From 1976 to 1988, the Nordstrom family of retail clothing fame owned the NFL Seahawks. Family members shunned the sports spotlight and deferred nearly all questions about football to club management. As a partial result, the team was highly successful, playing weekly in the fall to a packed Kingdome with a season-ticket waiting list that exceeded 20,000. John Nordstrom became one of the NFL's most influential owners partly because he cared so little for public glory.

The family was the personification of the Scandinavian Lutheran reticence that had been a prime element of the Seattle leadership character for many years. Humorist Garrison Keillor, although he was speaking of his fellow Minnesotans, also captured old-school Seattle when he once described the standard response to an invitation to join in the bright lights and good times: "You go ahead. I'll be fine."

"Whether that's how Nordstrom did it exactly or not, we adopted the model," Perry said. "That's where you let the baseball people talk about baseball, and all the ownership group should say is, 'Go team!' You don't say anything about pulling the lefty to face the next hitter, or say how you hope we trade so-and-so."

The approach also dovetailed with the Japanese cultural influence from Nintendo, which emphasizes group over individual, as well as the aversion of major investor Chris Larson to publicity and attention.

"If we pulled out sodium pentothal and had gone around the room, there were some who would have liked to run a different model," Perry said. "They might have viewed themselves as a mini-Steinbrenner. But Howard, Chris, and I were big advocates of the Nordstrom way. You got a sense that's what Nintendo wanted, so it was adopted by consensus."

❧

The time came to approach Major League Baseball with the proposed Mariners deal. A Seattle delegation led by Mayor Norm Rice was quietly assembled and booked to meet January 22 in the New York office of baseball commissioner Fay Vincent, who had been publicly supportive of finding local ownership in Seattle. The Seattle group figured that approaching a more sympathetic Vincent first instead of making a direct offer to Smulyan would help their chances, especially since the issue of Japanese investment would have to be dealt with quickly at baseball's highest level.

After the meeting, the purchase plan would be announced publicly.

The plan quickly evaporated.

On January 21, Rice was preparing to travel to New York from a conference in Washington, D.C., as was Slade Gorton. John McCaw was already in New York, and Frank Shrontz was on his way in a Boeing corporate jet. John Ellis was rolling up to Sea-Tac Airport a little after noon when his mobile phone rang. It was Howard Lincoln, with bad news.

"They don't want to meet with us," he said. "You'd better get back here to my office right away."

Lincoln knew that majority Japanese ownership would be a tough sell, but he thought the group would at least get an audience with Vincent to explain the plan. Instead, the commissioner called Nintendo's New York law firm to say any meeting now was inappropriate, because the offer should first go to Smulyan.

"Fay figured out what was happening, and somehow Smulyan, who was back there, found out too," Lincoln said. "It was clear we were not going to go about it the way we wanted. So we had to think about going public right away."

Ellis drove to Nintendo's headquarters in Redmond, where he was hustled into the Donkey Kong Room, named for the video game that launched Nintendo's astounding success. Usually populated by casually dressed, youthful Nintendo employees, the conference room quickly filled with a rush of suits, followed by the drawing of shades.

"Something big was going on, but we didn't know what," said Perrin Kaplan, a Nintendo vice president for marketing.

Ellis was joined by Lincoln, Minoru Arakawa, Chris Larson, John Bauer, and a handful of attorneys and executives. Included was Bob Hartley, a former newspaper publisher working for Jay Rockey Company, Seattle's premier public relations firm. Hired three weeks earlier to help direct the public presentation, Hartley and his staff would make things happen in less than twenty-four hours.

"There was a lot of tension in that room—some very unhappy people," Hartley said. "We got Slade on teleconference, and he was really steamed."

After his experience in the 1970s with the Pilots lawsuit, Gorton knew the owners of baseball would operate in their own self-interest unless extraordinary pressure was brought to bear. As a federally protected, unregulated monopoly, supported by a 1922 Supreme Court decision that conferred the status, the American and National Leagues were not accountable to either market forces or governmental supervision. Besides having exclusive power to determine which cities and which individuals would be allowed into their exclusive club, the team owners were not obligated to explain publicly their standards for acceptance or rejection.

Until the New York Giants and Brooklyn Dodgers moved to San Francisco and Los Angeles, respectively, in the late 1950s, major league baseball did not exist west of Kansas City. Until the first expansion in 1961, baseball had only sixteen teams. By 1992, there were twenty-six clubs. Any ownership change, franchise relocation, or further expansion was subject to review by a committee of owners, who would establish their own standards of suitability, then make a recommendation to the entire group. The commissioner, appointed by the owners, typically had only modest influence as an administrator and figurehead. Policy was the province of the owners.

Standard practice for ownership transfers involved backdoor inquiries by prospective purchasers to the ownership committee, which could quietly discourage an unsavory bid before any public embarrassment. But the Seattle bidders for the Mariners figured the back door had just been slammed on them, so they would go through the front door the next day. Gorton and the group agreed that public pressure would be the only way to get the upper hand in what was presumed to become a high-profile legal and political fight.

There was apprehension that the Major League Baseball (MLB) rulers would thwart the maneuver by announcing rejection of the Seattle group before it had a chance to make an offer. But as the 6 P.M. news passed without any such report from New York or Seattle, some of the pressure eased. Hartley had already prepared remarks for all of the speakers at the pending news conference, so he and his staff made a round of phone calls to community leaders and VIPs informing them that the event had been moved up by twenty-four hours.

Lincoln, working with a few others in the Donkey Kong Room until 10 P.M., cleared up a final piece of business. Baseball required that any prospective purchase group designate an owner's representative, an investor authorized to speak for all. Since Yamauchi would not be in Seattle, and his Nintendo designates Arakawa and Lincoln were not eager, Lincoln turned to Ellis to take on the additional task.

"Why don't we put you down as owner's rep?" Lincoln said to Ellis.

"What does that mean?" Ellis said.

"Well, it's no big deal. We just put you down for this kind of stuff we're doing tomorrow. We just have to move quickly."

"OK, put me down."

Without realizing it, Ellis, the retiring utility executive with a $10,000 stake and no particular passion for a game that was a joke of a business, suddenly went from planner to titular head of the infant organization. In a few months he would find himself the one Seattleite with full authority over a controversial international enterprise owned by some of the world's wealthiest entrepreneurs. At the moment, however, he knew none of this.

"Hell, I didn't know what a scouting system was," Ellis said. "I didn't know anything."

The ballroom of the Madison Hotel in downtown Seattle was overflowing the next morning with media, civic leaders, and some curious fans. They heard that, in contradiction to all that passed for conventional baseball wisdom in Seattle, a group of mostly local investors would pay Smulyan the agreed-upon $100 million to keep the Mariners safe at home.

"What got me as I walked out there," Lincoln said, "was I realized, damn, this thing was being broadcast live on all the television stations. As I was making my remarks, I saw a TV monitor with my face on it—God, this is really big!'"

Lincoln, Nintendo's senior vice president, may have been the face on TV, but it was the specter behind him—Japanese businessman Hiroshi Yamauchi—that drew immediate opposition from MLB and criticism elsewhere in the country. Not long after the fiftieth anniversary commemoration of the Japanese attack on Pearl Harbor, and following on the heels of President George H. W. Bush's failed trade mission to Japan, Yamauchi's offer to fund 60 percent of the $125 million deal represented to some Americans yet another predatory Japanese incursion into U.S. business and culture.

At his own press conference in Kyoto, Yamauchi attempted to make clear that he hadn't gone looking. Seattle came to him, and his offer "is the result of a request from the local community, Washington state. I have received requests from the state governor and senator. After careful study, we made the decision because we felt we had to respond to the state."

Before the day was out, baseball commissioner Fay Vincent issued a statement in New York saying baseball "has a strong policy against approving investors from outside the U.S. and Canada," declaring that approval of the deal "was unlikely." Other national political and business leaders chimed in with negative views. The conflict sent the story to the top of that night's *CBS Evening News* and to the front page of *The New York Times* the next day.

But as the story moved ahead over the next few days, reaction grew decidedly more mixed nationally. Japan for years had been the state of Washington's No. 1 foreign customer for airplanes, timber, and agricultural products, and the state was actually running a trade surplus. Investing in baseball was little different in Washington than the $300 million a Japanese company had invested in a paper plant in Port Angeles, or the $250 million another Japanese company spent on a semiconductor plant in Puyallup, all without international controversy.

It was also disclosed that Japanese investors already owned minor league teams in Vancouver, B.C.; Birmingham, Alabama; and Visalia, California. It wasn't long before the words "bigotry" and "racism" were aimed at Vincent and team owners. *New York Times* columnist Dave Anderson called baseball's thinking "narrow as a bat handle." It was learned that MLB had nothing in its charter that precluded foreign investment, only "a recommended policy" adopted a couple of years earlier that was much closer to a gentlemen's agreement.

Sentiment was shifting rapidly against baseball's xenophobic objections, particularly since the Baseball Club of Seattle—the owners' group—made it clear that Yamauchi's investment would be operated locally.

The change in public opinion wasn't strictly spontaneous. Lincoln approved a national media campaign, run by PR man Hartley, which targeted political leaders and commentators on politics and sports. "We were attempting to bring pressure on the owners to come to the table," Hartley said. "We tried everything we could think of to get hold of people. It went on for a month, and the drumbeat didn't quiet at all. At one point, some of the owners insisted we not fan the flames. So we sort of called off the hounds, because there was a point where irritation could have gotten in the way."

Meanwhile, in the back room, political arm-twisting was under way. Gorton was given the specific assignment of contacting perhaps the one owner who wasn't predisposed to hate him from his history of baseball battles—George W. Bush, the Texas Rangers' managing director. The Republican ties between Gorton and Bush's father, the president of the United States, were well established. The emotional investment of the Bush family in baseball didn't hurt Gorton's pitch, either. The previous summer, George H. W. Bush became the first president to attend a major league baseball game outside the United States when he visited Toronto for the All-Star Game.

"We had two phone conversations," Gorton said of Bush the younger. "I called him on the basis that his father knew me and would vouch for me as a good guy, and to tell him that I was a part of this [baseball plan for Seattle]. I told him it wasn't part of some underground plot. What you saw was what you got."

As to whether the information was passed to the White House, Gorton said, "It would astound me if the younger Bush didn't call his father. I would imagine President Bush would not want his son voting against Japanese ownership of a major league team. He was an internationalist and Japan was one of our great allies. He would not want his son accused of xenophobia."

In his 2002 book, *The Last Commissioner: A Baseball Valentine*, Vincent wrote that he was taking a public flogging over his stance against Japanese ownership in Seattle until Bush the younger intervened with his fellow owners. Vincent quotes Bush: "Wait a minute. Why are we letting Fay get killed for this? We took the

Nintendo of America senior vice president Howard Lincoln, Senator Slade Gorton, and Seattle Mayor Norm Rice enjoy the remarks of John Ellis (far left) at a press conference on January 23, 1992, announcing the bid to purchase the Mariners from owner Jeff Smulyan. ©1992 SEATTLE POST-INTELLIGENCER/PAUL JOSEPH BROWN

vote. It's our decision, and not his. We should speak up. This has nothing to do with Fay."

By March, Vincent and the owners, who also had heard from others in the Washington congressional delegation, including Speaker of the House Tom Foley, began downplaying the Japanese issue. Confirmation that the political pressure had been effective came in a startling phone call for Chuck Armstrong, the former Mariners president who was now working with the owners' group.

"Mr. Armstrong?"

"Yes?"

"The president would like to talk with you."

"The president of what?"

Quickly realizing his folly, Armstrong sat straight up and began apologizing. He had met President Bush in Seattle in 1987 when, as vice president, Bush was stumping for Gorton's election. Armstrong had invited Bush to a Mariners game in the Kingdome. The visit was going well until a Mariner hit a home run, which was greeted in those days by a loud, fake-cannon shot from the hokey "Good Ship Mariner," which rose on a platform beyond the center-field fence.

"Somebody," Armstrong said, "forgot to tell the Secret Service."

Apparently no long-term harm was done, because Bush was eager to know about the progress of Seattle baseball since he last found himself nearly pressed to the floor of the owner's suite by large, panicky men in dark suits.

"He asked me my view of the ownership group, and the chances for baseball success in Seattle," Armstrong said. "It was a brief, friendly call."

Soon it was obvious that sentiment about Yamauchi's role had shifted from "hell, no" to "well, maybe." The ownership committee agreed to meet with Ellis and the ownership group in Chicago to hear the Seattle proposition.

"The outside political pressure was sufficient that baseball felt it couldn't turn us down," Ellis said. "On the other hand, they felt they couldn't let this get out of control. They wanted to make sure that this deal wouldn't open the floodgates to foreign investment."

What remained undiluted was a deeper resentment on the part of club owners toward baseball in Seattle. The Mariners' long-term inability to make progress on the field or at the turnstile greatly annoyed the owners, who generally agreed with their compatriots Argyros and Smulyan that baseball would never work there.

"The American League owners hated us and they hated Slade," said Armstrong, who was working the baseball phones on the group's behalf. "They thought it was a terrible town. They said the Mariners got here not because of a groundswell of public sentiment; they got here as a quick-fix settlement of a lawsuit."

Bud Selig, the car dealer who brought the Pilots in 1969 from Seattle to Milwaukee, said the objections to the purchase were not grounded in xenophobia.

"We were more concerned about Seattle than foreign ownership; after Danny Kaye, Argyros, and Smulyan, it looked like mission impossible," said Selig, who would succeed Vincent as commissioner. "It was historical skepticism."

The contempt went back years. Armstrong recalled a conversation with Bill Dwyer, the Seattle attorney who in 1975 won the breach-of-contract case that produced the Mariners, and who later became a highly respected federal judge. Owners were recording their meetings back then, Nixon-style. Dwyer told Armstrong he heard one tape in which owner Charlie Finley of the Oakland A's could be heard saying of the Seattle baseball stewards, "Let's lead 'em on, then we'll fuck 'em."

Armstrong got his own earful during a conversation with Chicago White Sox owner Jerry Reinsdorf, the most outspoken of the current anti-Seattle group of AL owners and a key member of the ownership committee. Reinsdorf was also owner of the NBA Chicago Bulls, who were about to win the second of six championships with Michael Jordan, so he had no shortage of sports-business swagger.

"I don't know whether he felt he needed to deliver a team to Tampa," Armstrong said, "but he said to me, 'Look, you've been out there. George is a great guy. Jeff's tried. It's not going to work. When are you going to get it in your heads? It's never going to work in Seattle. The Pilots didn't work. There wouldn't be a team there now except for the lawsuit. It's too far to go, and you play in that awful Kingdome.' "

In late April, Reinsdorf fired another broadside, this one publicly questioning Nintendo's monopoly business practices that were punished in 1991 by the Federal Trade Commission, as well the company's minority-hiring record, the subject of a 1990 complaint by Seattle civil-rights activists. He also lamented that he had yet to meet any of the principal investors.

"How can I vote when I haven't met with Mr. Yamauchi, Mr. Larson, or Mr. McCaw?" he said. "Nobody on the committee, to the best of my knowledge, has had a conversation with them."

Howard Lincoln said Reinsdorf and the committee had agreed to confidentiality, and he was furious with Reinsdorf over the public discussion of the purchase attempt. "I'm very disappointed in his conduct," Lincoln said. "It doesn't appear he followed the rules at all."

Finally, in early June, five of the prospective Mariners owners—Lincoln, Arakawa, Ellis, McCaw, and Larson—flew to Chicago for their long-delayed audience with the MLB ownership committee. Gathering in the hotel lobby before the meeting, members of the Seattle contingent were surprised to see Chris Larson show up in a dumpy-looking shirt. A feverish collector of baseball memorabilia, Larson was wearing a Detroit Tigers jersey that had once belonged to Ty Cobb. The shirt was complete with holes, dirt, and seventy years of history.

"I thought it would be an ice-breaker in a meeting in which we had no idea how we would be received by Major League Baseball," Larson said ten years later. "We had never met any of these people before. I have never seen them since."

Lincoln was momentarily aghast. "I thought, 'What the hell is that thing?' When he told me, I started chuckling, because it was Chris's way of making the point that we were really serious baseball people."

The committee was not impressed. Nor did the committee care for any ownership proposal that left Yamauchi with control. The committee insisted that a single individual—not a corporation, as was proposed—had to be the club's managing general partner. At one point, Lincoln gestured toward Minoru Arakawa and asked the committee if Yamauchi's son-in-law, a longtime Seattle-area resident, was acceptable as the managing general partner. Told no, Lincoln said, "What about me?" Same answer.

Lincoln was stunned.

Vice President George H. W. Bush attended a Kingdome game in July 1987 at the invitation of Mariners president Chuck Armstrong. Five years later, President Bush called Armstrong with questions about the proposed purchase of the club by Japanese businessman Hiroshi Yamauchi. PHOTO COURTESY OF CHUCK ARMSTRONG

"It was the first time that I had experienced what I felt was discrimination," he said. "It really pissed me off. I knew Mino wouldn't say anything. We'd been partners through so much, I knew if anyone would do any talking it would be me. He's a gentleman. I made it clear I found it offensive."

Lincoln unleashed a tirade that chastised the owners for their apparent attempt to create a second-class citizen of his good friend. "He exhibited total outrage," said Ellis. "It quieted them down." The would-be Seattle purchasers walked out, apparently no closer to a sale.

On the flight back, Lincoln had a better idea: John Ellis. He was unaffiliated with Nintendo money, yet he was the one guy from Seattle that the ownership committee had come to know and like over the previous four months. Lincoln, as Nintendo of America vice president, had responsibility to protect his boss's investment, but he saw no threat in a structure that would give Ellis binding control of the franchise. "Not only did we know John wouldn't go to Bolivia, we knew that if worse came to worst, we could stop him before he got on the plane."

Arakawa consulted with Yamauchi, who agreed to reduce his ownership share to 49 percent while shifting part of his investment into the $25 million in operating capital the purchasers agreed to put up. A seven-member board of directors made up of U.S. residents was created (Lincoln, Arakawa, Larson, McCaw, Watjen, Ellis, and Shrontz), with Ellis as managing general partner. Ownership was divided into classes of A and B stock that precluded Yamauchi from having majority control, even though he had 60 percent of the total investment.

At least one insider viewed the concessions as an insult.

"The final requirements were, I thought, outrageous and humiliating to Yamauchi," said Gorton, tracking the maneuvers from the Senate. "Here was a man who made this civic gesture, and as soon as it's public he's excoriated as one of these grasping Japanese businessmen trying to take over everything.

"At one level, you would have thought the guy would have said the hell with it. 'You don't want me? I'm out of here.' "

That didn't happen. No insult was taken, in large part because of the trust and regard in the partnership that had developed over months in the foxhole.

"We were all kind of steeled by the difficult fight, and we had become awfully comfortable that we were all in this together," Lincoln said. "We [Nintendo] figured we could be flexible and everything would still be OK. This was a good group of people and everybody trusted each other. We realized we were going down a path of group endeavor, that there wouldn't be a majority owner who would run everything while the minority owners would have nothing but a nice seat at the stadium."

⁂

Over the weekend, Ellis called Jerry Reinsdorf with the revised ownership structure. As the one owner on the committee who was actually reading the Seattle documents, Reinsdorf was in position to pass quick judgment on the proposed changes. After hearing the proposal, Reinsdorf said Seattle had done it: The clear lines of local control were sufficient to win his endorsement. He asked Ellis to return to Chicago, alone and quietly, for final approval. At their Chicago meeting, Reinsdorf tossed one more curve: Ellis

To celebrate approval of the Baseball Club of Seattle as purchasers of the Mariners, a second opening night was held July 16, 1992. Among the invitees were numerous political leaders, including Slade Gorton (far left), and Seattle Mayor Norm Rice (second from right). ©1992 SEATTLE POST-INTELLIGENCER/ELLEN M. BANNER

must put up a significant financial interest beyond his token $10,000 stake.

"This came totally out of the blue; I had no idea I was even going to continue," Ellis said. "I started to laugh. I looked at this group of billionaires and said, 'You'd better define what you mean by significant financial interest.' "

They asked for $250,000. Ellis reluctantly agreed, pending approval in Seattle. Lincoln and others quickly endorsed Ellis's leadership role, and teased him into breaking into his retirement fund. The hit cost him his annual summer boat trip to Alaska, but Alaska wasn't going away. Neither were the Mariners, as of June 10, 1992, when MLB's ownership committee voted to recommend ownership transfer to the Baseball Club of Seattle. While all major league clubs had to vote, and terms with Smulyan had to be negotiated, the deed was all but done.

The irony lay thick: The city without apparent love for baseball had its franchise saved by a man who had no love for the game at all.

Finally over was the controversy that drew the curiosity of millions of non-baseball fans as it sprawled over half a year and the politics of two nations. If it hadn't been so contentious, so public, and so much larger than a baseball story, it might have worked out another way.

"If we had done it the 'right' way—approaching Smulyan and the ownership committee quietly—who knows what would have happened?" Ellis said. "But when we were rebuffed, we thought this meant that those goddamned people in major league baseball weren't going to give us the time of day. By God, we'll get them!"

A key asset was that the group was filled with relatively young men used to building successful empires by getting their way.

"We were not going to lose," Lincoln said. "We were going to win, and they were not going to wear us out. Nobody wavered. Nobody said, 'Enough—let's get out of this.' "

The same relentless resolve would show up four years later. The opponents then would not be the leaders of baseball, but the leaders of Seattle.

CHAPTER FIVE

George, Marge, and the New Lou Crew

On the left were the sheep. On the right were the cows. Every day, the Mariners' bus would pass the same Arizona tableau. Although blacktop was winning in the land of renegade sprawl northwest of Phoenix in 1993, not every acre was asphalted. The occasional sheep ranch or cattle farm still held bare ground between The Gap and the Whopper.

Pleasant as the visual diversions might have been, the Mariners saw only monotony. They were homeless in spring training. Forced out of their original spring digs in popular Tempe before a new stadium complex in the remote Phoenix suburb of Peoria was ready, the team was playing all twenty-eight exhibition games on the road in the Cactus League. The team had a clubhouse and training facilities in Peoria, but without a finished park, the bus was the players' alternate spring home.

If the daily route was maddeningly familiar, the daily baseball results were just plain maddening. At the moment, a traffic jam made everything more annoying. Finally, Lou Piniella saw something different: A handful of kids were playing Wiffle ball in a field next to the freeway. The moment was perfect for a manager who ached to send an early message to his new team.

"Stop the bus!" he barked to the driver. "Stop the fucking bus!"

Startled, the driver slipped the bus onto the shoulder. Sitting at the front, the manager stood up, moved into the aisle, turned his cap backward, and addressed the players.

"I oughta let some of you sons of bitches off the bus and see if you can go over here and beat these kids in a game," he bellowed, "because you sure as hell can't beat anybody else!"

Piniella sat down, muttering. The bus moved on. Some players were bug-eyed. Others snickered. All were certain they hadn't been talked to like that before, especially by a Mariners manager.

"He was kidding," said eyewitness Jay Buhner. "But he was serious."

Buhner, beginning his fifth year as a Mariners outfielder, summarized the wariness in the clubhouse: What's up with this dude?

All knew his reputation—Yankees hero, World Series champion manager, temper measured in megatons—but few knew his tactics. After an 0-5 spring start following a 64-98 season in 1992 that ended predecessor Bill Plummer's major league managerial career, the players were experiencing the early portion of the full arsenal.

"When I got here, I said I couldn't understand how this team lost 98 games last season," he said. "The reasons are becoming very evident."

Piniella suffered neither fools nor losses easily, and the Mariners historically had both by the boxcar-load. That's why almost no one in baseball believed he would take on the job of turning around such a misbegotten franchise. When word was out nationally the previous October that he was the Mariners' top candidate, Bill Madden, the respected baseball writer from the *New York Daily News*, who had grown close to Piniella from his days as a Yankees player and manager, was succinct.

"Don't do it, Lou," he said. "Your career will die there."

Confounding all, Piniella took the job and the initiative, shattering the club culture right in front of the sheep, cows, kids, and bus driver.

"I think everyone realized right there we weren't dealing with a nice guy," said relief pitcher Norm Charlton, who played for Piniella when he managed the Cincinnati Reds to the 1990 championship and became his first player acquisition in Seattle. "He had a job to do—turning a franchise around and winning ballgames. He basically said, 'I don't care how things were done here in the past. It's my way or the highway.'"

Piniella's way, at least at the outset, could have had a bit part in Mel Gibson's *Mad Max* movies. Piniella made it deliberately cruel: That was a big reason the club started 0-5. At the beginning of camp, he summoned the coaches and trainers to explain the new regimen.

"Work their asses off–I want to kill these guys," he said. "I want them in the best shape of their lives."

Nearly every day prior to the start of exhibition season, Piniella would end workouts with a corner drill, a fifty-yard square in which each of the four legs was run with a different stride–shuffle, backward, forward, etc. The drill was mandatory for all the ambulatory. One early day, after what seemed an endless series of corner drills, two players staggered over to a fence and threw up.

"That," said Piniella, "is what I want to see." Even though it was just spring training, Piniella poured on the pressure.

"That's one of the reasons we didn't start the spring so well," said trainer Rick Griffin, who had been with the club since 1983. "They were tired. We ran them down, let them rest, then built them back up."

The pressure wasn't confined to the field. Piniella was eager to emphasize discipline and sacrifice. After another early loss, Piniella ordered clubhouse man Henry Genzale to lock up the food room at the new clubhouse in Peoria. The small room just off the locker room had fruit, cereals, sandwiches, coffee, and cold drinks, along with a couple of tables. It was hardly sumptuous, but it was a convenient perk. It also became convenient for another purpose.

When word reached him that some players were grumbling about the denial of food privileges, Piniella burst out of his nearby office and unloaded.

"I'm tired of this," he said to a clubhouse full of silent players. "This isn't a fucking country club. We got the motherfucking sandwiches and the motherfucking pizza. We got the fucking mini-bars. I'm sick and tired of this shit."

Griffin said, "I thought to myself, 'What the hell is going to happen when the season starts?'"

The room stayed locked for almost a week. The episode stayed frozen for years in the minds of numerous witnesses. It would become obvious later that Piniella was making a stand now so he wouldn't have to establish standards during the season.

"Lou had done his homework and knew what had gone on here," Buhner said, referring mostly to the '92 season under Plummer. "Guys would do anything, especially showing up late, and get away with everything. Players were intimidating the manager, saying, 'I'm not going to play today.' Nobody was being held accountable."

The locked door to the food room was a vivid demonstration of what Piniella said in a talk that opened camp.

"We're going to play like professionals and conduct ourselves like professionals," he said. "When we walk out on the field people are going to know who we are. We're not going through the motions. I'm going to weed out everyone who does, and I promise you your ass won't be here."

Results were almost immediate. Not only did the Mariners, despite being homeless, finish spring with a 16-14 record, they returned in that first Piniella season to the winning side, improving 18 games from the previous year to an 82-80 mark. They also established a culture of winning that would carry them for much of the next nine years.

"Lou was very demanding of staff and players—they all learned to play a different way," said Griffin, who continued as head trainer into the 2003 season. "They respected him right away, and would run through walls for him. They didn't want to let Lou down. It wasn't just a matter of letting themselves down; they didn't want Lou to think less of them."

After his success in New York and Cincinnati, Piniella knew the requirements. He quickly realized that the Mariners, despite their abysmal history, weren't that far away from winning big. Griffin remembered hanging up from one of his first phone conversations with Piniella in disbelief.

"He said we're going to struggle a little in the first couple of years, but we're going to be in the playoffs in three years and the World Series in five years," Griffin said. "I couldn't believe he said that. No Mariners manager ever talked liked that."

Piniella was right on the first forecast and close on the second. To the disbelief of the baseball world and nearly everyone in Seattle, the Mariners would reach the postseason for the first time in 1995. In that season and in 2000 and 2001, they advanced to the American League Championship Series. Many factors contributed, but no one observing the ascent would deny that Piniella's sheer force of competitive will was paramount.

"Hiring Lou," said Buhner, "was the greatest thing that could have happened."

Yet by all that was conventional wisdom in baseball, Piniella's hiring in Seattle should haven't happened. If not for one last-minute, desperate phone call, it wouldn't have happened.

⚜

A charity golf tournament was about to begin at West Seattle Municipal Golf Course when a clubhouse boy ran down Woody Woodward to tell him he had a phone call waiting in the pro shop. Although he was passionate about his golf game—his critics would say it came at the expense of some of his baseball work—the general manager of the Mariners attended such functions mostly out of obligation. In this summer of 1989, the public appearances of the laconic Woodward, a former shortstop who played eight years in the major leagues, were frequently compromised by fans' questions about why the team was so lousy. But the Mariners' front office was happy that someone out there believed a team personality would enhance a public event, so Woodward gamely mixed with the dwindling knot of people who still cared.

Hustling over to the pro shop, he discovered the call represented the general state of things Mariners: It wasn't really for him.

Pat Gillick, general manager of the Toronto Blue Jays, was trying to find Lou Piniella. He figured Woodward, one of Piniella's best friends in baseball, would be able to track him down, since Piniella was in Seattle as an announcer to broadcast the Yankees' series with the Mariners. Gillick wanted to know if Piniella, despite having been fired twice as Yankees manager by George Steinbrenner, was ready to manage again.

As the Yankees' director of scouting and player development from 1974 through 1976, Gillick watched closely the first seasons of Piniella's eleven-year New York playing career, in which Lou took a modest amount of talent and stretched it as far as human sinew can be pulled. Later, from a distance in Toronto, where Gillick helped open the expansion Blue Jays franchise in 1977, he was even more impressed with the job Piniella did managing the Yanks in 1986-88, during some of Steinbrenner's most turbulent years.

"Lou has passion and he likes to win," Gillick said. "At the major league level, he evaluates players very well, and strategically is a very smart manager."

Woodward passed Gillick's request to Piniella, which wasn't hard since they were in the same golf foursome. But the favor was nevertheless dismaying, because about a year earlier, Woodward sought Piniella for the same reason—filling a managerial vacancy.

Hired halfway though the '88 season to replace the fired Dick Balderson, Woodward was eager to end the club's perpetual chaos by creating some managerial stability. His first choice was Piniella, his old buddy from their days together in the Yankees front office, where Piniella had succeeded Woodward as GM in October 1987.

Piniella was in a mood to listen, because his time in New York was coming to an unceremonious and volcanic end. Since his 1984 retirement as a player, he was a coach, a manager, and a general manager. Midway through 1988 he became manager a second time, replacing Billy Martin, whom Steinbrenner had just fired for, unbelievably, the fifth time.

But after finishing out the year with a 45-48 record, Piniella quit, furious with Steinbrenner's relentless interference. An episode early in his second tenure as manager stood out. As baseball's trading deadline approached in late July, Steinbrenner called to tell Piniella that he was set on acquiring from the Mariners a designated hitter, Ken Phelps, a power-hitting left-handed bat he thought would be a good fit for Yankee Stadium's short right-field porch. For Phelps, the Mariners wanted an outfielder—either Roberto Kelly, a young veteran who was starting in center field, or a prospect named Jay Buhner, a wild-swinging Texan with a good arm and serious right-handed power.

"You need a left-handed hitter, and you need to give up either Kelly or Buhner," Steinbrenner told Piniella.

"George, we don't need Phelps," Piniella said. "You're going to cause me problems here. I already have a full-time DH in Jack Clark."

Lou Piniella's baseball history with Seattle began in 1968, when he was taken in the expansion draft from the Cleveland Indians by the Seattle Pilots.
©1969 SEATTLE POST-INTELLIGENCER

"But you need a left-handed hitter."

"Yeah, but in New York we need one who pulls the ball, not one who hits straightaway or to left like Phelps does."

"I'm going to make the trade. Who do you want to give up?"

"I wouldn't give up either."

"I didn't ask you that."

"Well, Roberto is my everyday center fielder, so that leaves Jay. He's got problems, but he's got power and he's going to be a fine player."

Steinbrenner wasn't interested in the future. And it turned out he really wasn't interested in Phelps, either. But Detroit was, and given the tightness of the AL East race, Steinbrenner wanted to deny the Tigers. He didn't care what Piniella thought about his blocking move.

Nor did Piniella have recourse within the organization. He learned from his time as Yankees GM that the Mariners were one of four teams that Steinbrenner handled personally in trades. Whether it was because he liked the owner, George Argyros, or because he thought he could take him, Steinbrenner worked the trade independently of his baseball advisers.

Piniella remained as furious as he was helpless. With the Yankees, The Boss wins. Or at least, he won this round. Years later, Piniella would get his revenge. He unexpectedly followed Buhner to Seattle, where they teamed up to deliver a stunner to Steinbrenner and the Yankees in the 1995 playoffs. But all Piniella knew in the summer of '88 was that a promising young talent was taken from the Yankees for no good reason.

The 1988 season deteriorated for the Yankees so rapidly that by the end—a fifth-place finish, three games behind Detroit and four behind champion Boston—manager Piniella refused to take Steinbrenner's phone calls, either in the dugout or at home. Even when word reached Steinbrenner that Piniella was going to quit, The Boss would have none of it, insisting Piniella fly to his Tampa office to get fired. Piniella balked.

"Don't make me fly down there," he insisted after they hooked up by phone.

"Look," Steinbrenner said, "this doesn't have anything to do with the job you did or didn't do. But nobody quits on me. Besides, don't you want to know who's replacing you?"

"I really don't care."

"Well, let's sit down and talk about the ballclub."

"You're firing me! Talk to your new guy about the ballclub. Don't talk to me about it."

Eventually, Piniella gave in. He flew to Tampa and went to Steinbrenner's office at the Legends Field spring training complex so he could be handed his managerial head—"just to show me up," he said. But by the end of the conversation, amazingly, Piniella found himself obligated to the Yankees for another three years. Unwittingly, Piniella earlier signed a personal-services obligation as part of his original contract to manage the club. Steinbrenner had him again—although on the same financial terms, with less stress. Piniella chafed, but accepted the new job.

For years afterward, Piniella would have to explain the complicated relationship between himself and Steinbrenner, both Tampa residents. They hit New York almost together in 1973. Steinbrenner led a group of businessmen who purchased the Yankees from CBS for $8.8 million. Six months later, pitcher Lindy McDaniel was traded to Kansas City for Piniella. The arrivals in Gotham of Lou and George helped revive one of the great franchises in American sports—often at each other's expense, as well as to each other's credit.

"I have a special relationship with George," Piniella said. "We've had a love-hate deal at times—from both sides. I'm fully aware George made my managing career possible. I wouldn't have gone to the trouble of managing in the minors. But he took a chance on me after some coaching work at the major league level.

"I wanted to reward George. I have a lot of admiration and respect for the man. But it was disappointing that he didn't have the patience to allow me to continue."

Steinbrenner's admiration for Piniella was just as deep. In a 2002 interview with the *New York Daily News* as he approached his thirtieth year owning the club, Steinbrenner was asked by reporter Wayne Coffey to choose his all-time top Yank. "I wouldn't want to pick," he said. "I will tell you I've had some great warriors—and that's a title of honor for me. Lou Piniella was a great warrior."

❦

Even though Piniella was given a cushy job with the Yankees after his second managing stint, he missed being in the dugout. He wanted to manage—but not just anywhere. The first outside opportunity, however, came from nowhere, or least baseball's version of nowhere: Seattle.

Woody Woodward wanted Piniella to manage the Mariners. Mostly as a favor to his pal, Piniella agreed to fly to the Orange County offices of George Argyros, where he met with the owner as well as Woodward and team president Chuck Armstrong. As they talked, Piniella picked up on what most people in Seattle had already known about Argyros and his ballclub.

"I saw an operation that was really run more on a shoestring," he said. "The chances were that it wouldn't work. At the time, I didn't feel Seattle was the right situation for me."

Nor was it the right situation for anyone, apparently. About a year after the firings of general manager Dick Balderson and manager Dick Williams, the star pitcher, Mark Langston, was traded and the club was quietly put up for sale by Argyros. When the buyer turned out to be the owner of a radio network from Indianapolis, many assumed the Mariners were destined to move. Piniella's antenna accurately had picked up on low-boil chaos.

He politely said no. He moved into his new Yankees gig in 1989: public speaking, scouting, and TV work for the Yankees' cable show. He was enjoying the work—"a great way to stay in the game without the everyday headaches," he said—when Gillick found him playing golf in Seattle and asked him to take on another everyday headache.

Piniella left Seattle that night for Vancouver and a red-eye to Toronto to talk about the vacancy created after Gillick fired manager Jimy Williams. Having secured permission from Steinbrenner, Gillick met Piniella at an airport hotel. Piniella liked the idea of managing the Blue Jays sufficiently that Gillick called The Boss to say he was going to offer the job.

Steinbrenner surprised Gillick by demanding compensation—in the form of starting pitcher Todd Stottlemyre, who was in the second of what would be seven solid years with the Blue Jays. Recognizing how he would look if he traded a well-regarded pitcher for a guy who was then a broadcaster, Gillick said no.

"When I told Pat I was on a personal-services contract [to the Yankees], he thought I was putting him on," Piniella said. "But if I could have gotten out of it, I would have been Pat's guy."

Gillick recovered well from the Steinbrenner block, giving the job to a Blue Jays coach, Cito Gaston, who took Toronto to world championships in 1992 and 1993. But Steinbrenner had a reason for thwarting Gillick. He called Piniella at six o'clock one summer morning to say he was about to fire Piniella's managerial successor, Dallas Green. It was time, The Boss said, for Piniella to manage the Yankees a third time.

"Look, I appreciate all you've done for me," Piniella told Steinbrenner. "But if it hadn't worked twice, it surely isn't going to work a third time."

"I have you on a personal-services contract," Steinbrenner said, "and I stress loyalty."

"George. I'm the most loyal guy in the world, but this isn't going to work. I'm not going to do it."

Another return to the Yankees dugout would have made Piniella a New York punch line like Billy Martin. He wanted no more of the Bronx Zoo. It proved to be another wise decision. Not only was 1989 the first of four consecutive losing seasons for the Yankees, Steinbrenner in 1990 would be suspended by Major League Baseball for thirty-one months. He was forbidden from participating in team operations by baseball commissioner Fay Vincent for paying confessed gambler Howard Spira to dig up dirt on Dave Winfield, an ex-Yankees star with whom Steinbrenner was feuding. The decision came just a few months after Stein–brenner was pardoned by President Reagan for his 1974 felony conviction for illegal campaign contributions.

By the winter of 1989, when Piniella was approached to manage the Cincinnati Reds after the departure of local icon Pete Rose, it was clear to Steinbrenner that his guy wanted out of New York. This time Steinbrenner relented and sought no compensation, figuring Piniella would do little harm to the Yankees in the National League.

Instead he helped light up the NL. In his first season of 1990, the Reds started out 9-0 and became the first team to win a pennant wire-to-wire since the adoption of the 162-game schedule. In the National League Championship Series, the Reds won their first title in fourteen years with a 4-2 triumph over Pittsburgh. In the World Series, the underdog Reds stunned the baseball world with a sweep of the favored Oakland A's.

Following the celebratory bedlam in the Reds' clubhouse, Piniella couldn't wait to get to the press-conference podium: "George," came his first words, "I can manage."

Following the embarrassment of having been dumped twice as field manager and once as general manager in New York, Piniella was ecstatic. In just his fourth year as a big-league manager, with no minor league apprenticeship, and working for an owner, Marge Schott, as loopy as Steinbrenner was belligerent, he took a lower-payroll team to a pinnacle unseen in Cincinnati since the early-1970s dominance of the Big Red Machine. It was the sweetest of vindications.

"You get fired a couple times, and you wonder, 'Is the guy right?' " Piniella said. "That's probably why I went to Cincinnati—I had to prove it to myself."

At age forty-seven, he did it with a mix of volatility and sensitivity that seemed improbable to those who knew him only for his legendary outbursts. His notorious postgame fight in 1991 with Rob Dibble, in which he tackled the Reds' closer into his locker over a remark questioning the manager's honesty, has become a staple of many a sports-video anthology, but it obscured the larger attributes he brought daily to the clubhouse.

"Anybody can be a good manager, but Lou was a great motivator," Reds pitcher Jose Rijo told Hal McCoy of the *Dayton* (Ohio) *Daily News*. "I played for a lot of great managers, like Tony LaRussa and Yogi Berra, but Lou was the best. He had two rules: Don't be late, and play hard. Every day, he would talk to you and give you some kind of inspiration to take on the field. He was soft that way, but he never kissed anybody's rear end. He was his own man and a man's man, just a great human being.

"There's something about him. . . . He is just special."

Unfortunately for the Reds, Schott didn't have the same appreciation. Besides her eccentricities involving large dogs and Nazi memorabilia, Schott was recklessly cheap regarding the ballclub she inherited from her husband. Although she and Piniella got along well personally, Piniella grew irritated with her penurious ways. As he moved through his three-year contract—the Reds in 1991 fell off 17 games from the previous year, finishing fifth at 74-88, then rebounded to 90 wins and second place in 1992—Piniella came to a quiet conclusion that he wasn't going to re-sign.

The turning point came in August '91 when Piniella was outraged after an umpire, Gary Darling, took away a home run by the Reds' Bill Doran by reversing a ruling by another umpire. In a foolish postgame tantrum, Piniella publicly accused Darling of bias against the Reds. Darling and the Major League Umpires Association filed a $5 million defamation suit against the manager.

What really got to Piniella was Schott's failure to back him in the dispute.

"I went to Marge for help and she said, 'Darling, you're on your own,' " he said. "That left a bad taste. I had to hire personal attorneys. After about a year, we finally settled, with the help of Fay Vincent."

Piniella was required to pay a fine and make a public apology, write a check to the umpire union's designated charity, and do public appearances. He still didn't believe he was obligated to pay the attorneys' fees. He appealed to National League president Bill White, who persuaded the Reds to pick up half the bill. But the ordeal ended any chance he would stay on, much to the consternation of his wife, Anita.

"I liked Cincinnati, and so did Anita. I didn't realize until I got there how big the Reds are. We had a beautiful apartment ten minutes up the river from downtown. I got along well with Marge, and she and Anita had a great relationship. The Reds' spring training home was twenty minutes from my home in Tampa.

"Anita thought leaving was stupid."

But she knew that when her husband felt crossed, there was nothing anyone could do. In another ten years, Piniella would again feel crossed and would unexpectedly move on again.

❧

Though baseball came first, there were even more urgent matters on Piniella's agenda in the early 1990s. Not long after his 1984 retirement as a player, he joined some friends in investing in a variety of businesses—restaurants in several towns, a car dealership in Ossining, New York, and residential real estate in Connecticut. As the economy soured in the recession of the early '90s, the investments became a disaster. His partners declared bankruptcy, and Piniella was the only one among them with a substantial income.

Financial matters were so bad that he decided during his final season with the Reds that he would leave baseball for as long as it took him to run his businesses back into the black so he could sell them. "It's not that they were bad people," he said of the friends who left him holding the bag. "It's just that the economy went bad and my partners went bankrupt—all of them. So basically, I got stuck. "You know what I found out? What the phrase 'joint and severally' meant."

Out of stubborn personal pride, Piniella refused to use the bankruptcy route.

"You make mistakes, you pay for them. Learn from them. You don't duplicate them. Today you can offer me the best business in the world, and I have no interest. None."

Piniella plays the horses, and he plays the stock market. But he has refused active ownership in any enterprise, because it took nearly a decade to resolve his previous misjudgments. Some of his Mariners paychecks were garnisheed by court order from creditors, and he did not dispatch the last of the real estate holdings until 2002. "Many times I got up the middle of the night and hit my head against the wall. I don't know how many times I said, 'How can you be so stupid?' "

When asked, Piniella is forthcoming with young players who have suddenly come into millions of dollars. "I tell them I got burned. Be conservative, because you'll make enough over your career to not need anything else."

Leaving a disappointed fan base in Cincinnati and burdened by the specter of a cavalcade of lawsuits from his business creditors, Piniella in early October of 1992 was in no mood to listen to his pal Woodward again talk about baseball in Seattle.

"Woody, it's just not going to work," Piniella said. "I'm not looking for a manager's job. I have to get rid of some business headaches. Everything I hear is, 'Don't go. Seattle is a place where managers go to see their careers end.' "

Woodward interviewed other candidates, including former major league managers Davey Johnson and Doug Rader. But Piniella was clearly the most well-known, well-regarded veteran available; his name was quickly atop the speculative lists in the newspapers. A visit by Piniella also wouldn't hurt Woodward's credibility with the new ownership, which took over in July.

"It's quite an opportunity now," Woodward insisted. "We have some pretty good players and you're going to like the new owners, especially John Ellis."

Woodward figured Ellis and Piniella would hit it off. Both were tough, no-nonsense sorts who would give each other direct questions and direct answers. It wouldn't take long after any visit to know if there would be a match. Woodward finally prevailed on Piniella to give him twenty-four hours, as he did four years earlier under Argyros, as a personal favor. "Professional courtesy" was how Piniella put it.

⚜

John Ellis's company, Puget Power, owned one of the area's premier restaurants, Salish Lodge, a rustically elegant hostelry overlooking Snoqualmie Falls about a half hour east of Seattle. A large room at the lodge was reserved as the place for the Mariners ownership and Lou Piniella to get their first look at each other.

Ellis, Woodward, and Piniella were joined by Chuck Armstrong, Chris Larson, Jeff Raikes, Craig Watjen, and several others in ownership who were getting their first real action as baseball moguls. Ellis and Piniella met alone before dinner, then the group conversed over a sumptuous meal.

"I was up-front with them," Piniella said. "I told them I was here because of Woody. I wasn't here looking for a job, because truthfully I don't think I'm going to be involved in this situation."

As the evening wore on, the interrogation narrowed, getting more pointed—and awkward.

"They asked me some funny questions," he said. "They were all computer guys, so it struck me funny when they asked if I could use a computer to take out the lineups."

Then came a change-up, from software to hardball: Why, Piniella was asked, should we have interest in you when Cincinnati let you go?

Ellis nearly leaped out of his chair. Before Piniella could answer, Ellis said, "Let's stop this thing," and the meeting ended abruptly.

"They were the worst questions," Ellis said. "Chuck, Woody, and I sort of turned Lou over to them. And they start asking things that are simply unbelievable. Here we are recruiting this guy, and he's being exposed to these people who he'd view as the ones who would be running him—a bunch of wealthy young kids whose roles Lou didn't know.

"If I were him, I wouldn't have answered some of the questions, because in my view they were insulting. I thought the evening was a total disaster . . . almost the worst mistake known to man."

Ellis also admitted he wasn't used to that sort of give-and-take. But compared with fifteen years in the New York media meat grinder, Piniella heard nothing that put him off. And the rest of the diners heard things they liked.

"Lou said one thing that stood out," Watjen, the retired Microsoft treasurer, said. " 'If I'm your manager, you can be assured the inmates won't be running the asylum.' That's what we needed."

Ellis had a larger worry than the Q-and-A of the meeting: Would a manager of Piniella's résumé and accomplishments make a long-term commitment to a franchise that had done next to nothing? Piniella ended the visit without any commitment.

"Here's a big-time guy who lives in Florida and hasn't been out here. Is he just looking for a quick job and then he'll run out on me?" Ellis said. "How can we get him to stick around after he sees how difficult this job is?"

As important: How can his wife, Anita, be persuaded? As the couple flew home from Seattle the next day, Lou knew he liked Woodward and was impressed with Ellis. The playing roster had potential. But he just couldn't quite see himself in Seattle. By the time they returned to their home in Allendale, New Jersey, he was ready to say no—perhaps because that was the word that Anita pounded into his ear on the flight.

"No, no, no, no, no," Piniella recalled her saying. "She said, 'You're not going to Seattle. Just get that totally out of your mind.' "

Her reasons were obvious: too far from home, and spring training was in Arizona instead of Florida. The Piniellas had three children: Lou Jr., age twenty-three, was out of school and working on Wall Street, and Kristi, twenty-one, and Derek, thirteen, were still in school and needing a father closer than the West Coast.

Ellis had one play left in him. He knew Piniella to be a ruthless competitor. Watching his reactions over dinner, he knew Piniella could handle most anything. From all he had heard around baseball, Piniella checked out well; he was the guy to stop the bleeding on the field and in the box office.

Deciding he would "challenge him every way I could think of to see how he'd respond," Ellis called Piniella at home the day after his visit.

Piniella recalled three questions:

"Are you scared of the situation?"

"Are you afraid you can't make it happen?"

"You don't think you're good enough to get this going?"

Piniella burned. Nobody calls into question his guts and courage.

"He challenged me, and I've always loved challenges," he said. "I really happen to like John, and we hit it off right away. In Cincinnati, the challenge was for me to win the World Series, and that's what I intended to do. Then I intended to fix my businesses." But he also realized it would be easier to fix his businesses with income, rather than without income.

He turned to Anita.

"You're not going to agree with this, but I gotta do what I gotta do."

He promised that in return for her support, he would move them back to Tampa, where they had grown up, met, and married, and would build them a home on the beach. During the eight-month season while he traveled in and out of Seattle, she could remain in their Tampa hometown, where both sets of parents still lived. They could help with the kids, and the Mariners would pay for her visits to Seattle.

Reluctantly, she agreed. What Anita knew well, and what baseball found out over a quarter century, is that once ignited, the impulse in Lou Piniella is irresistible.

One last thing remained. Piniella had to talk to Armstrong about a contract.

"Look, there's no negotiating—I want $800,000 a year," Piniella said, knowing the previous Mariners manager had pulled $250,000.

"Well, I don't know, Lou . . ."

"Chuck, I don't know about 'I don't know.' "

Piniella got his money. The Mariners got their man.

After sixteen seasons of futility, Seattle was about to get its baseball groove on. In 1993 under Piniella, Chris Bosio would pitch a no-hitter, Jay Buhner would hit for the cycle, Ken Griffey Jr. would tie a major league record with home runs in eight consecutive games, Randy Johnson would win 19 games and strike out 300, and the Mariners on a warm June day in Baltimore would brawl with the Orioles for twenty minutes. Cal Ripken Jr.

As umpire John Shulock discovered, manager Lou Piniella was neither shy nor vague about making a point. ©1993 SEATTLE POST-INTELLIGENCER/KURT SMITH

hurt his knee and almost ended his consecutive-games streak.

The Mariners, perpetual doormats, suddenly were causing opponents to stumble.

When the season ended on the winning side at 82-80, there was no champagne as there was in '91. Instead, the Mariners watched a celebration. They were in Chicago as the White Sox clinched the AL West title and celebrated on the field. Afterward, Piniella closed the clubhouse door and talked to the players.

"People, that [celebration] is what baseball's all about. You're going to experience the same thing very soon."

He was right. He just had no idea how absurd the route would be.

CHAPTER SIX

When Every Everything Means Everything

Boiling with passion and contempt, Yankee Stadium seemed one unlocked door short of a prison break.

"Out of control," said Jay Buhner. "Everything that wasn't bolted down, they were throwing at me—golf balls, batteries, coins, darts. They were throwing full liter bottles of soda that would explode when they hit.

"Then there were the fights in the bleachers. Serious fists were being thrown. Fans would get the crap beat out of them by other fans."

Then there were the obnoxious ones.

Known in the Bronx as the Bleacher Creatures, many in the right-field crowd didn't have the arm strength to pick off the Mariners outfielders with objects. But they could reach them with a voice as unified as it was vulgar. The favored targets were the Mariners closest to their restless den—Ken Griffey Jr. in center field and Buhner in right.

After the usual "Griffey sucks!" and "Byoonah sucks!" the chants began evolving into singsongs of the schoolyard.

"Byoonah loves Joonyah! Byoonah loves Joonyah!"

Unable to draw the players into a response, the Creatures went deep.

"Byoonah takes it up the ass, doo-dah! doo-dah!

"Byoonah takes it up the ass, all the doo-dah day!"

Griffey and Buhner glanced at each other, then buried faces in gloves so fans couldn't see them laughing.

It wasn't as amusing elsewhere in the fabled ballyard. In the Mariners' bullpen, pitchers were showered repeatedly with beer, before and during the game. Warming up, starter Chris Bosio was ready to climb the wall after his suds-slinging assailants. Relief pitcher Jeff Nelson was worried about the impression he would leave on the mound entering the game. "I kept thinking Lou would ask, 'You been drinking out there?' " he said. "I reeked of beer." As Bobby Ayala warmed up, an empty bottle of Jagermeister missed his head by six inches. Fearing for their safety, the pitchers abandoned the bullpen seats against the wall.

In the grandstand behind and above home plate, in an open-air suite used by Mariners executives on the press box level, the first time the Seattle group applauded a play, fans in the rows just below the box turned around and began shouting obscenities and throwing cups. Beefy security guards, stationed on the front-row corners of the box, swooped down on the unrulies and ejected them.

The pregame warning from Woody Woodward was proving to be no exaggeration. As the execs got out of their cars at the stadium entrance, the Mariners general manager, who had been Yankees GM several years earlier, addressed the naive outlanders.

"You're about to enter Yankee Stadium," he had said. "You're about to know why clubs never want to play here in the playoffs."

That night of October 3, 1995, crackled and hissed in the Bronx in the manner of the emotional crescendo before a big-time heavyweight boxing match. The surprising Mariners were in their first postseason series after two barren decades. The storied Yankees were returning to the playoffs for the first time in fourteen years, a shocking drought whose end would draw the largest single-game crowd since the 1976 stadium renovation—57,178 mostly boozy belligerents bent on conquest. The American League Division Series was the first since labor strife voided the 1994 postseason, so baseball followers across the nation were itching for October electricity.

The sparks seemed hot enough to ignite the joint.

"For the first time, I was worried about being on the field," Buhner said. "What happens if five or six of these guys jump on the field? There's nothing I could do.

"Never in my wildest dreams did I imagine a night like that."

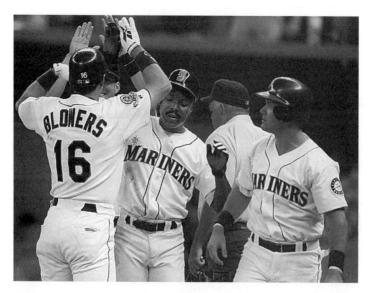

Tino Martinez, Vince Coleman, and Edgar Martinez greet Mike Blowers after he drove them in with a grand-slam home run, one of many big blasts that powered the Mariners' improbable drive to the AL West title in 1995.

©1995 SEATTLE POST-INTELLIGENCER/SCOTT EKLUND

Lou Piniella imagined it. In fact, this sort of October frenzy was what he had been planning for almost from the moment he came to Seattle three years earlier. Upon taking the job, one of his first phone calls was to trainer Rick Griffin, seeking an assessment of personnel from the '92 team that just finished a dismal 64-98.

"I trust trainers as much or more than scouts," Piniella said. "Be honest and don't sugarcoat—nobody knows we're talking."

In a conversation that lasted two and a half hours, Griffin spelled it out, saying there really was only one guy who didn't fit. A couple of days later, oft-injured, portly outfielder Kevin Mitchell was traded to Cincinnati for relief pitcher Norm Charlton, who would become vital in the Mariners' climb.

Piniella called Griffin again: "How do you like that?"

"Wow," Griffin said. "You work fast."

"From now on, we're going to work fast."

Speed was important, because he promised Griffin the playoffs in three years. The wild night in Gotham was delivery on that promise. Crucial in the execution were players such as Charlton, a warrior for such crucibles.

Piniella knew if he were successful in Seattle, it would lead to moments like Game 1 of the American League Division Series in Yankee Stadium, where lesser men might find warm water trickling down a leg. Piniella's demanding nature, blunt assessments, and occasional spittle-filled excoriations were not the product merely of an ill manner. The tirades, at least most of them, were part of a plan to make sure his guys learned to hold their water in big moments.

"I don't know exactly what Lou is thinking when he gets on a guy, but I do know he's trying to make him better," Charlton said. "He wants the player to prefer playing in front of 75,000 screaming people, because it would be better than getting yelled at by Lou."

Third baseman Mike Blowers was standing around the batting cage one day during the season when he overheard a conversation between Buhner and Piniella, who moments earlier chewed so hard on a teammate that Buhner had to ask why.

"He said, 'I need to have guys here who can handle what I give them, so they can handle the pressure of a race,' " Blowers said. "I was glad I overheard that." Many were the young Mariners who failed to grasp that subtlety, but Piniella had the history that backed the aggressive style. As a Yankees player, Piniella reached the World Series four times, winning twice, batting .319 in 22 Series games. So the big stage where the Mariners found themselves was a familiar one to Piniella. It wasn't the World Series, but given each team's long absence from the spotlight, reaching the ALDS was a big deal.

Piniella and club management assembled in three years a roster of young veterans in their primes, anticipating a moment when guts would be the highest requirement. Toughest of the tough was Chris Bosio, a barrel-bodied starting pitcher whose will was as stout as his knees were creaky. Signed as a free agent in 1993, Bosio was like Charlton—impervious to pressure and intimidation.

"Boz had a big influence," Charlton said. "He was no-nonsense. If he had a problem with you, he'd say, 'I'm not going to talk about it. I'm going to infringe on you right now.' Or, he'd tell the other team, 'If you hit one of our guys, we hit two of yours, and not when it's convenient with two outs—right now!'"

With players such as Bosio, Charlton, Buhner, Blowers, Griffey, Randy Johnson, Edgar Martinez, and Tino Martinez, Piniella had no doubts about his outfit's guts, not after what he had experienced with them in his time in Seattle. From the controversial change in ownership in 1992 to the preposterous regular-season finish of 1995, wrapped around yet another threat to move the franchise, the core group of players had been battered endlessly—up to and including the roof literally falling down upon them.

Blowers, who grew up in suburban Spanaway, forty-five miles south of Seattle, had an appreciation for Mariners history as a fan as well as a player. He also had a phrase for the seasons of 1993, 1994, and 1995: "A progression of ordeals." The travails created a hardness, a quality desperately tested in the fall of '95. All that was at stake was the franchise's continued existence in Seattle.

After a mostly upbeat 82-80 season in 1993, Piniella boldly asserted in November that the Mariners would win the AL West in '94: "I expect this team to win the division. I'll go on record as saying that. We've got a good nucleus of veterans. What I saw evolving was a team getting some good team chemistry and starting to develop some leaders."

What made Piniella's forecast at least a little credible came from forces outside the franchise. Owing to expansion in 1994, the American and National Leagues realigned into three divisions each instead of two. The Mariners were put in baseball's smallest unit, the AL West, which had in addition only California, Oakland, and Texas, none of which were considered powers. Also added to the playoff format was a wild card—the team with the best record apart from the three division winners. So these four teams in each league played a new round, called the Division Series, prior to the League Championship Series.

Instead of the Mariners going to the postseason mountain, the mountain was coming to the Mariners—perhaps the first break the lords of the game ever accorded the franchise.

After a 21-9 spring training record, the Mariners took the opportunity and ran with it—off the cliff. By midseason 1994 they had the second-worst record in baseball. Injuries and some flops by young pitchers were souring the optimism sufficiently that Griffey in late May told Larry LaRue of the *Tacoma News Tribune*,

"I want out." He had grown weary of the losing, and said he expected to be traded by season's end. While some teammates and club officials downplayed the remarks as simple frustration, the episode was one of several in which a Griffey impulse would send shock waves through the franchise.

In New York in early July, Griffey had another outburst, only this one didn't make it outside Piniella's office. In a tense series against the Yankees in which the Mariners won two of three, Griffey was hit by a pitch in retaliation for Mariners brushbacks aimed at Paul O'Neill, the Yankees' leading hitter. The inside shots came from a long-standing feud between O'Neill and Piniella dating back to their days together in Cincinnati. After the game, Griffey, uninjured, closed the door to Piniella's office and blew up, telling the manager that if he had issues with O'Neill, don't work them out at his expense. Piniella acknowledged Griffey's point, and asked him not to show him up in front of the rest of the team.

On July 7 came another sign of desperation. The club reached into its farm system to bring up an eighteen-year-old shortstop. The previous summer the Mariners took Alex Rodriguez out of high school in the free-agent amateur draft with the same first-round, first-pick selection they used on Griffey six years earlier—and with the same expectations. Rodriguez was thought of so highly by the Mariners that after the 1993 season they traded brilliant shortstop Omar Vizquel to Cleveland partly in anticipation of Rodriguez's arrival in the big leagues (as well as to save the club money).

Early in the '94 season, the Mariners dispatched Ken Griffey Sr., then an assistant to GM Woody Woodward, to scout the kid's readiness. Senior reported back that Rodriguez was superbly talented but too raw for the majors. He also advised against a call-up because of the larger threat that was hanging over all of baseball—a potential players strike. Labor negotiations were going nowhere. The owners, directed by one of their own, commissioner-without-portfolio Bud Selig, seemed particularly resolute about winning back control of the game, while the players union, which had come out on top in every previous conflict, saw no reason to step away from their accumulated wealth and power. An August deadline for a strike was likely.

Senior argued that in the event of a strike, it would be foolish to have Rodriguez gain major league service time in a fractured season going nowhere. The advice would prove prophetic, because in a few years the Mariners would find themselves in a bad business bind: Contracts of Griffey Jr. and Rodriguez would end up expiring at the same time, in part due to service time Rodriguez was granted for 1994.

But for Piniella, urgency prevailed for two reasons: the Vizquel trade, and the pathetic nature of the new, shrunken AL West. No division team had a winning record, so the Mariners were still in the hunt. That was enough for Piniella to demand that Woodward pursue another lightning strike with a teenage phenom. This time, it didn't work—Rodriguez played 17 games and hit .204.

But on July 19, the labor talks as well as the Mariners' desperation and crankiness fell out of first place as topics of travail. As the Mariners and Baltimore Orioles were warming up late in the afternoon for a game at the Kingdome, players were startled by a loud report, a clattering in the lower bowl grandstand along the third base line. A pair of wood-fiber tiles, 32 inches by 48 inches and 2 inches thick, each weighing 26 pounds, came loose from the Kingdome's ceiling and fell nearly 200 feet, breaking seat backs where they landed.

Tragedy was avoided because fans had not yet been allowed in for the day's game. Warming up in the Orioles bullpen was Jamie Moyer, a pitcher who would have a large impact on the Mariners' future but at the moment was standing and staring, baffled as everyone else.

"You think of all the events in that building, and what would have happened if the place had been full . . . a flat-out catastrophe," he said.

Randy Johnson was on his back in the outfield doing stretching exercises when he caught a glimpse of something falling. Sensing immediately the larger problem, he also saw into the future. "One way or another," he said wryly, "we'll get a retractable dome here."

While there was no catastrophe, the falling tiles became a civic disaster. The tiles were apparently loosened from their fasteners by water seeping through the concrete from a work crew that for weeks had been power-washing the Kingdome roof's exterior. These tiles were among thousands whose condition was almost unknowable because of inaccessibility. To be safe, the game was postponed. In short order, so was the home season.

Igniting a controversy about the Kingdome's increasingly cloudy future, King County officials decided to close the building until all tiles were removed and replaced with a spray-on material. The emergency repair would take nearly four months, kill two workers, and cost $70 million—$3 million more than it took to build the entire structure in 1976.

After looking at inadequate home-field alternatives in Portland, Vancouver, and Tacoma, Major League Baseball decided that the only way to assure proper game quality was to order the Mariners to play the rest of the season on the road—a loss of 33 home games. So the 1993 nuisance of spring training without a stadium in Arizona provided at least one virtue: practice for homelessness. The Mariners might have set a major league record for times orphaned.

Bad as the consequences were for King County and its taxpayers, the players turned the mess into an opportunity. The poor start and clubhouse friction that marked the season were swept away into what became a sort of rolling frat party.

"At first we said, 'Oh shit—it's going to be a loooong road trip,'" Buhner said. "But once we got over the initial reaction, guys started getting excited. We had a helluva road team, and we thought, 'Hey, we can hang out on the road, have a couple of cocktails, eat in good restaurants.'"

Adjustments were made for life on the road. The organization chartered an upgraded plane from the MGM Grand Hotel in Las Vegas and footed the bill for families to join players occasionally on the road. After a day game in Toronto, the entire team took over most of a restaurant for an evening. On an off day in Oakland, Griffey organized a couple of foursomes and paid for a round of golf at Pebble Beach, and Buhner picked up the tab for dinner afterward.

Walls came down. People under stress opened up. The usual distance between the coaching staff and players evaporated.

"The coaches were friendly, not the kind who would hide out in the coaches' rooms," said relief pitcher Jeff Nelson. "They went out of their way to be part of us. That was big for chemistry."

For Blowers, who attended the University of Washington, it was a flashback.

"With all games on the road, there was no place to hide, so we got to know each other well," he said. "We really had fun. It was like college again—sort of that us-against-the-world thing. The tiles were huge for us. It brought us together."

Players later would cite the extended road trip as the genesis for the success the team would have in 1995. But the hardship started to pay off sooner. Against all odds, the Mariners got hot. Starting in early August, the Mariners won 9 of 10 games to creep within 2½ games of the division lead, despite their 49-63 record.

But on August 12, the roof came down again, this time figuratively. The union-set deadline for a settlement on a new collective bargaining agreement passed without a moment of fresh negotiation, so after the Mariners beat the A's in Oakland in the final game that night, the players struck. For the eighth time in twenty-three seasons, baseball had a work stoppage. This one would prove to be the longest and most painful in pro sports history. A month later, the union's continued resistance to the owners' plan to implement a salary cap inspired Selig to cancel the rest of the regular season as well as the postseason. For the first time since 1904, there would be no World Series.

The widely condemned strike lasted for eight months, wiping out 669 baseball games in 1994 and 252 games at the start of the 1995 season. The fracture alienated millions of sports fans, some of whom never forgave baseball. The absurdity reached its height during spring training of '95, when owners opened camps with minor leaguers and replacement players, vowing to start the major league season with drywallers and firemen.

On April 1 a federal judge ruled against the owners' position, saying they illegally implemented a new set of work rules. The decision cleared the way for a truce. The strike's end came just three days before the "sub-Mariners" were to open the season in a minor league park in Dunedin, Florida, against the Toronto Blue Jays, who were denied use of their home park because Canadian labor law precluded use of replacements for striking workers.

⁂

The real players finally opened the real season on April 26—the first home game in the repaired Kingdome since July 18—after an abbreviated spring training of three weeks. The regular season was shrunk to 144 games from the usual 162, but it was an official season, complete with playoffs.

Just when it appeared safe to get back in the baseball waters, the Mariners found themselves wrapped up in yet another ordeal. "The tiles, the strike–they couldn't throw anything more at us," said Buhner. "Jeezus, what else?" They found something.

During baseball's biggest public-relations debacle since the Black Sox scandal during the 1919 World Series, the club's owners launched a public campaign to build a new, baseball-only stadium with an untested retractable roof, largely at taxpayer expense. In terms of timing, the maneuver ranked with stowing away aboard the *Hindenburg*.

Virtually since the new ownership took over in mid-1992, the Kingdome was seen more and more as economically obsolete by the Mariners, as well as the Seahawks. The Mariners' twenty-year lease with the county for use of the Kingdome would expire after the 1996 season, and the owners made it clear that they wouldn't sustain millions in annual operating losses without some hope of profit from a new stadium. The threat was disturbingly familiar to the ones made by previous owners: We'll sell the club to out-of-towners.

Early in 1994, King County Executive Gary Locke appointed a Stadium Alternatives Task Force, whose twenty-eight members were charged with determining whether a remodeled Kingdome or a new stadium was the wiser course for baseball. By January 1995, helped in no small part by the Kingdome's demonstrated physical vulnerability, the panel recommended a public-private partnership for a new baseball stadium. But it didn't specifically say where it was to be built, how it was to be funded, or what it would look like.

The next step was to present a case for funding to the state Legislature. The regular session began in January, when the baseball strike was still unresolved and replacement players were scheduled to substitute for real major leaguers.

"There wasn't a lot of sentiment to help the Mariners," said Paul Isaki, the Mariners' vice president for business relations. "They would ask, 'What are we watching, Kentridge High School?' "

After months of wrangling, the state gave a stadium finance plan to King County government leaders, who approved it in late July– an increase in the state sales tax from 8.2 percent to 8.3 percent in

King County alone. Expected to cost the average county taxpayer about $7.50 a year, the tax increase would raise $240 million for a baseball park with a retractable roof. But the legislation stipulated that the package must be subject to a public vote. The proposition was put on the ballot for the September 19 primary election.

From the Mariners' view, the deal was weak. It consigned the financial burden to one county, whereas the Mariners drew fans from many counties—and the amount seemed insufficient for a project that hadn't been sited or drawn up. The vote was almost doomed to fail because a sales-tax increase, in a state without an income tax, is usually highly unpopular regardless of beneficiary.

"It put us in a position where it was not winnable," Isaki said. "But it was all we could get. The legislators knew that it wasn't going to fly, but it got us out of their hair."

The vote would occur within the easy memory of an electorate disgusted, if not furious, with baseball for canceling the World Series. And the money would benefit one of the most inept franchises in sports history.

Initial voter polling by Bob Gogerty, a longtime Seattle public affairs consultant hired by the Mariners to help direct their "Home Town Fans" committee for the stadium, showed almost 70 percent against the measure.

The odds were so stacked against the proposition that some players began assuming the club was moving to Tampa, where the 43,000-seat Suncoast Dome had been sitting empty for five years. "It was bad," Buhner said. "On plane flights, guys were looking at pamphlets sent by the chamber of commerce about apartments. Envelopes were full of locator guides for houses and schools."

With the crucial political brawl as backdrop, all the Mariners had to do on field was create some stadium momentum by winning ballgames at a pace unprecedented in their turgid little stay on the planet.

Which they proceeded not to do.

Griffey slammed into the Kingdome's center-field wall during a game in late May, making a spectacular running catch—and breaking his right wrist in two places. Crippled by Griffey's injury that kept him out of the lineup for nearly three months, the Mariners failed to gain traction. Bumping along around .500, the team drew only eight crowds above 21,000 in the first half of the 1995 season, including a tidy gathering of 9,767 for a game against

Oakland in June, the lowest in three seasons. When in late July they fell behind the West-leading California Angels by double digits for the first time in the season, it appeared the urgency of the budding stadium campaign was no match for the Mariners' irresistible, incorrigible legacy of losing.

Tension was building. Buhner, slumping in his performance at the plate, showed up one afternoon at the Kingdome to discover on the lineup card posted outside the manager's office that he had been moved from his usual fourth spot to sixth. Fuming, he burst into Piniella's office.

"What the fuck?"

Piniella looked up from his desk and fired back: "Who the fuck are you to tell me what the fuck?"

"I've been your cleanup hitter all year. You losing confidence in me? At least let me know what the fuck is going on."

Piniella walked up to Buhner and the two were quickly chin to chin. The conversation was loud enough that a coach, Lee Elia, hustled into the room to step between the two.

"Lou said he wanted me to have a breather, take some pressure off me," Buhner said. "I told him I didn't need it. That night I was back to hitting cleanup.

"But that's the way Lou was—he was hard on some guys because he wants to see you pissed off. By the next day, it's forgotten."

In the front office, however, things were going in a different direction. General manager Woody Woodward was making his usual midseason pitch to CEO John Ellis, hoping that the new wild-card berth, allowing four teams into the league playoffs for the first time, might give him the leverage to take on veteran players and their bigger salaries for a long-shot stretch drive.

"I told John you don't often get a chance to get into a pennant race, so don't pass on the opportunity," Woodward said. "Spend a few extra dollars to get it done."

Ellis said OK.

⁂

Woodward was stunned to hear Ellis giving the go-ahead to hire new players—as were his fellow baseball execs Roger Jongewaard and Lee Pelekoudas, along with Piniella.

"When I told them we could add payroll at the trading deadline, it was like it was Christmas," Woodward said. "They asked me what happened? Why? I said ownership wanted to be in the race. I gave them the same pitch I always used, but this time it fell on concerned ears.

"The wild card kept us in it. If there had not been a wild card, the way California was playing, we might not have gone out and made the moves." But with the wild card, the M's had a chance to grab a playoff spot even if the Angels won the AL West as expected.

On July 31, Woodward swapped two minor league prospects to San Diego for Andy Benes, a twenty-seven-year-old right-hander who was 4-7 with a 4.17 earned-run average with the Padres, and in the final year of his contract. The 6-foot-6, 240-pound Benes, a power pitcher, was the third starter added by the Mariners, after Tim Belcher and Salomon Torres in May.

Benes cost them outfielder Marc Newfeld and relief pitcher Ron Villone, both of whom had something in common with Shawn Estes, traded for Torres, and Roger Salkeld, traded for Belcher. They were former first-round draft picks who became expendable. The deals reflected management's urgency, prompted by the stadium campaign needing public support, to win now—a first in franchise history.

Two weeks after the Benes acquisition, the Mariners traded another youngster with promise, pitcher Jim Converse, to Kansas City for veteran outfielder Vince Coleman, thirty-three, a top-of-the-lineup hitter with the kind of speed that was sorely missing from a cast of heavy hitters. With the Royals, he had a .287 batting average with 26 stolen bases in 35 attempts. When he played with the St. Louis Cardinals earlier in his career, they twice made the World Series. Among the Mariners regulars, only Norm Charlton and second baseman Joey Cora had postseason experience.

The news of Coleman's hire sent a jolt through the clubhouse.

"We needed a leadoff man, and [ownership] showed they were paying attention," said catcher Dan Wilson. "That was huge." Woodward said the positive reaction caught him off guard: "It surprised me. It was like somebody threw a light switch. It was, 'C'mon, let's go! They do want to win.' "

It was the second dose of good news that day. The first was that Griffey, a metal plate in his repaired wrist and a fire in his belly, was returning from the disabled list. Still, the club was 51-50 and 12½ games back of the Angels. Things didn't start to change until August 24, the night The Kid found the ignition for a burn that would last for six weeks.

Against the Yankees in the Kingdome and facing ace closer John Wetteland with two outs in the bottom of the ninth, Griffey shattered a tied game with a two-run homer for a 9-7 triumph. It was the first win in what would be a three-game sweep of the Yanks, and the first of what would be many late-game stunners. The streak of quality play stretched to six wins in eight games; by September 1 the Mariners had cut the Angels' lead in half, to 6½ games. The 16 wins in August were a club record for any month. So were the 182 runs scored—by a margin of 30. The offense, agitated by Coleman and Cora, and powered by Griffey, Buhner, Blowers, and the Martinezes, Edgar and Tino, was crackling.

"We had a good lineup in its prime," said Edgar Martinez. "The right guys at the right time, ready to take off."

On the mound, Randy Johnson was unhittable; he would finish the season 18-2. The arrival of Benes, who would win seven of nine decisions as a Mariner, took some pressure off aging vets Bosio and Belcher, who nevertheless were the sort of gritty gamers that Piniella loved. In the bullpen, Charlton had become "The Sheriff," locking up the ninth inning, backed by Jeff Nelson, Bill Risley, Bob Wells, and occasionally the most publicly abused member of the team, Bobby Ayala.

"Quite honestly, I could do no wrong," said Charlton, who was released from Philadelphia and reacquired in July, becoming a crowd favorite with his disarming honesty, stone face, curly blond hair, and a pitching routine of many twitches, grabs, and pulls. "I'd throw the wrong pitch, but it would work. Or someone would make a great defensive play behind me, like Junior climbing a wall."

A slogan, old in sports but new in Seattle, caught on quickly with the public: "Refuse to Lose." In the clubhouse, it became "Refuse to Go Home."

"We'd be in the clubhouse all day—we'd have slept there if we could," Buhner said. "My wife went from pissed off to resigned. The clubhouse was the greatest place in the world to be. Couple times I got there at 1 P.M., and I was late. We'd order pepperoni sausage pizza for lunch. At least fifteen of us would be there, hanging out and having lunch—an absolute blast.

"Our chances were slim and none, but we were having a helluva time."

Contributions were coming from all over the roster, not just the big guns. Backup outfielder Rich Amaral, subbing for a sore-wristed Griffey, hit a three-run homer to beat the Orioles September 3. Rookie pitcher Bob Wolcott, age twenty-two, beat the Red Sox August 31 and the Yankees September 5. The light-hitting Cora hit a game-winning double September 10. On September 15, Coleman had four hits in four at-bats; a week later, he hit a game-winning grand slam, a career first.

"The biggest thing about that September was you never knew who it was going to be, but it was going to be somebody," Charlton said. "We had no idea who was going to get the postgame shaving-cream pie in the face."

In the stadium campaign, polls showed a growing shift toward a "yes" vote for the tax, thanks not just to the play on the field. A clever, million-dollar TV ad campaign funded by the Mariners and orchestrated by Gogerty, the savvy strategist, began around Labor Day.

"A lot of these campaigns tried to show economic development and all this bullshit, and it just doesn't sell," Gogerty said. "People can see right through it because it's not true."

Instead of the specious economic argument, the campaign went for the baseball heart. The four thirty-second commercials showed little kids playing sandlot ball while the narrator asked viewers to spend $7.50 annually for a place "open to the sky ... and open to dreams," with final fades to dramatic action moments featuring Johnson, Griffey, and Edgar and Tino Martinez.

"You don't get people to raise taxes logically—it has to be emotional," Gogerty said. "There has to be something there to convince them it's for a higher good. We were hyping the team and hyping the connection between family values and baseball. The narrative was 'We all need dreams, and dreams need a place to grow.'

"They were some of the best ads I've ever been involved in."

If it were possible for a dream to have a dream finish, it happened September 19, the night of the primary election that would settle the stadium issue. The Mariners had cut the fading Angels' lead to two games, making the wild-card berth secondary to a sudden race for the division title. Hosting the Texas Rangers, who themselves were in the wild-card race, the Mariners were behind 4-1 in the eighth inning when Griffey stirred things with a solo home run. But the Mariners' season record when trailing after eight innings was 1-51.

After a walk opened the bottom of the ninth, Piniella decided to pinch-hit for catcher Dan Wilson. The manager made a somewhat surprising choice—Doug Strange, who had played in only three of the Mariners' previous ten games, batting twice. That season the reserve infielder would play in only seventy-four games, hitting .271 in 155 at-bats. He was a Ranger the previous two seasons, and was a late add to the Mariners roster in spring training, just for a little bench insurance.

In the ground-level, glass-enclosed box behind home plate at the Kingdome, known as the bunker, the baseball brass and a few of the team's minority owners were watching intently as Strange stepped to the plate. Wayne Perry, a member of the McCaw group of owners, was also watching the baseball execs.

"I think Strange was 0-for-his-career in this situation," Perry said. "They looked at each other, and I expected them to say something like 'He's a guy who can hit a slider low and away'— you know, some tremendous baseball insight that no ordinary fan would know.

"They said, 'We don't have a clue.' "

Strange would say later that he had two objectives: "I told myself to be aggressive, and, if possible, get him before he gets me. After sitting on the bench for two hours, I didn't want to have an 0-and-2 count on me."

A lefty replacing the right-handed Wilson, Strange took one pitch from Texas closer Jeff Russell, a right-hander, then provided the clue—a soaring home run to right center that forced the game into extra innings. The conclusion came two innings later, when Strange, after hitting a single, scored on Griffey's liner into left field. Moments before Griffey's at-bat, the scoreboard screen showed the Angels losing to Oakland.

If ever absurdity was an orphan, it had a fine new home in the concrete shed on Occidental Avenue.

The 5-4 triumph rocked the house and devastated the Rangers. "I don't know how we recover from a loss like this," said Johnny Oates, the craggy Rangers manager. "I don't reckon I know."

Absurdity wasn't done. The game concluded around 11 P.M., just in time for the local TV news. In an extremely close vote, the anchors were saying on Kingdome monitors, the stadium measure, which had zero chance of success in July, was passing.

Not only were pigs flying, they were building dams, curing diseases, and making world peace.

At the edge of the Kingdome's north parking lot, a venerable sports bar, F.X. McRory's, was the site of the postgame, postelection party. Hundreds jammed into the joint, including owners, players, and fans, swirling in a stink of sweat, cigars, and booze. Among the celebrants was Paul Isaki, the Mariners' business vice president, who had done much to engineer support of the stadium campaign. He had just walked from the game through the parking-lot pandemonium to the bar.

"When Strange hit that home run, I just knew we would win the vote," he said. "With all the improbable things that were occurring, and the impact it was having on the community, it just had to be a fairy-tale ending."

As is sometimes the case, fairy tales need Angels. Their collapse was as crucial a part of the story as the Mariners' rise. After holding steady through the first couple weeks of September, they were defeated nine straight games. The night after the Strange events, they lost sole possession of the AL West lead to Seattle when Oakland beat them 9-6 while the Mariners were having their way again with the wasted Rangers, 11-3.

One of the Angels' stars, outfielder Tim Salmon, could feel the fates all the way down the coast.

"You'd look at the out-of-town scoreboard and the Mariners would be losing, then by the time you'd get in the clubhouse, they'd have won the game," he said. "We'd had a big lead in the division, and we weren't looking over our shoulder, but they were making such news with their comebacks. You could hear them coming. We weren't playing bad, just losing a few one-run ballgames.

"It was almost like destiny. There was nothing we could do to stop it."

After an off day for both teams, Salmon's point was underscored in improbable fashion again. While the Angels lost at Texas when ace starter and ex-Mariner star Mark Langston gave up seven runs, the Mariners won in the Kingdome against the A's. Coleman hit his first career grand slam for a tie at 7, then Alex Diaz, a little-known backup who did well in center field during Griffey's injury absence, followed with a pinch-hit, three-run homer off another former Mariners pitcher, Rick Honeycutt, for a 10-7 triumph.

The Friday-night victory was the first in a three-game sweep of the A's over a weekend series that drew more than 150,000 fans. The Mariners' dubious past, represented by Langston and Honeycutt, no longer was a drag on the future. For the first time in the season—and for only the twelfth day in their eighteen-year existence, not counting April standings—the Mariners were alone in first place.

Prosperity proved difficult to sustain, on two fronts. After nine losses in a row, the Angels rallied to win six of their last seven regular-season games, including a four-game sweep of the A's. The Mariners, who had a three-game lead September 26, lost their final two contests in Texas by 9-3 scores. Unused to the high altitude of the standings, they momentarily swooned.

"That was the one time we choked," Buhner said. "We felt the pressure like a knife. I'd never experienced pressure like that."

The political victory was also in full swoon. The election-night celebration turned out to be premature. A surprising number of absentee ballots, always a large portion of King County vote counting, went against the tax measure. By less than 1 percent of the final tally, the apparent victory became a defeat.

So the end of the regular season brought twin astonishments. Because the Mainers and Angels each finished 78-66, an unscheduled, single-game playoff was required to break the tie to determine the AL West champion. It would also keep the loser out of the postseason. Since the Yankees, who finished second in the AL East to Boston, had a better record (79-65) than Seattle or California, they were entitled to the wild-card spot that the Mariners had been targeting for months. So in the frenzy of the final week, second place in the West suddenly became meaningless. What became

Besides backing their team in October 1995, Mariners fans at the Kingdome also had a message for the state Legislature in Olympia that was debating whether to fund a new stadium. PHOTO BY BEN VAN HOUTEN

meaningful was a coin flip in the AL offices a couple of weeks earlier, which determined that Seattle would host a tie-breaker game against California.

Meanwhile, the fate of the franchise was back in the hands of the owners, who originally vowed to sell the team if the ballot measure lost. News reports that a group in northern Virginia had already made contact with Mariners representatives to purchase the club were met with an angry denial by CEO John Ellis.

"I'm not trying to sell the damn team," he told the *Post-Intelligencer* in late September. "That's the last thing I want to do. I'm not Jeff Smulyan. I don't want those sons of bitches [in Virginia] to end up doing this to me." A week later, Ellis announced the club was putting off any decision about a sale until October 31.

On October 1, as their final loss in Texas ended with the Angels' last game still under way in Anaheim, the Mariners literally did not know where they were going—to Seattle for the one-game playoff, or to New York to begin the new Division Series against the Yankees. Nor did they know if they would be back in Seattle next season.

But after three years of ordeals, the Mariners had learned to be comfortable on the precipice.

"Once the Angels won their last game," Buhner said, "we said, 'It's been tough to get this far, but what the hell. One more game—we can do it.' We had a great flight back, laughing, joking, ready to go."

As the team flew home, the front-office staff went into an all-night frenzy to create tickets and prepare for a game that hadn't been scheduled. The 1:35 P.M. start, to allow the winner travel time to New York for the start of the ALDS the following evening, forced Kingdome operations to double its workforce to more than one hundred to quickly convert the building from its football configuration, in which the Seahawks had beaten the Denver Broncos on Sunday.

Broadcaster Dave Niehaus, who had spread his syrupy baritone over nearly two decades of baseball dreck, was so fired up for the big game he was at the park by 8:30 A.M.

"I wasn't tired at all," he said. "The teams were running on adrenaline. This day was for the whole damn year."

Or as Buhner put it a little earlier, trying to capture for interviewers the significance of something he and Seattle had yet to experience: "Every throw, every pitch, every at-bat . . . every everything means everything."

Never had the sports crucible been described with more loopy eloquence.

Seven Days in October

C onfidence radiated around the Mariners. They had been forced into a one-game playoff against the Angels, but there was a noisy hometown crowd in the suddenly intimidating DinDome, with the ultimate intimidator on the mound, Randy Johnson. The Angels beat Johnson two months earlier, for his second and final defeat of the regular season, but since then the Big Unit was practically unscored upon.

"What better pitcher in baseball would you want out there at home?" said Piniella. "This is the way baseball should be: Winner goes on, loser goes home."

Pitching for the Angels was not intimidation, but irony. The Angels called on Mark Langston, the former Mariner who in 1989 was sent to Montreal in the trade that brought Johnson to Seattle. Gone six years, Langston's 74 wins with the Mariners were still the second-most in club history. No. 1? Johnson, with 95. Both would pitch on three days' rest, one less than usual.

Not long after the Angels arrived in town Sunday night, Langston was visited at the team's downtown hotel by Dave Henderson, his old Mariners teammate. In their early Seattle days, the two bought homes near each other in a prosperous Eastside neighborhood. The club's original No. 1 draft choice, Henderson retired after the '94 strike but remained a fan of ball and a neighbor of Langston's.

He discovered in his visit that Langston's left arm was so sore he couldn't comb his hair. He had been on heavy doses of anti-inflammatory drugs for the previous ten days to minimize his season-ending soreness. "I told him, 'Don't comb your hair—pitch,' "

Henderson said. " 'Your team needs you. You gotta go. You can't care that your arm is sore.' "

Even if Langston could comb his hair, the coif was destined to be messed up. The next afternoon, more than 52,000 fans played hooky from work and school to contribute an audio riot to the biggest moment in club history.

At first, Angels outfielder Tim Salmon thought he and his mates, winners of five straight, were up to the task.

"After our sweep against Oakland, we felt we had momentum and we were going to win," he said. "We knew the Mariners didn't want to fly all the way home from Texas for one game. We were all fired up. But I remember that first at-bat against the Unit—oh, man, we were in for it. I was overmatched. It was a terrible feeling to have. I had no chance against that guy in the most important game of the year."

Langston, once derided by a former Mariners manager, Dick Williams, for not having "gut one," dueled resolutely with Johnson through six taut innings. In the seventh, ahead 1-0, the Mariners loaded the bases for Luis Sojo, yet another of the Mariners' below-the-radar heroes. The backup infielder had an ungainly batting stroke and was an awkward runner, but he had an inexplicable knack for delivery in the clutch.

A Langston fastball was hard enough and tight enough to break Sojo's bat, but the ball took a billiards-style spin down the first-base line that somehow escaped first baseman J. T. Snow, squirting all the way into the bullpen bench in right field. By the time the ball was excavated, two runs scored. The throw went to Langston, whose relay was wide of catcher Andy Allanson, allowing Joey Cora to score a third run. As the ball bounded to the wall behind the plate, a huffing Sojo rounded third and headed home, where Langston was covering.

Allanson's throw was late. Sojo was safe. Langston sprawled on his back atop the plate for the better part of a minute as the Northwest exulted. In the press box as Sojo crossed the plate, radio color man Rick Rizzs shouted a phrase that became a part of the local sports vernacular: "Everybody scores!"

In the Angels clubhouse afterward, Langston was inconsolable. "Everything," he said, "unraveled all at once."

So had California's season in the run-up to this playoff game, although it took six weeks. In mid-August, the Angels led the

Mariners by 13 games. Then they produced what was calculated to be the third-biggest single-season collapse in baseball history, which ended with Langston prone on the Kingdome infield, a metaphor too corny even for B-grade Hollywood sports movies.

In the next-to-last inning of that descent, the humiliation became complete with another four Seattle runs. As he stood in right field in the ninth, Buhner looked around at the party for 50,000, full of chants, high fives, and hugs, and let his imagination drift over the past six years in Seattle.

"Are you kidding me?" he thought. "Is this the same Seattle Mariners?"

Buhner was among a handful of players with a full appreciation of the moment. Acquired in a trade with the Yankees in 1988, he became the starting right fielder in 1991, as well as a key figure in the franchise renaissance. Perhaps more than any other player in club history, Buhner bridged the changing times and the club's growth, and did it from the driver's seat as a clubhouse leader.

A quick-tempered Texan, Buhner in his early years would break bats and verbally blister teammates and managers, often more

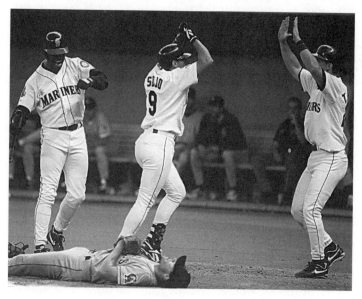

Luis Sojo's bases-loaded double drove in three runs to break open the one-game playoff against the Angels. Sojo scored on a throwing error by Angels pitcher Mark Langston, a former Mariner, who sprawled on the plate in exasperation.

©1995 SEATTLE POST-INTELLIGENCER/GRANT M. HALLER

angry with his propensity to strike out than with anything said or done to him. Then he would pull a profane prank in the clubhouse that would leave all aghast and laughing.

As success came and superstars went, Buhner and Edgar Martinez became the comfortable, familiar franchise bedrocks who made Seattle their permanent homes. With his shaved head and goatee, "Bone" was distinctive in looks as well as character. His fourteen years in Seattle would endear him to teammates for his passion and to fans for his accessibility.

One of the weirdest, most successful promotions in club history was "Buhner Buzz Cut" night, in which fans would gain free admission if they were shorn to their scalps by barbers outside the gates. The event became an annual fund-raiser for a breast cancer foundation, and over the years more than 22,000 fans proudly displayed their unadorned scalps in right field behind Buhner's position, sporting "Bald Is Buhnerful" T-shirts.

Ironically, the player for whom he was traded in 1988, Ken Phelps, was a Seattle native and graduate of Ingraham High School and a community stalwart too. But he was mostly a bust in New York, playing in just 131 games and hitting 17 homers over parts of two seasons before being dealt again. The Buhner-Phelps trade became so notorious in New York baseball folklore that it was part of an episode of the TV comedy hit *Seinfeld*. Upon meeting the Steinbrenner character for the first time, Frank Costanza, father of Yankees employee George Costanza, confronts him: "What the hell did you trade Jay Buhner for? He had 30 home runs, over 100 RBIs last year. He's got a rocket for an arm. You don't know what the hell you're doin'."

Over the next week, the Costanza wisdom was about to play out in real life. But at the moment, the ninth inning of a do-or-die game, the tension for Buhner became nearly unbearable.

"I was standing in the outfield thinking, 'I wish it was over. I wish this was the last out.' It was the most nervous I've been, getting through the last inning."

Johnson insisted on closing out the game himself. Although he allowed a run in the ninth, he gave up only three hits and struck out 12 in the 9-1 win. As the last batter of the Angels' season, Salmon entered the batter's box almost helpless from the noise.

"I never experienced anything that loud," he said. "I was trying to talk to Dan Wilson, trying to tell him congratulations. But he couldn't hear. My ears were ringing. The noise was echoing in my helmet. I took a couple pitches, but I don't even know if they were strikes or balls. My one indication I had struck out was the crowd's roar."

Squatting behind him and closer to the umpire, even Wilson couldn't hear the final strike call. He was so adrenalized that his breathing was labored. At the third strike, he burst from his crouch. Johnson thrust up both arms and pointed to the roof. Wilson sprinted up the mound and wrapped himself around the Big Unit.

"By the time I got to him," Wilson said, "I was out of breath, it was so exciting."

Eighteen seasons of basset-faced history ended. From the middle of nowhere, the Mariners had come to the midst of everything. Earlier in the week, *Dallas Morning News* columnist Randy Galloway described the Mariners as an "armpit forever" franchise. Now, on national TV in a do-or-die moment, the Mariners were offering sweetness.

In the bunker suite behind home plate, hugs and tears prevailed as owners and execs who paid large coin and poured heavy sweat over the past several years saw the first rewards play out in front of them. Lee Pelekoudas, the senior director of baseball administration, embraced his wife, Terri, as their eyes fell upon the club's teenage ballgirls who were sobbing joyously on the field.

"They have no idea why they're crying," said Terri Pelekoudas, her thoughts drifting over the sixteen years the couple had been with the club. "No idea."

The players scrambled off the field and to the clubhouse for a party eighteen years in preparation. Cigars were lit, champagne flew, and silliness exploded. Edgar Martinez, Johnson, Griffin, Griffey, Buhner, Blowers, and Charlton jumped into the training room whirlpool tub, uniforms, cleats, and all. Part-owner Chris Larson, spotting Piniella doing a TV interview, grabbed a ten-gallon bucket of ice water, and, with the help of 6-foot-8 Jeff Nelson, poured it over the manager's head so forcefully it nearly knocked him off his feet.

Taking in the scene along a wall, out of the way, was former first baseman Alvin Davis. The American League's 1984 rookie of the year carried on so nobly in the dark years that he was nicknamed Mr. Mariner. He left after the 1991 season, before the

Catcher Dan Wilson embraces Randy Johnson after the Big Unit's complete-game triumph in the one-game playoff over California. PHOTO BY BEN VAN HOUTEN

good times, but the club thought enough of his contribution that the retired Davis was flown in from California that morning so he could throw out the game's ceremonial first pitch.

"I still can't believe I'm here," he said, damp from many sopping hugs. "I'm so happy I can't even explain it. You know what? I believed this would happen. That's the honest truth. When I see Junior, Jay, Tino, and Edgar, guys I played with, succeed . . . it

SEVEN DAYS IN OCTOBER | 121

means so much to me. The hard times make these times that much sweeter." Four years earlier in the visitors' clubhouse in Texas, it was Davis who embraced trainer Rick Griffin in celebration of the first winning season. This time, the hugs held no awkwardness.

Much in the clubhouse was still sticky when the AL West champion Mariners (79-66) cut short the revelry. A charter flight was waiting at Seattle's Boeing Field to take them to New York, where the Yankees, led by manager Buck Showalter, had closed their season at 79-65 to become the AL's first wild-card team. The supremacy of the Mariners' division title would prove crucial in the best-of-five ALDS: It gave the Mariners the home-field advantage for the series' final three games. The Yanks finished second in the AL East Division to Boston (86-58), which would play AL Central Division champ Cleveland (100-44) in the other Division Series.

As he packed for New York, Johnson paid tribute to what he felt was a difference in the game and in the final home games of the regular season, and what would become the foundation of future success.

"The fans really helped me," he said. "When I first got to Seattle, if you wanted to see a lot of people, you had to go to a Seahawks game. But this season, they came out and supported us. They are a big part of this. I had a lot of emotion built up because of them, and I pitch on emotion anyway.

"You couldn't write a better story."

The story was not finished. Over the next six days, five more chapters would render the game against the Angels mere background music. The fans at Yankee Stadium—batteries, beers, and bad intentions in hand—were ready to rumble with the Mariners.

⁂

After beating the Yankees nine times in the clubs' thirteen regular-season meetings in '95, the Mariners didn't fear their division-playoff opponents. In fact, compared to what they had just experienced against the Angels, a playoff series seemed almost leisurely to Dan Wilson.

"We just got out of a one-game playoff," he said. "Three out of five is so different. There's almost a sense of freedom. We were in a series, not a do-or-die game."

A bigger series issue was fatigue. Game 1 was the Mariners' third game in three cities in three time zones in three days, all of which came after the climb of an extraordinarily steep hill in September. And because the Division Series was best-of-five instead of best-of-seven, Johnson would have enough rest to start only a single game.

"I had never been more exhausted," said Blowers, the third baseman and former Yankee. "The first day in New York, I was so tired I couldn't even focus. It was really weird."

The rambunctious crowd did its part, however, to keep everyone alert. As the coins began to pile up in the outfield, Buhner and Griffey plotted to annoy the beery masses. They began picking up quarters and inserting them in the leather folds of their gloves, infuriating the Bleacher Creatures, who couldn't believe millionaires were pocketing their change.

"Bosio asked me what the hell we were doing out there," Buhner said. "I told him when the riot breaks out, I'm up the stands and out of here with subway fare back to the hotel."

At the plate in Game 1, Griffey did what he could to supply some real annoyance, hitting two home runs in his first postseason appearance, including a 401-foot shot off the third-deck fascia in right field. But a bullpen collapse led by Bobby Ayala gave the Yankees a 9-6 triumph. The Mariners' top reliever in the first half of the season, Ayala began pressing in the second half and lost his mental toughness. In the seventh inning, he gave up four hits and three runs while getting just a single out. Afterward, Piniella shifted Tim Belcher, a starter who hadn't relieved all season, into the bullpen for the rest of the series. Ayala was no match for either the Yankees lineup or the crowd, which spiked its game-long badgering with an increasing number of projectiles. It was a night where no hair rested on the back of anyone's neck.

"There was just such electricity in the air," said Yankees manager Showalter. "Seattle is a tough place to play. They certainly can be very loud there. But I can't imagine a more electric ballpark than there was here tonight." Soon enough, his imagination would be tested.

Piniella was so concerned that, before Game 2, he met with the stadium's security director to demand more crowd control and better protection for his team. The increased security worked until the sixth inning, when back-to-back homers off Andy Benes by Ruben Sierra and Don Mattingly, in what would be his last game at Yankee Stadium after a storied fourteen-year career, gave the Yankees a 3-2 lead. The euphoria prompted a wave of debris to pour from the stands—tomatoes, grapefruit, cups, Frisbees, souvenir bats, stereo headphones, golf balls, batteries, softballs, toilet paper.

Enraged, Piniella, the former Yankees hero, pulled his team off the field for five minutes until matters calmed. Upstairs in his suite, George Steinbrenner stomped and fumed, figuring Piniella was pulling a gamesmanship stunt to blunt the Yankees' momentum. Already furious over umpiring calls regarding balls and strikes and safe/out plays, Steinbrenner had invited reporters into a video-replay room in the press box to show the purported errors. He even said that one of the umpires, a resident of Portland, had a Northwest bias against the Yankees. After the series, Steinbrenner was fined $50,000 by the American League for his words and actions.

The drama had just begun. The Mariners scored twice in the seventh for a 4-3 lead, but Paul O'Neill tied it again in the bottom half with a solo home run off Norm Charlton—his only mistake in an unusually long four innings of relief. The contest drifted into extra innings.

Griffey, bidding to become a new Mr. October, shocked the Yanks with a solo home run in the twelfth inning. It came off John Wetteland, the same pitcher who surrendered the homer to Griffey on August 24 in the Kingdome, the trigger event that began Seattle's astonishing run to the division title. In the bottom of the inning, Belcher, the former starter, relieved Jeff Nelson and was one out away from a split of the New York games when Sierra drove in the tying run with a double.

Four hours old, the game passed midnight into a second day. The temperature dropped and a light rain began, but few at the stadium preferred warmth and comfort over the drama in front of them. Belcher dueled ace reliever Mariano Rivera pitch for pitch for three innings until the fifteenth. With one on and one out, Jim Leyritz, a second-string catcher with a touch for the clutch moment, lofted a fly ball that a leaping Buhner, back to the right-field wall, tried to bring down. He came up empty-handed. After five hours and twelve minutes—the longest game in playoff history, by a half hour—the game ended on a walk-off home run for a 7-5 Yankees victory at 1:22 A.M. EDT.

Instead of bed, the Bronx turned to bedlam. As police horse patrols trotted onto the field to intimidate the crowd, the

Mariners appeared devastated. Belcher lashed out at a TV cameraman on his way into the clubhouse, where silence lay heavy. After all the onerous, exhilarating effort to get to the playoffs, the Mariners were abruptly down 0-2 and physically and mentally spent, with a cross-country flight in an hour. They would arrive in Seattle at 7 A.M., having logged more than 6,500 flight miles in five days.

"I'll never forget that night," said Dave Niehaus. "I just knew it was over. We have to fly back 3,000 miles and there's no way you beat New York three straight games." Still, the Mariners had spent an entire season, as well as most of the last three years, tied to the railroad tracks. It wasn't as if they had no experience in imminent peril.

⚜

On the off day in Seattle between Games 2 and 3, the Yankees helped out with two mistakes, one emotional and one tangible.

As Yankees officials made arrangements for arrival at the Kingdome, one made a request for a suite at the Kingdome for Steinbrenner and his entourage. Mariners president Chuck Armstrong obliged, booking for three games. Responded a Yankees' executive, "That's OK—we'll just need the one night." Word about that traveled fast.

The same hubris was displayed by Showalter, who decided to use his best veteran starter, Jack McDowell, in Game 3 against Johnson, the Mariners' ace. The Yankees were looking for more than a series win. They wanted a sweep.

"If they had held McDowell until the fourth game, it would have been advantageous to them," said Piniella. "The mistake was matching McDowell against Randy, because Randy was going to win, no matter what. We'd played very well at home, where we had a huge advantage in the Kingdome. A win would open the door."

Nelson, the relief pitcher who would find himself traded to the Yankees next season, saw Showalter interviewed on TV and picked up on the vibe that the Yankees weren't as confident as a 2-0 lead would seem to merit.

"He was asked if he was comfortable, and he said, 'Nothing's over,' " Nelson said. "He only had to win one of three, but the way he said it, it was clear he wasn't convinced."

The Mariners were 47-26 at home, including the last seven in a row, and had beaten New York six times in seven Kingdome games during the season. Seattle fans, having seen the rowdiness at Yankee Stadium, were particularly eager to participate in the club's first playoff series. Paying up to $350 for a $50 seat behind home plate, the crowd arrived early, bearing attitude and signs: "Welcome Back to Civilization" and "Even 25 Yanks Can't Beat Our Johnson." The Mariners played one more emotional chord: Broadcaster Dave Niehaus, the club's most enduring figure, threw out the ceremonial first pitch.

"Even down 0-2," Edgar Martinez said, "we had confidence we could win three straight."

Again pitching on three days' rest and tired from the emotions of Monday's game against California, Johnson relied more on breaking pitches instead of his fastball. He would have to go deep into the game, because the bullpen had largely spent itself in the 15-inning defeat. The Yankees' McDowell (15-10), the 1993 AL Cy Young Award winner, had no issue with fatigue: He sat out September to rest a sore back.

The largest crowd in Seattle baseball history (57,944) was so torqued that some fans began to emulate their Gotham counterparts. Yankees right fielder Gerald Williams was hit in the lip with a quarter, and in the fifth inning was targeted with a tomato.

"The crowd had the ability to disrupt you," center fielder Bernie Williams said. "It was very intense." Said Nelson, "Yankee Stadium is the loudest outdoor stadium, and the Kingdome was much louder. You had to scream the whole nine innings. Unbelievable."

Meantime, in the Mariners clubhouse after the game started, Charlton was sound asleep. Years earlier he learned how to complete his preparations, then nap to get ready for his late-game appearances. "I can't ride the emotional ups and downs of the game," he said. "I can't get involved. These people [Kingdome fans] are giving standing ovations for the third strike in the first inning."

A two-run homer from first baseman Tino Martinez gave Seattle a 2-1 lead in the fifth inning, but the Yankees loaded the bases in the sixth. The only left-handed bat in the Yankees lineup, Don Mattingly—others, such as All-Star Wade Boggs, wanted no part of Johnson—stepped in. Three hard sliders later, he stepped out. As he walked away from his third whiff of the game, Mattingly, used to the adoring four-syllable chant "Don-nie

Base-ball!" in New York, instead heard "Don-nie Strike-out!" from the Seattle wise guys.

A four-run sixth inning against McDowell and reliever Steve Howe for a 6-1 lead was cause for a great exhalation in Seattle—a Game 4 seemed imminent. Although Bill Risley relieved Johnson (four hits, two runs, ten strikeouts) after seven innings and gave up back-to-back homers, Charlton was awakened to get the last four outs of the game, just two days after he had pitched four innings in Game 2. It was exactly the moment, requiring a veteran's guts on the mound and in the clubhouse, for which Piniella had twice acquired Charlton.

"They beat the piss out of us twice in New York, we fly all the way back, and guys are wondering what's going on," said Charlton, a clutch performer on the Reds' 1990 champions who in September saved 11 games in 11 tries. "Most hadn't been to the playoffs before. Hey, some of them thought we got a ring for winning the division: 'No, you dumb-ass—that's the World Series.' "

❦

The 7-4 triumph was the second do-or-die victory in a week. But both had Randy Johnson on the mound. Now the Mariners had to do it two more times without him.

The Yankees' Game 4 starter, Scott Kamieniecki, who had a solid September (3-1, 2.48 ERA), looked a lot less of a "mistake" than his Mariners counterpart, Chris Bosio. Shaky in Game 1 and worse in Game 4, Bosio and his sore knees left after two innings and five runs. But this was not much of a night for pitchers. The Mariners' offense, which hadn't exactly been bashful in scoring six, five, and seven runs in the series' first three games, shifted into Incredible Hulk mode after the 5-0 New York lead that stunned another sellout crowd.

In the third, Edgar Martinez rocked Kamieniecki with a three-run homer that refired the masses. He knew that a special evening was upon him.

"I really felt it going around the bases," he said. "I was having a lot of good emotions. We were coming back from 5-0, and that's when I thought we were going to win the series."

As Nelson pitched four shutout innings of relief, the Mariners added another run in the third, then single runs in the fifth and sixth innings. It was 6-6 in the bottom of the eighth when the

Mariners loaded the bases and Martinez stepped up again, this time against Wetteland, the closer who had been drilled steadily by the Mariners.

"The Yankees never shied away from pitching to me," Martinez said. "I was looking for a fastball early in the count. Once it got to 2-2, I told myself just to put the ball in play. I didn't try to do too much, and I had my best swing."

He launched a soaring shot into the blue drape above and beyond the center-field wall. The man who would be called later in the weekend "the best hitter in baseball" by Mr. October himself, ex-Yankee Reggie Jackson, brought the house to its feet, plus a foot or so, with a grand slam. Martinez would later call the game the best of his life: an AL playoff record 7 RBIs in a four-hour spectacle featuring 30 hits, 11 pitchers, and an 11-8 Mariners triumph that began from a 5-0 deficit.

Spectacular as it was, it would prove the lounge act for the real show the next night—what they call on Broadway a high-kick finish. Game 5 would become one of those seminal moments in sports where a thousand times more people will tell you they were there than actually were there.

⁂

For the series decider the Yankees sent to the mound veteran David Cone, who won Game 1 with eight survivable innings (six hits, six walks, four runs), to match up against Andy Benes, the Game 2 loser, who gave up three runs in five innings. Cone, who began the season in Toronto before coming to New York, did nothing to discourage his big-game reputation through seven innings. He held the potent Mariners offense to eight hits while the Yanks pulled out to a 4-2 lead, thanks to a two-run homer by O'Neill in the fourth and a two-run double by Mattingly in the sixth.

After striking out six of the previous nine hitters, Cone in the eighth was gassed. Griffey got to him first, sending a fastball into the second deck in right field for his record-tying fifth homer of the series, to cut the lead to 4-3.

After Edgar Martinez grounded out, Tino Martinez walked and Buhner singled. Piniella then sent up two pinch hitters, Alex Diaz and Doug Strange. Each worked one of the game's best pitchers for a walk, the latter on a 3-2 forkball that barely missed low, forcing in the tying run.

Finally, Showalter pulled Cone after an unusually high number of pitches, 147, signaling that the Yankees' bullpen was as depleted as the Mariners'. While Mariano Rivera finished the inning without further damage, another extra-inning game loomed. But Piniella was in the dugout, contemplating the diabolical. Before the game, he had approached Johnson, his ace who supposedly was unavailable.

"I'm not sure we'll need you," the manager said. "But if I need to get the crowd into the game, if it's close. . . . By having you walk out there, whether we use you or not, will really get this place alive."

"I'll do whatever you need," Johnson said. "I'll take the walk, and you can use me."

Between the seventh and eighth innings, Johnson gathered up his gear in the dugout, then walked to the bullpen down the left field line. The crowd nearest the dugout noticed right away, and burst into mad cheers. Then the buzz began to grow, sweeping the building. Was it possible? Was the Big Unit, after just a single day's rest after his Game 3 victory, actually going to pitch in relief?

As Charlton, who relieved Benes for the last out of the seventh and pitched a scoreless eighth, began warming up on the mound for the ninth, Johnson slipped off his warm-up jacket in the pen.

"I thought it was a scare tactic," said Buhner, watching from right field. "Then you heard Randy hit the catcher's glove in the pen—crack! crack! The crowd started going ape-shit."

After Charlton allowed the first two batters aboard, Piniella came out to fetch his exhausted closer and gave the signal for Johnson. Around the Kingdome, fists pumped, eyes bulged, voices howled, and mouths dried.

Eastwood-style, the gunslinger ambled in slowly, the only quiet figure in the decibel festival.

"It was an extremely emotional moment," said Niehaus, who was describing the drama from the radio booth. "When he walked to the pen, everyone stood and cheered. Then he came into the game. . . . It was one of the signature moments in Mariners history."

Despite trotting out the three best hitters in their lineup, the Yankees had no chance. Boggs struck out, and Bernie Williams and O'Neill popped out to end the inning. As Johnson walked off the mound, western Washington seismologists bent over their machines for a closer look.

But in terms of theater, New York would take second to no team. As soon as Johnson entered the game, Showalter, having seen Wetteland battered senseless by the Mariners, sent down to the pen his own gunslinger. Jack McDowell, who lost the Game 3 duel with Johnson, was ready to answer the tactic. After Rivera got the first out in the bottom of the ninth, McDowell was called upon, and he dispatched the Mariners as readily as Johnson did the Yanks.

Extra innings, extra drama, extra audio. It would become only the fifth postseason series in baseball history to be decided in overtime.

Cone, the '94 Cy Young winner as the AL's best pitcher, was slack-jawed at the developments. Johnson, who would win the '95 award, and McDowell, the '93 winner, were taking high risks with their valuable arms. Coming back on such short rest ratcheted up the chance for injury. The stakes, apparently, were worth it.

"Randy and Jack—what can you say?" Cone marveled later. "Those guys are putting their careers on the line. Any one pitch could have blown out their careers."

The pitchers sailed through the tenth inning, Johnson striking out the side—his last pitch to O'Neill was recorded at 99 mph. But in the eleventh, the Unit's emotional tank ran empty. Leading off for the Yankees, Mike Stanley walked and was sacrificed to second, from where he scored on Randy Velarde's single. Johnson, pitching for the third time in seven days, then retired the side, but the 5-4 deficit momentarily sucked serious wind out of Puget Sound.

But as was the case throughout a stupefying season, there was always another chance and another way. This time, rather than the Mariners' usual Paul Bunyan act, they went the Tweety Bird route. Joey Cora, the little second baseman who homered unexpectedly earlier in the game, was aware that McDowell, a former teammate with the Chicago White Sox, was not the most agile of pitchers. Cora surprised the Yankees and Piniella—"I had no idea," he said—when he squirted a leadoff bunt down the first-base line that forced Mattingly to come a long way. Running almost out of the baseline, Cora eluded Mattingly's tag and flopped safely on first base. An emotional wind was back.

Up came Griffey, exuding confidence from a spectacular series debut on the national stage. He ripped a high fastball to center for a single that advanced Cora to third. That brought to the plate the last man in the world the Yankees wanted to see in that spot–Edgar Martinez.

The player whose reputation within baseball far outstripped his public profile was about to reverse that order, with what Piniella would describe later as "the hit, the run, the game, the series, and the season that saved baseball in Seattle."

Anonymity suited Martinez well. Although he won his first batting title in 1992, he had little recognition outside Seattle. "It has a lot to do with my personality," he once said. "I just try to do my job and stay quiet. I do what I'm told, and not cause problems." That sort of approach won over a lot more teammates and fans than it did headlines, which made him happy. Raised in Puerto Rico by his grandparents, Martinez would watch his grandfather, Mario Salgado, fuss over every task until it was done to near perfection. A truck driver, Salgado would not accept any imperfection in his vehicles.

"He hated to do mediocre stuff," Martinez said. "If he did a thing wrong, he would do it right until it was perfect. When I was younger, a lot of times I didn't understand it. But as I got a little older, I found myself doing things the way he did them.

"My friends would complain a lot about me."

He applied the same relentless attention to detail to his job as designated hitter. His perfectionism would annoy the Yankees as much as it did Martinez's childhood pals. His .356 average that won the batting title was the highest for a right-handed hitter since Yankee great Joe DiMaggio hit .381 in 1939. For the ALDS against New York, Martinez would hit .571, tying a major league record for most times on base in a playoff series (18, including 12 hits and six walks).

A moment before he stepped into the on-deck circle, Charlton came up to him, knowing Martinez had struck out in the ninth.

"He kept repeating that I was going to be the one again–I was going to do it," Martinez said. "I told him, 'This is my chance again.' "

As the concrete shed trembled, the chance came on a 2-1 count, when McDowell served up a split-finger fastball that hung instead of sinking.

"I got one up in the strike zone. I just wanted to put the ball someplace where we could get one run."

He chose the left-field corner. His line drive wasn't such a screamer that left fielder Gerald Williams was going to get a hard carom off the wall; as with Mattingly on the Cora bunt, he had to come a long way. As soon as it bounced, the game was tied, Cora walking home easily. As Williams ran down the ball in the corner, all eyes shifted to Griffey, who was under way like a Derby Thoroughbred, perhaps lifted by the identical command from 57,000 voices:

"GO! GO! GO!"

Or, as his good buddy Buhner put it in his own earthy fashion, leaping from the dugout to the edge of the field:

"Run, motherfucker, run!"

As Martinez rounded first, he was simultaneously tracking the ball and Griffey.

"When I hit it, I thought Junior would get to third, but I didn't think he would be able to score," he said. "As I got toward second, I saw he was going to try to score. I said, 'Oh!' I'd never seen him run the bases like that."

Ever the clinical analyst, Dan Wilson, out of the game after being pinch-hit for in the eighth, was on the bench and figured the sensible thing was to send Griffey all the way around.

"The worst case would have been a tie game with one out and a runner on second," he said. "But I didn't think he was going to make it. Hey, I didn't even think he was going to try."

As Griffey churned in perfect sprinter form toward third base, he looked at Williams and third-base coach Sam Perlozzo, and made his decision.

"I saw that Williams was playing towards left center," he said. "When I saw the ball land near the line, I ran as fast as I could for as long as I could. When I got to third, Sammy said, 'Keep going!'

"So I did."

The throw from Williams was relayed to catcher Jim Leyritz, but it was late and wide. Griffey slid across the plate with the sweetest baseball goods ever brought home to Seattle—the game's best player scoring on a double by the game's best hitter, in the eleventh inning of the final game of a playoff series they had once trailed 0-2 and were losing ten seconds earlier, to beat the ace of the sport's most legendary team.

In a phrase inserted by Niehaus into the lexicon of the Northwest, never in a grander fashion: "My, oh my!"

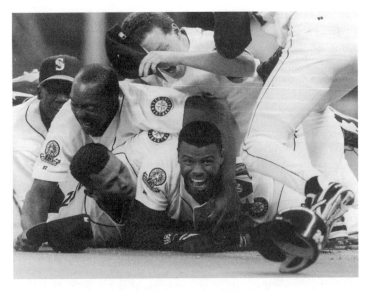

One of the most electric moments in Seattle sports history ended in a delirious pileup at home plate after Ken Griffey Jr. scored the winning run in the 11th inning of Game 5 of the 1995 American League Division Series to beat the Yankees.

©1995 SEATTLE POST-INTELLIGENCER/ROBIN LAYTON

In the stands, Dave Henderson, the Mariners' first drafted player in 1977 and now retired and a ticket buyer like all the mad folk around him, lost the professional cool carefully crafted after seventeen years in baseball. He was as dippy damn delirious as just about everyone else packing a Washington driver's license.

"For the first time, I was seeing baseball like a fan," he said. "It was the most exciting thing I'd ever seen in my life."

Greater plays of more significance have been made in the game's long chronicles. But for the Seattle Mariners, it was the epochal moment in the rise from the baseball sorrows. The 2002 *Biographical History of Baseball* described Martinez's shot "as one of the most dramatic hits in the history of postseason play." ESPN would rank the play as the No. 1 moment in Division Series play.

As he popped up from the plate, the jubilant Griffey was knocked to the dirt by his teammates, flashing from the bottom of the pig pile a soul-deep smile that created perhaps the most memorable image in Northwest sports photography. Years later, when the Mariners visited Cincinnati for the first time in interleague play, club broadcaster Rick Rizzs asked Griffey to recount the moment. "If [Perlozzo] was going to give me the stoplight, I was going to run through it anyway," he said. "It's hard to stop 210 pounds, especially going full speed. The inning lined up perfectly—a bunt, then a hit for [runners on] first and third, then Edgar hits the double, and I get to slide home and everyone jumps on me. I'll never forget looking in the paper the next day [to see] my smile on the bottom of the pile."

The Yankees, devastated, trudged from the field as the Mariners' bench and bullpen stormed past to the melee at home plate. The Kingdome crowd, as with many in town, and in the region, and many parts of sporting America still fighting to stay mad at baseball for the debacle of '94, became industrial-strength sloppy at the sight of the team from nowhere coldcocking the behemoth. The moment, and the series, was the perambulating paradigm of Yogi Berra's irrefutable wisdom: "It ain't over 'til it's over."

In the only place of peace, the visiting clubhouse, Cone was as inconsolable as Langston a week earlier. He couldn't forgive himself for walking in the tying run in the eighth, despite his otherwise gallant effort. The game was the toughest loss of his baseball life. But he saved his final remark for a tribute.

"The bottom line," he said, "is that's a helluva team over there."

He was nodding in the direction of party central—the Mariners clubhouse. For the second time in a week, after going 0-for-18-years, the Mariners were engaged in another champagne-and-hugs festival. In the din, Wilson was trying to grasp the achievement of the last seven days.

"If we do make the playoffs in the future, there's no way to equal this energy," he said. "It's never going to be like this again." Added Buhner, "You know how they say there's no crying in baseball? Bullshit!"

The brawny brawl with the Yankees set major league records for home runs in a playoff series with 22 (11 each) and combined batting average at .288 (Mariners .315, Yankees .259). Griffey's five homers—he was still operating with a plate and seven screws in his wrist—tied Reggie Jackson for the individual mark. The overarching achievement was expressed by Johnson:

"Who would have ever thought that the Seattle Mariners would be playing to go to the World Series?"

⁂

The deliriously improbable outcome needed a happy-ever-after curtain, but as is almost always the case in baseball, there was another game. In this case, at least another four. The reward for vanquishing the Yanks was a chance to play the team with the season's best record. There may be crying in baseball, but surely there are no favors.

After a day off, the Mariners joined the Cleveland Indians in the American League Championship Series starting in the Kingdome. At the beginning of the strike-shortened season, a $1,000 Vegas wager on a Seattle-Cleveland matchup in the ALCS would have earned the successful bettor a lavish retirement fund. Unlikely as was the Mariners' rise, the Indians had not been to the postseason since 1954. But with large revenues from a new ballpark, Jacobs Field, the Indians created a powerhouse that won 100 games in a 144-game season and easily secured the Central Division, which they would do five more times in the next six seasons. Both teams were helped by an odd slippage in the rest of the AL: The teams that, combined, had won the previous seven league championships (Oakland, Minnesota, and Toronto) each finished last in their respective divisions.

The Indians reached the ALCS far more easily than the Mariners, sweeping Boston in the Division Series. That meant their veteran starting rotation and bullpen for a best-of-seven series were rested.

The Mariners, meanwhile, were so desperate for pitching help that they added Bob Wolcott, the rookie, to their ALCS roster and promptly put him on the mound to start Game 1 against the AL's most formidable lineup. The development was another sign that the Mariners were not prepared for their success in the first season that demanded a third tier of playoffs. The addition of the Division Series put a premium on pitching depth, which the Mariners did not have.

In their season-long fight to reach the playoffs, the Mariners went through forty-six players, including a club-record twenty-four pitchers. Belcher and Salomon Torres were acquired in May, Charlton in June, Benes in July, and Wolcott was called up from the minors in August. Now Wolcott, left out of the Yankees series for an extra bench hitter, was thrown into the fire at age twenty-two against Indians legend Dennis Martinez, forty. Johnson's dramatic relief

Vanquished Yankees pitcher David Cone congratulates Edgar Martinez in the
Kingdome clubhouse after his series-winning double beat the Yankees.

©1995 SEATTLE POST-INTELLIGENCER/MIKE URBAN

appearance against the Yankees, only the second of his career,
meant the ace would be unavailable to pitch until Game 3.

Fatigue would prove to be the difference in the series.
Magnificent as it was, the joust with the Yankees took a toll.

Said Jeff Nelson, "It was a series that really kicked your butt
emotionally and physically."

The flickering flame was masked well in Game 1. Wolcott, with
three major league wins compared with Martinez's 231, acted the
part of stage-frightened kid, walking the first hitter, Kenny Lofton,
on four pitches; the second, Omar Vizquel, on five; and Carlos
Baerga on four. In 13 pitches, he threw one strike, had three men
on, none were out, and next up was the AL's leading home run
hitter, Albert Belle.

Piniella went to the mound. Instead of a typical rant about
throwing strikes, he caught Wolcott off guard.

"He said, 'Even if we get beat 11-0, it would be a good off-
season,' " Wolcott said. "That was kind of amusing."

Knowing the kid had to breathe to laugh, Piniella walked away.

Belle struck out.

Eddie Murray popped out foul.

Jim Thome grounded out to second.

No runs, no hits, no errors, and nobody believing what they just saw.

"That," said Indians manager Mike Hargrove, "was the game right there."

Said Wolcott, "I felt like Houdini."

The unlikely 3-2 triumph, helped by a two-run homer from Mike Blowers, gave more assurance to the Refuse to Lose crowd that the Mariners weren't going to be denied the World Series. If a win by Wolcott could be pulled out of the Mariners' hat, then sawing the Indians in half couldn't be that difficult.

But in Game 2 against another savvy Indians starter, Orel Hershiser, it became apparent that magic was not infinite. Hershiser was matched against an old buddy, Belcher; they were teammates on the 1988 Los Angeles Dodgers team that won the World Series. Despite being thirty-seven, Hershiser showed he was closer to his prime, giving up four hits and one run in eight innings for a 5-2 triumph. Only the third home loss in the last 25 games, the defeat deflated the biggest Kingdome baseball gathering yet, 58,411, and sent the series to Cleveland with a split in Seattle the Indians desperately needed.

"The prospect of being down 0-2 and facing Randy Johnson is not one that would cause your appetite to stay with you very long," Hargrove said. "This was a very big win for us."

Game 3 found Indians fans at Jacobs Field far more civilized than the fans in New York, and Johnson no less inhospitable than he was to the Yankees. As advertised, he disturbed dinners across the Midwest with eight innings of four-hit, one-run ball. But he left the game tied at 2-2, thanks to a misjudged fly ball by Buhner in right field—just his second error in 145 games. Charlton picked up for Johnson again with three more innings until Buhner atoned for his goof with a three-run homer in the top of the eleventh for a 5-2 win.

Despite the 2-1 series lead, signs were ominous. In the last seven Mariners games, three went extra innings. Besides having temporarily used up their two best pitchers, Johnson and Charlton, they had accumulated just 22 hits and 13 runs in the first three ALCS games. Martinez, the Yankees killer, was 0-for-11. He would finish the series 2-for-23 (.087); Vince Coleman would hit .100, Tino Martinez .136.

"In most games, you pick up a second wind, but as that series went on, it was tougher and tougher to get that second wind," Buhner said. "The bat was heavier, the shoulders more tired, the legs were harder to get going."

Supporting evidence was everywhere in the fourth and fifth games. In Game 4, lightly regarded Indians starter Ken Hill shut down the Mariners on five hits through seven innings of a 7-0 clubbing. In the final series game at the Jake, Bosio summoned the last of his guile to duel Hershiser through five innings and a 2-1 lead. But he was left in an inning too long, and Thome's two-run homer was the difference in a 3-2 win that provided a 3-2 series lead.

"Lou never let Chris go past five innings," Nelson said. "But he let him pitch into the sixth, gave up the home run, and that was it."

The series returned to Seattle, where for the fifth time in the past fifteen days, the Mariners faced elimination. They had a full Kingdome, they had Randy Johnson on the mound, and they had the belief. The flesh, however, was weak. The Mariners scratched only four hits off Dennis Martinez, and for the second time in three games were shut out, this time 4-0.

As he had done in Game 5 with Bosio, Piniella left his starter in too long: After battling magnificently, Johnson gave up three runs in the eighth. As Piniella came to the mound to replace him with Charlton for the final four outs, Johnson's first step to the dugout was greeted with a deafening roar, a salute to his courage in four do-or-die performances. As he took his hat off in salute, he and the crowd knew the party was over.

After scoring 35 runs in five games against the Yankees, the Mariners scored 12 in six against the Indians—a record low for a six-game playoff series. They hit a collective .184, the lowest post-season number in twenty-one years. Pitching was so dominant in the series that the teams' 35 runs combined was a new postseason low—by 14 runs. The results left no doubts that Cleveland was the superior team, just as there were no doubts the Mariners had spent themselves numb.

As the Indians gang-tackled each other on the Kingdome turf in celebration of Cleveland's first trip to the World Series since 1954, the stunned crowd watched for a few moments, disbelieving.

Then, from the upper deck in the outfield, from below the press box, and along the first- and third-base lines, scattered pockets of people started to do what they had become used to doing the last six weeks—cheering.

The Indians ambled off to their clubhouse to talk of the Atlanta Braves, their National League foe in the upcoming World Series. The Seattle fans began celebrating the immediate past. The cheering did not cease. Almost fifteen minutes after the game ended, someone entered the Mariners clubhouse with news:

"Lou, no one's left the building."

Startled, Piniella went into the clubhouse and asked the players if they wouldn't mind returning to the field. As they trickled back one by one, the ovations grew. The game was over, the season not quite.

"I have never," said Piniella of the many thousands who lingered, "seen anything like that."

As Piniella waved with both hands, tears streamed down his face. Bellicose and belligerent as the highlight videos claim him to be, Piniella has a heart as soft as Fourth of July ice cream. He was moved by the moment, as well as by the transformation of the city's sports history—an electric bonding between team and fans that moved governments, altered taxation and work schedules, interrupted classes and weddings, blistered hands, ravaged throats, and lifted spirits.

"To see this ballpark filled is what it's all about," he said, still emotional afterward. "It basically starts with the fans. . . . Everything has to start somewhere, and this organization has started its own tradition."

It was a tradition the lords of baseball said would never happen. For twenty-five years they were convinced there was little possibility baseball would be well received in Seattle, especially in an indoor ballpark that shunned the glorious Puget Sound summers. It hadn't occurred to them that Seattle, rather than a bad baseball town, was merely a town of bad baseball.

Offered some good baseball, funded by the region's new prosperity, evidence was incontrovertible that the Northwest would refuse to lose its baseball team. As the Mariners were dueling with the Yankees and Indians, public sentiment linked with some powerful lobbying pushed Governor Mike Lowry into calling a special session of the state Legislature to deal with funding a new baseball stadium. On the final weekend of baseball in 1995, the Legislature, after rancorous debate, approved a tax package providing $320 million for a stadium with a retractable roof.

Hard to know which was more implausible: the Mariners coming from nowhere, or the fans and their politicians coming from everywhere to embrace them.

It was probably a dead heat.

But not a dead end.

As Griffey, the star whose arrival changed everything, said in the clubhouse following the final loss to the Indians, "This is not the end. It's the start."

The baseball renaissance was upon Seattle.

So, too, as the old tradition would have it, was another crisis.

CHAPTER EIGHT

Field of Screams

Framing the southerly vista of Seattle that rolls out from the office windows of the King County executive, forty-two stories up in the Columbia Tower, are the Cascade Mountains and Puget Sound. Dead center in the panorama is Safeco Field and Seahawks Stadium, Seattle's immense, side-by-side temples of professional sports. Ron Sims's gaze falls every day upon the sports district, a visual reminder of events that almost caused him to quit his position as county executive, the job he long had coveted.

"It was the worst six weeks of my life," he said, recalling with little animation another baseball cigar that exploded in the face of King County government. In December 1996, for the third time in five years, the county's major league baseball tenant made a move to leave Seattle. This time the public perception was that the latest imbroglio was induced not by the manipulations of Major League Baseball, but by local politics, led principally by Sims.

On the same day, and the same hour, that Sims was appointed county executive by the Metropolitan King County Council to finish the term of Gary Locke, who a month earlier had been elected governor of the state of Washington, Mariners ownership put the club up for sale. Frustrated by delays and opposition to its agenda for the new Legislature-approved ballpark, CEO John Ellis abruptly called a press conference at a downtown hotel to say the fed-up owners were done talking, done writing checks, and done with baseball. G'bye.

Besides grinching a Christmastime weekend for sports fans, the Mariners' shocker spoiled the best day of Sims's professional career. After his appointment ceremony, attended by family,

The opening of Safeco Field in July 1999 allowed the Mariners to move outdoors from the Kingdome and into revenues that would make the franchise one of baseball's most profitable. ©1999 SEATTLE POST-INTELLIGENCER/DAN DELONG

friends, well-wishers, and county employees, a jubilant Sims drove to his home in the Mount Baker neighborhood of Seattle to discover a TV truck waiting on his street, and protest signs in his yard. One of the signs said, "Save your job," a job he would not be sworn into for three weeks.

"I'll never forget it," Sims said. "The culmination of eleven years of being in political office, becoming executive of one of the largest counties in the U.S., and I was hit with the Mariners' departure.

"I had no idea."

Nor did he have a clue about the size of the searing controversy that was about to disrupt his life.

"You would not believe the e-mails," he said quietly. "You would not believe the phone calls to my house. You would not believe what was happening to me in restaurants. My kids were baited at school: 'Your dad's the reason the Mariners are leaving.' It was awful."

A few days later, just before Christmas, matters grew worse. An old political rival, Slade Gorton, who beat Sims, the

Democratic challenger, in a rancorous 1994 race for the Republican incumbent's seat in the U.S. Senate, demanded a meeting. For the third time in his political career, Gorton was charging in to save baseball in Seattle, and Sims happened to be in the way.

In the 1970s, Gorton helped embarrass baseball into replacing the Seattle Pilots, hijacked after one season to Milwaukee, with the Mariners. In 1992 he helped find an owner in Japan and some local partners from the high-tech boom to keep the club in Seattle. Now that same group, after spending almost $200 million to buy and keep the Mariners going, wanted to bail out.

Having asked them to play ball originally, Gorton figured he owed it to the group to take a few swings on their behalf. To Sims, who put up a stout fight against Gorton in the Senate race, winning a surprising 45 percent of the vote, he owed less than nothing. The three-term senator confronted the rookie county executive–designate with a list of nonnegotiable demands from club ownership about the stadium project that would remove the for-sale sign.

"Slade came in and told me what the deal was going to be," Sims said.

Told, not asked?

"Correct."

After the meeting, a distraught Sims sought out Norm Rice, an old friend and the mayor of Seattle. The pressure from Gorton, the Mariners, and the public was so intense that Sims was considering turning down his appointment to the executive's job. Rice helped convince him that the issue was resolvable without sacrificing a career.

Sims hung in, and over the next month presided over yet another return from the precipice by the Mariners, thanks to a nearly complete capitulation by the municipal governments and the Public Facilities District (PFD), the seven-member agency created by the state Legislature to manage the ballpark project.

But the Mariners' decision to return didn't necessarily make Sims's life much easier. County voters who strongly opposed providing public money for a private enterprise such as a ballpark began to weigh in.

"The people who wanted no public subsidy began to hate me," he said. "They said I caved."

He did. So did nearly everyone who had standing to object to the stadium and its potential costs and consequences to the public. Two members of the PFD, Shelly Yapp and Ruth Massinga, quit shortly after the board agreed, on a 4-3 vote, to a stadium lease with the Mariners that included the demands presented by Gorton, estimated by the county to be worth around $50 million to the Mariners over the twenty-year life of the lease.

"The job of the board is not to be baseball fans or advocates of the Mariners," Yapp wrote in a statement announcing her resignation. "Their job is to be fans of the public and to protect the public purse." As always in the fight between public rights and private interests in sports stadiums, the line will never be as clear and straight as the line to first base.

The display of bare-knuckles power politics was only the beginning of the ballpark brawl. By the time it opened as Safeco Field in July 1999—a Seattle-based insurance company paid $40 million over twenty years for the naming rights—mistakes, cost overruns, and change orders added almost $100 million to the cost, making the final tab of $517.6 million the most expensive toll ever paid for a stadium in the U.S. By agreement with the PFD, the Mariners were responsible for costs above the eventual $380 million supplied by the public.

The financial upshot was that by Safeco's opening, ownership had invested $322 million in baseball—$100 million to purchase the club, a claimed $77 million in operating losses over six years, an initial $45 million for ballpark construction, plus the overruns. They took no annual dividends, because there weren't any.

"We were members," said Wayne Perry, speaking of himself and his fellow owners, "of the dumb club."

There were other costs too. Paul Isaki, the Mariners' vice president for business relations and the club's point man on the project, suffered a stroke in August 1998, around the time the Mariners began to understand the enormity of the cost overruns. Chief among the contributing factors for Isaki, who was fifty-four, was job stress associated with a project virtually out of control. No major physical impairment resulted from the stroke, but he lost some memory and vision. The stroke contributed to kidney failure and subsequent dialysis. In 2001 he received a transplant.

"That part of my life was a direct function of the three years spent on the ballpark project," said Isaki, who left the Mariners in early 1999 to return to state government. Appointed by Governor Gary Locke as his special trade representative to promote the export of state goods and services, he returned to a business world known for its hardball politics and international wrangles. But Isaki, born to Japanese-American parents in a World War II internment camp, never experienced anything as rugged as the ballpark project.

"It was absolutely the toughest in my experience," he would say later. "Nothing even rivals it."

※

Conceived from sudden passion for baseball by the public and equally urgent lust for profit from the businessmen who owned the club, the rush for a new ballpark was born out of major league baseball's arrogantly inefficient economic system and a failing Kingdome, abetted by a municipal government overmatched as an entertainment provider, and nearly killed by the historical enmity in Seattle between the baseball club and the pro football team.

As enjoyable a sport as it is aggravating as a business, baseball— and its economic chaos—has been the subject of numerous books, studies, analyses, congressional hearings, public protest, and law-suits. Its contentious business history sweeps over parts of three centuries and eight work stoppages, and remains largely unre-solved today, despite a modest truce achieved through a collective bargaining agreement with the players union in August 2002. But rather than revisiting these macroeconomic vagaries, it's possible to begin explaining Seattle's harrowing foray to the frontiers of public stadium mayhem, and another near-departure by the club, with a more simple human experience than bond debt, revenue sharing, and change orders:

Peeing.

In July 1993, a year after the Hiroshi Yamauchi–led group was approved as the Mariners' new ownership, part-owner Perry attended the All-Star Game at Baltimore's Camden Yards. The Orioles' new ballpark, with its retro look and modern, spacious amenities, was not only the gem of baseball, it abruptly trans-formed the way ballparks could generate big revenue.

Without looking at a single income statement or balance sheet, and without comparing and contrasting the aesthetic virtues,

Perry knew there was something vastly different about the Camden Yards baseball experience from the one at the Kingdome. His wife went to the rest room and came back in the same inning.

"It didn't take twelve innings," Perry said. "In the Kingdome, women stopped drinking after the fourth inning."

Among the Kingdome's many shortcomings for baseball, it lacked sufficient toilets, especially for women. Among all the weighty issues that had compromised baseball in Seattle, ease of peeing doesn't seem like much. Unless one really has to go. Then, of course, nothing in the world is more important.

Of simple needs are battles made.

"Baltimore is a nothing city versus Seattle, but it had a helluva lot better stadium," Perry said. "It was comfortable and beautiful, and it was clear they were going to derive significant revenue. I sat there thinking, 'We better get one of these, or we're toast.'

"We were going to war, and we were flying prop planes and the other guys are flying jets."

A year later, when two water-soaked tiles fell from the Kingdome ceiling a half hour before fans were admitted for a Mariners game, the issue of discomfort was leapfrogged by safety. The ensuing public debate about accountability and responsibility for a repair that ended up costing $70 million revealed design and construction flaws, as well as a long-standing neglect of maintenance, that left the then eighteen-year-old building vulnerable. It was already vulnerable to the criticism of baseball people.

"The Kingdome was a nightmare from day one. It was a very difficult place to attract pitchers," said Woody Woodward, the club's general manager from 1988 through 1999. "It made it harder to build a club.

"You know those great artists' renderings of the old-time ballparks? Tell me when you see anyone sketch the Kingdome."

The dominoes that began toppling toward Kingdome death and ballpark birth began at least as far back as 1975, when the Kingdome was under construction. A young engineer for the contractor that would supply the roof's insulation, Adrian Jenkins, stood atop the partially completed concrete roof as a crane accident punched an eighteen-inch hole in a bay between two of the umbrella-like ribs. Jenkins made his way over to inspect the minor damage. His first glimpse made him gasp. He felt his knees weaken. Having studied the building blueprints, Jenkins knew the roof specifications called for a five-inch thickness. The hole exposed the fact that the roof was less than half of that.

"I had the impression I was nearly walking on tissue paper," Jenkins said. "I was 250 feet off the ground walking on damn near nothing."

Although the roof structure never did falter, the thin pour of concrete indirectly helped bring about the 1994 tile travail. In 1991, Jenkins, then his company's international sales manager, was hired by King County's insurance company to survey the roof's condition. His report disclosed nearly ninety leaks and concluded that condensation inside the Kingdome could contribute "to the hazard of falling structural components" from the building's ceilings or roof.

His report never gained the attention of top King County officials until he was summoned to a hearing three weeks after tiles fell. Because of the lack of a proper vapor barrier, Jenkins contended that condensation from the Kingdome's interior penetrated the wood-fiber tiles and the porous, thin concrete roof as well as eighty-six miles of roof seams. The vapor eventually helped rot the exterior insulation, which allowed rainwater leakage.

"The roof was a disaster," he said in 2002 of his inspection eleven years earlier. "If it didn't leak today, it would leak tomorrow. It was gone. There were leaks from day one. There had been warnings that the problem existed and was going to get worse. Nobody knew, including me, how bad it would get how fast.

"By the early '90s, it got to the point where there wasn't a helluva lot you could do to save the whole roof."

After persistent complaints and warnings about the Kingdome roof's leaks and dirty looks, Tim Hill, elected King County executive in 1986, agreed in 1993 to authorize a $3.9 million resurfacing, for which Pacific Components of Seattle was the low bidder. Instead of using more expensive but more efficient techniques of sandblasting and mechanical devices to remove the old roofing materials, water and small pressure washers were deployed.

In the year after the project began, less than a quarter of the Kingdome's forty bays were cleaned. Some of the ceiling tiles were so water-saturated they could be seen bulging, but county workers were ordered to rebolt the offending tiles from the outside. Water from the washing leaked onto the playing field and stained the artificial turf, while in the seating areas, baseball fans complained of showers. Once the two tiles fell that summer, years of told-you-so warnings echoed throughout county government.

The neglect, superficial fixes, and bad calls were typical episodes in the building's sorry history. A succession of executives and King County Council members, avalanched by often-contradictory solutions from experts, didn't want to write the big checks to fix an eleven-acre roof and ceiling that were not built properly the first time.

"We had quite a few meetings with management at the Kingdome," Jenkins said. "We were talking to people who could not act. They were hamstrung by county politics."

In the end, the leaders and public paid dearly. Including interest and make-goods to displaced tenants such as the Mariners and Seahawks, the roof cost more to fix in 1994 (absent inflation) than the Kingdome cost to build in 1976–and the fix, as well as the entire building, would last for only six more years. In 2000 the Kingdome was demolished, a unique architectural creation gone to waste largely because a municipal government was ill equipped to balance the needs of pro-sports tenants, taxpayers, and customers in the construction and maintenance of a one-of-a-kind entertainment and assembly venue.

⁂

The Kingdome's political and economic demise began in earnest in 1994, when Gary Locke succeeded Tim Hill as county executive and appointed a task force to analyze the Kingdome's future for baseball. As the panel reached the predictable conclusion in 1995 that a new, baseball-only stadium was the best solution, the Seahawks chirped that they needed a new place too.

Seattle's National Football League team was owned by Ken Behring, who was about as popular as another California real-estate developer who earlier fled the Seattle sports scene, Mariners owner George Argyros. The Seahawks, however, had been far more successful on the field in the ten Sundays a year they used the Kingdome than the Mariners in eighty-one dates. The NFL was also more enlightened economically than Major League Baseball, sharing national revenues so equally that smaller-market teams were on a roughly similar competitive footing with big-market teams.

Nevertheless, Behring insisted that he was not making money operating in the Kingdome because of its revenue inadequacies.

Once the state Legislature in 1995 authorized a public vote in
King County for a new baseball stadium, Behring went into me-
too mode, seeking more than $100 million in public money for
renovating the Kingdome to better suit football. But the
Seahawks made a tactical public relations mistake. The franchise
deliberately did not support the baseball stadium campaign. Since
the ballot measure lost by fewer than a thousand votes, many stadium advocates passed some blame to the Seahawks.

It was the latest in a long line of resentments between the
Kingdome co-tenants that began from the mid-'70s birth of both
teams and continued into the new century. A helpless parent, King
County could not get the quarreling sports siblings to play nice.

"They just didn't like each other," said Ron Sims, who was
elected to the King County Council in 1985. "There was no
bridge."

In fact, the situation in Seattle was similar in almost every city
that had a multipurpose stadium serving football and baseball.
From 1960 to 1971, all twelve stadiums built in the U.S. were
designed to accommodate both, but made neither happy, just as
with the 1976-model Kingdome. The sports were forever at odds
over leases, concessions, premium seating, scheduling, field conditions, and access.

Co-tenancy also left fans poorly served. The round shape of
the Kingdome left midfield football seats far from the action,
while many of the Kingdome's baseball sideline seats were canted
away from the infield. Players on both teams universally hated
the hardness and friction of artificial turf, deemed a necessity by
building operators because of heavy use. As far back as 1985,
baseball commissioner Peter Ueberroth declared that baseball's
objective was to get all teams into single-purpose stadiums. By the
mid-1990s, the Kingdome and the Metrodome in Minneapolis
were the only domed stadiums hosting both sports.

Back in Seattle politics, the Seahawks early on enjoyed a better
relationship with the county. The Kingdome served football better
functionally and aesthetically, and put fewer physical demands on
it. For the team's first twelve years, until it was sold to Behring in
1988, the Seahawks were owned by the Nordstrom family of the
retail-clothing empire. The family and the business were longtime

Seattle icons, held in higher community regard relative to the early baseball ownerships. Seahawks games were consistently sold out and entertaining, with a waiting list for season tickets said to number more than 20,000.

There was also a distinctive difference in the way the two sports cultures related to local governments.

"They're so diametrically opposite—I don't know if you want to call it light-years—from the top of the leagues on down," Sims said. "The NFL believes that it can't endure long periods of public hostility. Major League Baseball believes it can persevere past it. The obvious reason is that in this country, baseball has played a much bigger historic role. It's been inculcated in the American professional sports mind. Baseball believes that 'We were here before you came, and we'll be here after you leave.' They can endure huge dropoffs in the numbers of fans showing up.

"In football, there's a kind of 'We try harder' aspect. Are they tough negotiators? All these people are tough negotiators. But they are easier to deal with because they are unwilling to threaten or shed light on the tensions between the parties. They try to work it out without cameras and a lot of public debate."

The enterprises did have something in common, however.

"Every single meeting was about money," Sims said. "I never had a meeting that wasn't demanding more general-fund money from taxpayers to subsidize them. They saw themselves as almost a single defining benefit of living in the region. You'd hear about how many people would move here or visit, or how much money they'd generate. They even wanted a share of the flat show revenues [home, car, boat, and outdoors exhibitions] and we had to push them back on that.

"Government simply cannot meet the insatiable appetites of professional sports."

In the years when the Mariners began to get good, the once-beloved Seahawks, under Behring and his son, David, the team president, went bad. Besides reversals of fortune on the fields, there was a Kingdome difference: The Mariners' lease expired in 1996, while the Seahawks' agreement went through 2005. The Seahawks may have been more reasonable tenants, but by the time Sims began leading the county, the Mariners had the public and business leverage. The narrow 1995 election defeat of the plan for a new baseball stadium underscored the point. Despair at the defeat was plain among the big backers of baseball. That included the downtown Seattle business community and the media, which suddenly discovered that good baseball was also good for street sales, ad revenues, and ratings points. Prior to the election, a rather mundane afternoon meeting of the county council's budget subcommittee, in which a stadium item was on the agenda, drew the publishers of the region's three largest daily newspapers. Only *The Seattle Times*' Frank Blethen (known in his newsroom as Ballpark Frank) testified on behalf of the stadium proposal, but the buzz around the halls of county and city governments that week was that no one could remember when Blethen, the *Seattle Post-Intelligencer*'s J. D. Alexander, and the *Tacoma News Tribune*'s Kelso Gillenwater had ever shown up alone, much less together, for a local government subcommittee meeting.

Besides the editorial championing of the stadium by the newspapers, Microsoft was already on board with some of its current and former managers in club ownership, as was Boeing, the region's biggest employer and most influential industrial player. In addition to having CEO Frank Shrontz as a token member of ownership, Boeing's chief lobbyist, Bud Coffey, suddenly loomed large.

For many years, Coffey, a vice president, had been the most influential lobbyist at the state capitol, not only because of Boeing's big foot, but also for his uncanny ability to win over legislators and fellow lobbyists with a rare combination of honesty, charm, integrity, and a judicious use of corporate muscle.

"People trusted him," said Paul Isaki. "They didn't always like what he was doing, but they respected him. He was good, he delivered, and he never lied. Simple as it sounds, that isn't typical."

Those virtues, after nearly forty years working the state halls for Boeing, translated into considerable power. Shortly after the stadium's election defeat, a meeting took place that included county executive Locke, Mayor Rice, lobbyist Coffey, Isaki of the Mariners ownership group, and Bob Gogerty, the public affairs consultant who helped rally the stadium campaign from as far back as the Mariners were behind the Angels. After a short exchange of hangdog looks, Coffey said, "Well, it looks like we're going to have to call a special session of the Legislature."

Isaki looked at Coffey.

"Who," Isaki said, "is 'we'?"

He soon found out. Locke, Rice, and Gogerty were longtime friends and Democratic brothers with Governor Mike Lowry, and Isaki had worked as an international trade representative for Lowry's gubernatorial predecessor, Booth Gardner, another Democrat. Since Gogerty ran Lowry's successful 1992 campaign for governor, it wasn't difficult to get Lowry to pick up the phone that evening in the governor's mansion in Olympia. As the group sat around a speakerphone in Gogerty's Seattle office, he told Lowry, "We all want to come down and talk to you. We think we really need to talk about this baseball situation."

The next day the governor's helicopter ferried the group to Olympia.

"Mike's not what you'd call a baseball fan or a football fan or any fan," said Gogerty. "He's a policy wonk. But he said he'd take it under advisement, and he did."

Lowry's liberal instincts told him, as did several members of his staff, not to get involved in what amounted to a public subsidy for a private business. But his political instincts told him something else: A lot of people, including a lot of important

Boeing lobbyist Bud Coffey (second from left), and Mariners vice president Paul Isaki (right), strategize during a break in a session at the state Legistature in Olympia.

©1995 SEATTLE POST-INTELLIGENCER/GRANT M. HALLER

people, wanted the stadium to happen. And he considered the franchise sale threat real.

"It wasn't a negotiation; I definitely thought it was not a bluff," Lowry said. "They had a hot product to sell and they were losing a lot of money. They were saying, 'It's been nice, but it's going to happen.' "

After a talk with Mariners CEO John Ellis to confirm intent, Lowry convened, on the day of the one-game playoff with the California Angels, an impromptu "sports summit" that included legislative leaders. Amid widespread political skepticism that was almost equal to the widespread public delight over the ballclub, Lowry began preparations to call for a special session of the Legislature, which normally meets in January—too late for the Mariners, who had hoped that with passage of the King County measure, a new stadium would be ready for the 1998 season.

"Frankly, I was going to have to go out on a limb, or it wasn't going to happen," Lowry said. He began to make his case for a tax plan with legislators as well as the public. Reflecting on it years later, Lowry explained his rationale.

"A stadium is not as important as quality of education, quality of environment, or the overall economy, but it's a small part of the picture," he said. "As I've said about eight thousand times in my life when people are shouting at me, it's not an either or question of whether we do a stadium instead of supporting education. That's never been the question. The state appropriation for education is more than $4 billion a year—and that's just the state.

"You can spend forever analyzing sports' economic impact. But in my view the activity generated by 45,000 people at a ballpark and related activities, relative to a twenty-year taxation that includes user taxes, will come out somewhere between a wash or just a small benefit. And that's not including the community goodwill issue, because putting a number on goodwill is always difficult to do."

He also freely admitted to the axiom that prevails among his elected contemporaries in every state facing the same pressure from sports teams for public subsidy: No politician wants a team to leave on his or her watch.

"There are reasons for old bromides," Lowry said, smiling. "I'd like to think that reason was down lower on the list, but it's absolutely true."

Pressure built on legislators too. Coffey corralled at least a dozen of his fellow lobbyists to work without charge on the campaign. The week of the division series with the Yankees, the Home Town Fans organization funded by the Mariners took a leftover $10,000 from the failed election campaign and began a phone-bank operation to instruct voters around the state to call hot lines and urge legislators to support stadium funding.

Given the baseball entertainment that voters were being provided that week, the sell was not a tough one. The state hot line received 27,000 calls on the topic after October 1, and calls and letters to Lowry numbered nearly 5,000. Reluctant legislators faced a changed, and charged, circumstance from the past spring when they approved the sales-tax increase for the King County vote that they knew to be virtually doomed.

"They thought if the vote lost, the Mariners would disappear," said Isaki. "It lost, but the issue didn't disappear. Not only that, they faced a thousand-fold more troops than the first time. The mood was very different. It was 'We have to give them something different, because we now care that it works.' "

On the day the Mariners began the American League Championship Series against Cleveland, Lowry announced that legislative leaders had created a workable tax package that authorized a $320 million stadium with a retractable roof.

The negotiations, described as "gruesome" by Senate Majority Leader Mark Gaspard, produced a series of taxes: a 0.5 percent surtax on food and drink sold at restaurants, bars, and taverns in King County; a 2 percent surcharge on car and truck rentals; and a 5 percent admissions tax on all Mariners tickets in the new park. The state agreed to divert 0.017 percent of state general sales taxes collected in King County to the project. A new sports-theme lottery scratch game and commemorative stadium license plates were also authorized.

The state share amounted to $107 million, the Mariners would contribute $45 million (and were allowed to keep revenues from stadium naming rights), and the county tax increases on restaurants, car rentals, and tickets would supply the rest of the money.

The day before the ALCS moved to Cleveland for Game 3, Lowry summoned the entire Legislature for a special session to debate the package. After three days of threats, near-collapses, and twisted arms, the Senate voted 25-16 and the House voted 66-24 to approve the package just as the Mariners were eliminated from the playoffs by the Indians.

The package was authorized without the requirement of a public vote, something that opponents never forgot. In subsequent years, public initiatives became laws that curbed the state Legislature's ability to raise taxes for any project. The baseball stadium's tax funding was frequently cited by critics as an example of unchecked government spending for special interests.

The stadium tax plan had the virtue of keeping tax consequences to one county while drawing from optional spending sources, not general tax funds. But critics, including a Tacoma-based government watchdog group, Citizens for Leaders with Ethics and Accountability, claimed the package was a misuse of public funds that was unconstitutional, and filed a lawsuit.

The legislation did not include financial aid for the Kingdome. Going into the session, there was a plan endorsed by the King County Council to create enough taxation to also cover the Kingdome's $70 million repair bill as well as up to $100 million in improvements that would satisfy the Seahawks. But the state told the county and the Seahawks to drop dead, which infuriated both parties since the Seahawks were an annual moneymaker for the Kingdome, while the building, thanks to previous lease concessions, actually lost money on each Mariners game.

Adding to the county's anger was the creation of a Public Facilities District board to own and operate the stadium and oversee its construction. The board members, four appointed by the state and three by the county, would have total control of the project, including siting, design, management, and financing. But if something went haywire that would jeopardize the $320 million in bond sales, the county would be the responsible party. The state's rationale: The Kingdome was screwed up by county politics, so it will be forbidden by law to compromise the new park.

Faced with no reasonable alternative and under enormous pressure, the County Council, angry but helpless, voted to approve the issuance of bonds for the project. Approval for public funding of a new stadium completed a reversal of fortunes for the Mariners that was no less astonishing than the players' turnaround from the short, fat kids of baseball to contenders.

Despite the triumph, the crossroads moment at the state capitol was not the final resolution for baseball in Seattle. Remember, this was the Mariners, a team created by litigation and nurtured by complaint and chaos. The OK for public funding was merely a respite between crises.

Over the next fourteen months, the relationship between the club owners and the ballpark agency, the Public Facilities District (PFD), would take center stage as the parties wrangled over almost every aspect of the new stadium, all before ground was broken. The intense, complicated triangle between the public agency, the private businesspeople who owned the club, and the King County bond issuers heaved apart on December 14, 1996. That was also the day Ron Sims was named King County executive, but the Mariners undercut the biggest moment of his political career as John Ellis shocked Seattle and baseball with the decision to pull out.

"Reluctantly, after more than three years of work toward fulfilling the dream of thousands of fans," Ellis read from a prepared statement at a press conference, "the Baseball Club of Seattle has concluded there is insufficient political leadership to complete the ballpark project in 1999."

At an impasse with the PFD for nearly a month over terms of a twenty-year lease, the Mariners said the trigger event was an advisory letter sent two days earlier to PFD chairperson Joan Enticknap from four of the County Council's thirteen members: Sims, Pete von Reichbauer, Larry Phillips, and Cynthia Sullivan. The four wrote that they were alarmed at the breakneck pace of the proposed construction schedule as well as the unresolved legal challenge to the constitutionality of issuing the bonds.

"Frankly, we think the public would be better served if the PFD were to adopt a more realistic schedule," said the letter, backed with advice from county staffers who said there was a high risk no one would buy the bonds until the legal challenges were resolved.

The council members' anxiety had been ratcheted up by another sports development—the Seahawks' demand for a new stadium, too. In February 1996, Ken Behring caused a firestorm of his own when, frustrated by alleged operating losses and the lack of progress on improving the Kingdome, he abruptly announced he was moving the franchise to Southern California.

Almost immediately he began trucking some of the team's equipment to Los Angeles, which had recently lost the Raiders to Oakland and the Rams to St. Louis. The NFL, however, had a bigger say. Disliking Behring nearly as much as the average Seahawks fan, football commissioner Paul Tagliabue forced Behring to keep the team in Seattle, citing a valid lease as well as an agreement Behring and all other owners signed to keep the Los Angeles market vacant until the league collectively chose a course.

By midyear, Behring's boondoggle was over. But a plan was afoot in Seattle to disconnect Behring from the Seahawks. In the spring, Microsoft co-founder Paul Allen, owner of the NBA Portland Trail Blazers, emerged as a willing purchaser for the Seahawks, but only if the same demand made by Behring was granted to him—a better facility.

The plan favored by Allen was a renovated Husky Stadium at the University of Washington. But when the surrounding neighborhood, loaded with the politically influential, objected, the favored priority became the demolition of the Kingdome and replacement with an open-air football stadium on the site, across the street from the now-imperiled new ballpark. If Allen, said to be worth more than $20 billion, didn't get a tax-subsidized deal like the Mariners, he would let his option to purchase the team from Behring expire, allowing him to sell to out-of-towners or move, this time perhaps with the NFL's blessing.

The Seahawks-Mariners animus flared anew. The Mariners were furious with Behring and Allen for complicating the county's decision-making. The Mariners saw Sims and von Reichbauer as champions of the Seahawks cause, and potential saboteurs of the Mariners deal. The pair was an odd political couple—a black urban liberal Democrat and a white suburban conservative Republican—but became friends and allies on the council who grew weary of baseball's incessant demands. It was von Reichbauer who parlayed friendly relations with Behring and an acquaintanceship with Allen into the deal that kept the Seahawks in Seattle until the stadium issue could be resolved.

Critics said the Seahawks' deal came at the Mariners' expense. Then came the December 12 letter to the PFD cowritten by Sims and von Reichbauer, which was seized upon by the Mariners as a smoking gun proving the plot against them. The four council members' request for delay was seen as the latest, and last, decision going against their interests because it jeopardized the club's No. 1 stadium goal: an April 1999 opening.

"Sending that letter was like throwing a stick of dynamite into the fire," said fellow council Republican Rob McKenna. "It was irresponsible."

Von Reichbauer countered that the Mariners' reaction to the letter was mere cover for a decision already made. "I can't imagine making a multimillion-dollar decision on December 14, based on a letter sent December 12—it's an extraordinary overreaction," he said. "I think there are some principles about fiscal responsibility that cannot be compromised when it comes to stadium issues."

As the fingerpointing grew intense, the Mariners had a political problem of their own: Ellis. During delivery of the club's drop-dead statement, Ellis, whose temper was legendary, showed his emotional flip side. He momentarily broke down, offering that he was hurt by the thought that his granddaughter would no longer be able to see her beloved Mariners.

The gesture was seized upon by columnists, opponents, and skeptical TV viewers, who interpreted the tears as a cheap, transparent manipulation to gain public sympathy for put-upon millionaire owners. The "granddaughter speech," as it quickly became known, has served since as a shorthand reference in local civic discourse for what not to do in a critical public moment. Cynicism was so strong that it created a civic myth: Just before taking the podium, it was said, Ellis was advised to tug out some nostril hairs, an old Hollywood trick to induce tears.

Years later, Ellis not only swore no such thing happened, he also admitted he was the wrong man to deliver the bad news.

"I was so fucking emotional," he said during the club's 2003 spring training in Arizona, which was attended by granddaughter Kerri, now seventeen, who has Down's syndrome. "I'd been so involved in this thing. People think I contrived the story, but I didn't. Baseball is the biggest damn thing in Kerri's life. Jay Buhner, her hero of heroes, used to take her for rides in a golf cart down here."

Ellis also said his recommendation to end the project, which was accepted unanimously by the other owners, was influenced by another experience in which he also became too emotionally involved. A couple of decades earlier, during the time he was president of Puget Power & Light Company, the electric utility that served much of the region outside Seattle and Tacoma attempted to build twin nuclear power plants on 1,500 acres in the scenic Skagit River Valley, about an hour north of Seattle. But the discovery of a geological fault, as well as large community protest, eventually stopped the $3.8 billion project in 1980, two years before the first plant was to have come on line. The company and its partners had invested more than $300 million in planning and equipment for the site.

When news of the geological problems emerged well into the project, Ellis said he was advised by some to abandon the controversial Skagit Valley site and move it to the Hanford nuclear reservation in eastern Washington. But he pushed on. He later conceded it was a big mistake. The experience haunted his judgment at a pivotal time for the ballpark project.

"I thought, 'God almighty, we have another one in baseball,'" he said. "This time, I'm not going to let it happen. I thought it would be the dumbest thing in the world to plow ahead again."

However sincere he was about his granddaughter, and however well-meaning his attempt to avoid another financial debacle, Ellis's community reputation would become another casualty of stadium politics, much in the manner of Sims's political standing and Isaki's health.

Public contempt for all parties was running deep throughout Puget Sound. The baseball club was up for sale for the third time in five years, and for the second time by the supposed good guys. The public's share of stadium funding was soaring—starting at $240 million, it would eventually wind up at $380 million—while no lease deal had been struck. Resentment toward baseball still lingered from the 1994 strike, and now there was football demanding its own subsidized playpen. Simultaneously, the Mariners and Seahawks were in play nationally—not just playing.

Wrote Steve Kelley of *The Seattle Times*: "I'm sick of personal seat licenses and luxury suites. Sick of $100 seats. Sick of free agents and holdouts. Sick of threats and broken promises. Sick of all of the owners and politicians and even some of the players. I'm sick of the irresponsible baseball owners, who let salaries spiral out of control, then ask us to bail them out.

"I'm sick of everybody protecting their turf and nobody working together."

Fury reached its apex in the person of Senator Gorton. Vacationing in Hawaii, he had known nothing of the Mariners' decision to pull out until his return, when he was surrounded by reporters at Sea-Tac Airport. He went into action almost immediately, using his bully pulpit to raise hell with Sims and all involved politicians—especially von Reichbauer, who fell into Gorton's crosshairs at least in part because of his friendship with Sims, Gorton's election opponent in 1994.

Less than twenty-four hours after Ellis's notice of sale, von Reichbauer's fellow council members, some of whom savored the chance to punish a powerful political rival, voted to strip him of his budget committee chairmanship, the council's most powerful post. Members were eager to show they could get back on the Mariners' side by putting von Reichbauer in the doghouse.

Gorton presented to Sims the nonnegotiable list of ownership demands for the lease, which was conveyed to the PFD members. Two days before Christmas, the PFD incorporated every one of the demands into a new twenty-year lease, including issuance of bonds regardless of legal challenges.

Within a week, pending a small deal with the city of Seattle, the new lease was done. The Mariners, again, were back from the precipice. The for-sale sign was down. Old-fashioned power politics had prevailed.

Shelly Yapp, who resigned her PFD board position a week later, was the staunchest advocate for the public interest and the most astonished at the naked manipulations. She said numerous PFD meetings were interrupted when Gorton would call board members, principally Tom Gibbs and Bill Gerberding, on their cell phones to discuss their positions.

"Slade was actively involved behind the scenes, not as a mediator but an advocate," Yapp said. Beyond Gorton's influence, she was stunned by the owners' approach throughout the yearlong negotiations.

"They had no understanding of public policy or politics," she said. "It was like an entirely different language. I absolutely believe the owners never had, with the exception of Isaki, any idea how a public agency operated."

Isaki said that aside from disagreement on issues of the lease, a deep resentment developed among the owners for the PFD's relatively late role in the stadium ordeal.

"For four years, the Mariners had given blood from every orifice, stood up under a massive dose of public scrutiny, had every aspect of our humanity challenged," he said. "Then we had to go through all these disputes and conflicts with a group of people [PFD] who just showed up.

"From the Mariners' perspective, it magnified a thousand-fold the disputes. After everything we'd been through, it was very difficult for us to accept this bullshit—they had no skin in the game. If we don't keep putting money into this, the team and the ballpark go away. All the public-safeguard things they were trying to impose on us would have materially affected the ability to run the ballclub. It went way beyond typical landlord-tenant relationships.

"In hindsight, the import of some of those things wasn't as significant as the Mariners took it. But the Mariners couldn't undo what they had been through. That's what got to them."

Perry, a minority owner, acknowledged shortcomings both ways.

"We probably should have seen it coming, that they were going to ask for stupid things," he said. "It's a political reality. Some things we were willing to give, but they were overreaching. And we could have done a better job in making them understand."

On the day the club signed the lease, Perry said, Chris Larson, the owner with the second-largest stake behind Yamauchi, cautioned his partners.

"Chris said, 'If we sign this lease, it's going to cost us $250 million, versus what we could sell the team for. I don't want anyone having any illusions.' To Chris's credit, he gave an honest assessment and galvanized everyone's thoughts; we were reupping again for another charitable contribution to the community."

Even then, Larson proved naive about the financial consequences of the next two years. Although the Mariners agreed to push back the opening to July instead of April 1999, the twenty-seven-month construction schedule remained the fastest for any modern ballpark, especially one with a retractable roof. For the task of general contractor and construction manager, the PFD accepted the low bid of Indianapolis firm Huber, Hunt & Nichols, which had done Cleveland's Jacobs Field and Phoenix's Bank One Ballpark among its twenty-two previous football and baseball stadiums. Hunt was partnered with Kiewit Construction Company of Omaha, an outfit that had worked on many other Northwest construction projects.

Against the wishes of the Mariners, the PFD chose as architect NBBJ, a longtime Seattle firm with little ballpark experience. Mariners CEO John Ellis was so concerned he had what he termed a "come-to-God lecture" with chief architect Bill Bain, an old friend.

"I told him I was very, very concerned," he said. "I wanted his personal assurance he would put his top people on the job. He assured me they would.

"Our concerns turned out to be right."

❧

At the height of the design phase in late 1996, NBBJ had about one hundred staffers spending days, evenings, and weekends on the project. Even after the owners temporarily pulled out in December, the design team kept working because a shutdown would have made a restart difficult and the new completion date of July 15, 1999, impossible. But the pace still wasn't fast enough to complete design elements before ground was broken in March 1997. Among the many issues complicating the fast-track project were slow decisions from ownership.

"We said the schedule was doable, but it would take everyone making decisions in a timely manner," said Dennis Forsyth, NBBJ principal and head of the stadium design team. "The thing that irked me was that we said yes to the client, but I don't think they had any idea what the schedule meant. They run a baseball team, not build buildings.

"Frankly, it was incredible what was done under the circumstances."

One of the most costly early examples was the late arrival of the specifications for concession stands. Due in March but delivered in December, the plans called for much more cooking equipment at each site, requiring more drain lines, water pipes, cables, and venting to be woven through completed construction.

"If you're building an office building, that's OK, but not for the confined spaces of this project," Forsyth said. "That cost everyone money."

Another large error concerned the estimate for concrete used for the main grandstand. PFD sources said the cost budgeted for $38 million, ended up around $60 million. Forsyth denied any design flaw accounted for the huge error.

New-Generation Ballparks

Ranked by Total Cost

Park	Opened	Cost	City
1. Safeco Field	1999	$517.6 million	Seattle
2. Miller Park	2001	$413.9 million	Milwaukee
3. Comerica Park	2000	$361 million	Detroit
4. Bank One Ballpark	1998	$349 million	Phoenix
5. Pac Bell Park	2000	$319 million	San Francisco
6. Minute Maid Park	2000	$265 million	Houston
7. PNC Park	2001	$262 million	Pittsburgh
8. Turner Field	1997	$235 million	Atlanta
9. Coors Field	1995	$215 million	Denver
10.Ballpark Arlington	1994	$191 million	Arlington, TX
11. Jacobs Field	1994	$180 million	Cleveland
12. New Comiskey	1991	$167 million	Chicago
13. Camden Yards	1992	$110 million	Baltimore
Total		$3.6 billion	

New-Generation Ballparks

Ranked by Public Money Spent

Park	Opened	Cost	City
1. Safeco Field	1999	$372 million	Seattle
2. Miller Park	2001	$323.9 million	Milwaukee
3. Bank One Ballpark	1998	$238 million	Phoenix
4. PNC Park	2001	$222 million	Pittsburgh
5. Minute Maid Park	2000	$180 million	Houston
6. Coors Field	1995	$168 million	Denver
7. New Comiskey	1991	$167 million	Chicago
8. Ballpark Arlington	1994	$135 million	Arlington, TX
9. Comerica Park	2000	$115 million	Detroit
10. Camden Yards	1992	$110 million	Baltimore
11. Jacobs Field	1994	$84 million	Cleveland
12. Turner Field	1997	$0	Atlanta
13. Pac Bell	2000	$0	San Francisco
Total		$2.1 billion	

"I don't know why it was spun as a misestimation," Forsyth said. "There was a lot of overtime paid, and there were concrete subcontractors who weren't properly running the job. Our estimates were almost exactly right."

The pace eliminated time for debate about who did what. As J. C. Brummond, the Hunt-Kiewit project manager, put it, "This job is like trying to change a tire on a car that's going seventy miles an hour."

By completion, the PFD estimated the Mariners made about ten thousand change orders from the original drawings, for which they paid 100 percent by terms of the agreement with the PFD. That was the cost of the prime directive—opening by July 1999.

"On any construction project, decisions are made whether to give on the schedule or give on the money," said Forsyth. "Since the Mariners weren't budging on the schedule, the money had to give."

"The change orders just kept cascading in," said Terry Carroll, a judge who was appointed to Yapp's vacancy and was chosen later as chairman of the PFD board. "The Mariners signed off on all of them. The board didn't know whether we needed to do this or that. The board can't know those kinds of details.

"At board meetings, whenever a change order came in, there was 'Carroll's rule': Always ask, 'Did the Mariners approve it?' "

The debates among architects, contractors, workers, the Mariners, and the PFD were endless, and mostly paid for on overtime, given the 24/7 requirements of the compressed schedule. By the end of 1998, the public money ran out. Cash for completion came from the Mariners' $100 million line of credit with Bank of America. Nearly every anxiety about costs, voiced earlier by County Council members and others, had come home to roost. Critics argued that if the Mariners had accepted an opening date in 2000, operational losses for another full year in the Kingdome would have been less than what they paid in cost overruns attributable to the relentless construction pace.

"I've asked myself that question over time, and I just don't know," Ellis said. "We had been assured at the time of construction by the architects, engineers, and contractors that the additional time [to a July 1999 opening] would be adequate. In my mind, more time meant more delays that would have given the project a chance to derail."

Isaki acknowledged that the criticism about the timetable was well-founded.

"No question, in some respects the final bill comes with an 'I told you so,' " he said. "From the standpoint of a good-government class . . . absolutely goddamn right. But at that point, the cash burn rate–after the initial investment by people who simply wanted to save baseball–left no choice. The only way the Mariners could see a way was to have that stadium become a reality sooner than later. Any externally or internally imposed delay would kill it."

❧

Unlike most public-works projects that spiral out of control, a ballpark that is completed has a remarkable way of overwhelming logic with sensory and sentimental delights. On July 15, 1999, fresh air, grass, and sunshine returned to major league baseball in Seattle for the first time in thirty years. None among the 47,000 customers was thinking about cost overruns or damaged careers. They were there to be dazzled by marvelous sight lines, wide concourses, a roof with enough steel to build a fifty-five-story skyscraper, varieties of good food cooked on site, and views of Puget Sound, the Olympic Mountains, and the downtown skyline–and, yes, plenty of toilets.

For half a billion dollars, peeing had better be easy.

In a different way, another marvel was the pricing of tickets. The best 382 seats behind home plate were part of the Diamond Club, whose price was $195–per seat, per game. Included was parking, an elegant pregame buffet, and other perks. The section sold out. Along the baselines, another 928 seats were designated for charter seat licenses. Available for twenty years for a one-time fee between $12,000 and $20,000 depending on location, the price did not include game tickets. These premium seats were in addition to sixty-nine luxury suites, the impetus for all new stadium projects, priced from $94,000 to $164,000 a season. The price range for tickets elsewhere in the park ranged from $5 outfield bleacher seats to $32 for a box seat along the baselines in the lower bowl.

One of thirteen "new-generation" baseball stadiums built in the majors between 1991 and 2002, Safeco Field was designed to create revenues that would keep up with the nearly uncontrollable upward spiral of players' salaries. The buildings also increase the net worth of each franchise, something club officials rarely bring up when discussing how much they pay out.

The members of "the dumb club," as Perry called the owners' group, saw a startling appreciation of their investment, at least by outside estimates. In 1991, the year before the Baseball Club of Seattle bought the team, *Financial World* magazine estimated the value of the club to be $71 million, lowest in baseball. In 2001, *Forbes* magazine valued the club at $373 million, baseball's sixth highest. Whether a sale would fetch such a price on the open market is unknowable, but a minimum assumption is that the Seattle franchise has value at least roughly equal to its owners' investment ($322 million), even including the egregious overruns.

By the end of 2002, the public's debt was being paid down at a far more rapid rate than forecast. Besides the $336 million in bonds for the stadium and garage, the county estimated in 1996 that interest payments on the debt over the twenty-year life of the bonds would add about $276 million to the public cost. But in the first six years of tax collection, thanks to a good economy in the late '90s and robust crowds–the Mariners led the major leagues in attendance in 2001 and 2002–revenues exceeded the deliberately conservative estimates by 20 to 35 percent a year.

The collection of $190 million through 2002 is about $50 million ahead of debt-retirement forecast through six years. The excess is applied by county policy exclusively to early debt retirement. If revenues were to stay around the same pace, the debt could be retired by 2012 or sooner, saving millions in interest. Additionally, once the Mariners make their operations and construction investment back, they share stadium profits with the PFD.

Tax revenues were so good that the club owners, still steaming from overruns that they blamed on mistakes and poor oversight on the part of the PFD, the architects, and contractors, began a campaign to be reimbursed from the excess. The club threatened to sue to get the county to refinance the bonds to give them $60 million.

Outrage from the PFD, county officials, and the public greeted the claim.

"What the Mariners got was a miracle," Vic Oblas, the PFD's project manager, told *The Seattle Times*, "and they are acting like it was a mugging."

With zero support in the community for the claim, the club in 2001 gave up the pursuit of public money in exchange for the right to pursue legal action against Hunt-Kiewit and NBBJ. Once the PFD and its public disclosure requirements were out of the way, the club, and the architect and builders, negotiated a settlement that included a confidentiality agreement precluding release of terms.

What is known is that by the summer of 2002, the Mariners made enough money from the settlement and ballpark operations to pay off the $100 million credit line the club took out in 1998 that covered the overruns. The Mariners reported to the PFD through the end of 2002 a cumulative Safeco operating profit of around $30 million. The club also received large up-front payments on their $250 million deal with Fox Sports Northwest for television rights and their $60 million deal with KOMO-AM for radio rights. Adding in the settlement payments, the club by the end of 2002 had the operational cash to be free of commercial debt.

Broadcaster Dave Niehaus, the franchise's most popular figure, threw out the ceremonial first pitch at Safeco Field. ©1999 SEATTLE POST-INTELLIGENCER/MIKE URBAN

"We're net investors," said club president Chuck Armstrong, shaking his head. "Amazing."

Credit for many of the ballpark's virtues was given to Chris Larson, who has actively shunned media attention and the public spotlight throughout his time as the top American investor in the Mariners. He had high visibility, however, as he marched for months around the construction site in his yellow hard hat.

"I guarantee you we would not have as nice a stadium as we have today, with as many amenities and forethought and anticipation of detail, if we hadn't had Chris," said Craig Watjen, a minority owner who worked with Larson at Microsoft. "He was all over the plans, and knows every nook and cranny. Owners and fans have to be grateful for what he contributed."

Larson, who has devoted a large room in his Highlands estate to his collection of baseball memorabilia, tolerated the financial hit on the overruns because he wanted Safeco Field to be an impressive legacy.

"We had only one shot in my lifetime to get it right," he said. "Unlike the Kingdome, we knew we weren't going to be able to do this again in twenty years."

※

Most of the political combatants in the fracas of December 1996 emerged with few visible scars. Sims, von Reichbauer, Phillips, and Sullivan, signatories to the infamous county letter, all won subsequent reelection bids, and von Reichbauer regained the budget committee chair. The healing was helped by the knowledge that their apprehensions about cost overruns because of the project's pace were proven legitimate.

Gorton in 2000 was defeated in his Senate reelection bid by Democrat Maria Cantwell, although the ballpark events were a negligible influence on the outcome of the vote. He entered private law practice. In late 2002 he was asked by President George W. Bush, with whom he had become acquainted ten years earlier in the bid to win approval for the Mariners' sale to Hiroshi Yamauchi, to join a national panel of experts investigating the September 11, 2001, terrorist attacks on the United States.

The Seahawks emerged from the imbroglio with what they wanted: a new stadium. Ken Behring sold the Seahawks for $200 million to Paul Allen, who conditioned his purchase on voter approval of a new publicly funded stadium on the site of the Kingdome. A referendum providing $300 million in tax money was put on a statewide special election, whose $4 million cost was paid for exclusively by Allen, an act by a private individual unprecedented in state history. In June 1997 the proposal passed with a 51 percent yes vote. In contrast to the baseball stadium wrangle, the open-air, 67,000-seat football stadium opened in July 2002 on time and within its $430 million budget. Allen paid the $130 million beyond the public share of the costs. Also included in the project was an exhibition center that hosts many of the flat shows (car, boat, outdoors, etc.) that made the Kingdome profitable. Nestled between the two giant stadiums south of downtown, the exhibition center was built and operated by Allen, who used its profits from more than two hundred event-days of rental to subsidize the little-used football building.

If the stadium story's numbers and politics seem overwhelming to the sports fan exclusively interested in the game, there was a baseball casualty too, one that also ends the debate about whether the for-sale declaration by John Ellis in December 1996 was a bluff.

Sitting at his home in Ventura, California, Jim Colborn, a former Mariners pitcher hired to the new club post of Pacific Rim scouting director, was talking with Shigetoshi Hasegawa. The young pitcher was attempting to follow Hideo Nomo, the 1995 National League rookie of the year for the Los Angeles Dodgers, to become the third pitcher from Japan to make it in the major leagues. Colborn, Hasegawa's pitching coach when each worked for the Orix Blue Wave of Japan's Pacific League, had moved back to the U.S. and invited Hasegawa to train in Southern California in the winters. Hasegawa, a free agent, made it clear he wanted to play for one of three West Coast teams: the Mariners, Oakland A's, or California Angels.

The phone rang. Someone from the Mariners' front office told Colborn that the club was for sale, and scouts were forbidden to sign players until the new owners took over. Stunned, Colborn passed the news to Hasegawa, who seemed to be leaning toward the Mariners because of his friendship with Colborn and the Japanese-led ownership.

"In a couple of weeks, it was announced the Mariners' owners were back in business," Colborn said. "Two days earlier, Hasegawa decided to go with the Angels."

Originally a starter, Hasegawa converted to relief and provided the Angels five substantial years in the bullpen. After he became a free agent in 2001, he signed with the Mariners. In '02, he was 8-3 with a 3.20 ERA.

The killer aspect of the deal for the Mariners was that in 1997 the bullpen melted down so frequently that general manager Woody Woodward made a trade of desperation. To acquire Heathcliff Slocumb, a reliever of surpassing ordinariness, Woodward sent the Boston Red Sox two top young prospects, catcher Jason Varitek and pitcher Derek Lowe. Slocumb did help the Mariners make the '97 playoffs, where they won a single game. But he lasted only one more undistinguished season in Seattle. In Boston, Varitek became a solid starter and Lowe became an All-Star in 2002 (21-8 with a 2.58 ERA, including a no-hitter).

The trade was indisputably one of the worst in club history. It likely wouldn't have happened if Hasegawa had been in Seattle to take the pressure off the 'pen. While the if/then game can be played with every baseball transaction, in this case the catalyst for the deal's failure came before the deal. The failure to sign Hasegawa, because of the threatened sale, forced the club into desperation. It cost them a prospect who, providing Piniella had the patience to wait, would have become a No. 1 starter.

Seems the owners in '96 were not bluffing about their intent to sell. They got their way with the ballpark. But the costs were many, in more than dollars.

Nor was the ballpark the universal draw they had hoped. Sure, millions of delighted fans poured through the turnstiles to make the Mariners one of the great financial powerhouses in sports.

But three important people couldn't wait to leave.

CHAPTER NINE

Who Let the Stars Out?

After Randy Johnson won the 1995 Cy Young Award as the American League's best pitcher, Alex Rodriguez in 1996 won the AL batting title and finished second in the Most Valuable Player voting. In 1997, Ken Griffey Jr. won the MVP balloting unanimously.

Star power? The Mariners had become baseball's version of the Big Bang: darkness followed abruptly by cosmic brilliance.

The game's three best players were on the same team. In those three years, Johnson, Griffey, and Rodriguez twice led the Mariners to the playoffs, and it probably would have been all three seasons if not for Johnson's herniated disk that required surgery, bringing a premature end to his '96 effort.

The dominant left-handed pitcher in baseball, Johnson in 1997 became the club's first 20-game winner. In one stretch of five games, he allowed one earned run. Twice he struck out 19 in a game. An article of AL faith was that hitters preferred a breakfast of gravel to an evening of fastballs from the Big Unit.

"Randy put the fear of God into other teams," said teammate Jay Buhner. "All that beanball crap would go away when Randy stood up on the top step and yelled, 'I'm pitching tomorrow!' "

Rodriguez burst into prominence when, at twenty-one, he hit .358 to become the third-youngest player to win a batting title. Selected by two news organizations as the major league player of the year, Rodriguez was dazzling in his first full season as the starting shortstop. At 6-foot-3, a sculpted 210 pounds, and blessed with grace in the field and power at the plate, Rodriguez was also handsome, articulate, bilingual, and a smooth operator for one so young.

"What people didn't appreciate was how hard he worked," said Rick Griffin, the club's longtime trainer. "He was gifted, but he made himself better."

In '97 there was one word for Griffey: astounding. He led the AL with 125 runs scored and 56 home runs, the latter the seventh-best total in history. His 147 runs batted in were a club record that led the majors. In one game, he hit two home runs off Roger Clemens and three total—part of a major league record 13 in April. He won another Gold Glove award for his defense, helping him complete one of the game's greatest individual seasons.

"He had a total disregard for bodily injury," said Dave Niehaus, the club's broadcast voice. "Crashing into walls, breaking bones, making spectacular catches. Lots of guys don't do that. He always took the risk. Once the game started, nobody played it any harder."

⁂

As different as they were spectacular, the superstars did share something besides the uniform—they were thirsty for acclaim and money. Which reward came first varied with the individual, but such a collection of talent in so remote a baseball outpost kept national speculation focused on how in the hell the Mariners could keep these enormously popular players in Seattle.

Despite fans' frequent laments about a lack of player loyalty, the fact of baseball life is that three such prodigious talents were destined for any port they desired. Besides the pull of such gravity, there was also the centrifugal force of ego that pulled them away from each other and the team.

"I think at times they were a little envious of each other; I think jealousy is a better word," said Buhner, a Mariner since 1988 who watched all three blossom—and collide. "Somebody wrote that there wasn't enough headroom in the clubhouse for these three guys."

Point well taken. Once the 1995 success established the Mariners in the baseball landscape, Rodriguez's ascension the next season ratcheted up the clubhouse pettiness. The jealousies didn't morph into fights or open feuds. No witness to the Mariners' scene at the time claimed to have seen a confrontation or physical clash among the stars. The tension was an undercurrent, not an explosion.

"It was accurate about the jealousy," said general manager Woody Woodward. "But I had a different view: Where is it said there has to be total harmony between great players in order to win? The great Oakland teams, the great Yankees teams, they managed to get through it. Winning was a way to keep Alex and Junior."

In an article for *Sport* magazine, writer Barry Bloom interviewed Rodriguez and Griffey separately and disclosed the cattiness. For them, the MVP voting among national baseball writers was a touchy subject, particularly since in '96, Rodriguez finished second by three votes to Texas's Juan Gonzalez, thanks in part to Seattle writers Jim Street and Bob Finnigan casting their No. 1 ballots for Griffey, who finished fourth overall.

"MVP and Junior were never mentioned once at all [in '96]," Rodriguez was quoted as saying. "It was Alex first and then Gonzalez. I didn't hear [Griffey's name] once."

Said Griffey, "Alex had a great year, but so did I. I'm expected to do what I did. He wasn't. It's ironic that somebody who has the same numbers as me gets all the credit."

Rodriguez, on Griffey's claim that he is underappreciated: "I don't think you would hear Michael Jordan talk like that. I would

Alex Rodriguez (left), and Ken Griffey Jr. powered the Mariners' offense from 1996 to 1998, but there was jealousy between them.

think that [superstars] would be picking up [teammates] and trying to bring them to their level. I got a lot of attention last year,
but I deserved it."

Griffey: "Other guys can have their share of the spotlight. It's
not important to me. But when they get more than their share,
then they say about me, 'You're not the star of the team.' But I'm
the one guy who has to take the responsibility."

Rodriguez: "I'm mature enough to realize it feels like I'm the
older one and he's the younger one."

As with most debutante balls, the backstage sneer didn't turn into
a hair-pulling contest. Both denied any feud, claiming they were
good teammates and friends. Not long after the story came out,
they doused each other with champagne in the clubhouse after the
Mariners won the '97 AL West with a team-record 90 wins.

"That [feud talk] really bothered Junior," said Brian Goldberg,
his Cincinnati-based agent. "There was no bad blood, but a
friendly competition. They went out together, and there was gen-
uine friendship."

Nevertheless, the location of clubhouse lockers in the new ballpark was no accident—Ken Griffey Jr. at one end, Alex Rodriguez
at the other. Said Niehaus, "Junior was king of the hill long before
A-Rod ever got here."

Meanwhile, Randy Johnson was harder to locate psychologi-
cally, given his moody remoteness. Always a sensitive sort prone
to slights, Johnson, as far back as Piniella's first year of 1993,
lamented his place in the Mariners' food chain. As he arrived at
spring training that year, he cited the club's failure to give him a
long-term contract extension, as they had done for Griffey and
Edgar Martinez, as evidence of their lack of concern.

"All I want is for them to show me some respect and appreciation," Johnson told the P-I's Jim Street. "I don't think that's asking
too much. I've done a lot for this organization on and off the field
but I haven't been treated like a member of the family here. It
bothers me and I'm hurt."

He claimed the club had not helped him enough with a calendar project featuring his photography that would have benefited a
charity. He was also hurting over an inadvertent gaffe. His father,
with whom he was very close, died in California on Christmas
Day. Since the club's offices were closed, no one received word.
Upon his return to Seattle in early January, Johnson's first

encounter with a club employee was president Chuck Armstrong, who said, "How were your holidays?"

Johnson never seemed to forgive.

"It's hard for me to say exactly, because I never brought that up with him, but it hurt him bad," Buhner said. "It pisses him off to this day. Randy definitely holds a grudge—no doubt about it."

Buhner, who used to room with Johnson on the road in their early days together in Seattle, was well aware of the big guy's small tolerances.

"I really think that Randy didn't feel appreciated," he said. "He felt like he didn't get respect from some people in the front office. He talked about that a lot. Some guys take that harder than others. Some of us are a little stronger and hide things better."

Said Armstrong, "Randy got it in his head that we were favoring Junior and Alex. It was weird. If we did a promotion, like a growth chart, for one of them, the others would be upset. And if we didn't do one, all three would be upset."

Some of the feelings stemmed from a starting pitcher's standard 30-plus appearances a year versus the 150 games of most starting position players, according to Lee Pelekoudas, the club's assistant general manager: "Randy was having a hard time with not getting the same attention that Junior and Alex got. But that's what happens when you're out there every five days."

In the summer of '93, the Mariners came perilously close to dealing Johnson. Piniella was irked by his petulance and the owners were worried about affording an increase from his $2.6 million salary. Offers from Toronto, Pittsburgh, Philadelphia, and the Yankees were considered right up to the July 31 trade deadline. But none were deemed worthy. In the off-season, the Mariners finally made him financially happy with a four-year extension, with a club option for a fifth season.

⁂

By the conclusion of the 1997 season, in which the Mariners made the playoffs but were ousted easily in the Division Series, three games to one, by the Baltimore Orioles, circumstances swirled together that pushed the club toward yet another edge. In Griffey, Johnson, and Rodriguez, the Mariners possessed the game's three most valuable jewels, but the club was still two years away from the safe-deposit box of the new stadium, which presumably would create the revenues that might sustain a potentially stupendous payroll. Yet the departure of one or more of the marquee players might annoy the newly formed, wildly enthusiastic fan base.

After drawing 1.6 million spectators in 1995, the Mariners drew 2.7 million in '96 and 3.2 million in '97 (so much for the baseball-won't-work-in-the-Kingdome bromide that served as a crutch for every Mariners ownership group). No longer threatened by the team moving away, fans bought almost totally into the team marketing motto: "You Gotta Love These Guys." The club's popularity in the Northwest soared past that of the Seahawks and University of Washington football, and was sharing the spotlight with the Sonics, who in 1996 reached the NBA finals.

But locking up the future services of Johnson, Griffey, and Rodriguez would require some serious cost overruns in payroll before the owners knew whether they had cost overruns with the stadium. The results of the '97 season also showed the club needed help in multiple areas if something more than distant contention was possible.

Hard as it was to imagine the Mariners without Johnson and Griffey (both had been in Seattle since '89) as well as teen-heart-throb Rodriguez, the difficulty of keeping them satisfied had become a mind-stretcher, too, especially given developments away from the field.

Griffey and Johnson detached themselves physically from Seattle by moving their off-season homes. Married with kids, each did what a large number of established major leaguers do when they get cash and leverage—head for the sun, particularly if they've spent a couple of winters around Puget Sound. Johnson, a Bay Area native who spent two years at USC, fell in love with the Arizona desert, where the Mariners trained in spring. After the '94 season, he bought a golf-course home in the Phoenix suburb of Glendale, and later built a home in Scottsdale.

In the same winter, Griffey, who as a kid growing up in Cincinnati was part of an annual family pilgrimage to Florida to be around his father during spring training with the Reds, bought a large lakeside lot in an exclusive golf-course development outside Orlando. His wife, Melissa, a Seattle-area native, was an advocate of the move because of problems within her family. Although Griffey still maintained a home in the Seattle suburb of Issaquah, club officials viewed the Florida move with apprehension.

Armstrong lobbied in vain to get Griffey to consider Arizona. The Florida move didn't make an immediate difference because in '96, Griffey signed a contract extension for four more years. But the notion of "home" would eventually loom much larger.

Johnson was an imminent concern, because his contract was up in '97, although the club held an option for one more year, which it

Taken out of Game 6 in the eighth inning of the 1995 American League Championship Series against Cleveland, Randy Johnson acknowledges the roaring ovation from the Kingdome crowd. Fewer than three years later, Johnson waved goodbye more permanently. ©1995 SEATTLE POST-INTELLIGENCER/GRANT M. HALLER

planned to exercise. Johnson was becoming high-profile in the Phoenix area, even beyond his 6-foot-10 stature. In the spring, he did a thirty-second TV commercial promoting tourism for the Phoenix Chamber of Commerce. He told a reporter for the *Arizona Republic* newspaper that he wanted to be the opening-day starter for the Arizona Diamondbacks when they began their first season in 1998. The D-backs' managing general partner, Jerry Colangelo, also happened to be the owner of the NBA Phoenix Suns, whose sideline seats were made available regularly to Johnson.

Another outside influence affecting Johnson's fate was a jump in the salary market for pitchers. Greg Maddux, the best pitcher in the National League, signed a contract extension with the Atlanta Braves that put his stipend at $11 million a year. "Maddux money" became the new benchmark. Johnson was scheduled to make $6 million in his option year.

In August, Armstrong and Pelekoudas, the assistant GM, were dispatched to Chicago and the offices of Johnson's agent, Barry Meister, to begin talks about an extension. The news wasn't good.

"Meister said, 'Don't even make an offer—you can't afford us,' " Pelekoudas said. "They didn't want to be here."

Woodward, the general manager, heard that report. But he also heard that Johnson wanted to stay. He wasn't sure what to believe. The mixed signals continued into the off-season, when Johnson told Steve Kelley of *The Seattle Times,* "They aren't interested in offering me a contract past next year, and that's the story. I didn't want to leave here, but now I think I do because I know how the Mariners feel. . . . I've seen their true colors. I do feel a little betrayed."

Howard Lincoln, who would succeed John Ellis in two years as club CEO, scoffed at Johnson's remarks.

"That was nonsense, disingenuous," Lincoln said. "He didn't want us to even pick up his option. We knew he didn't want to be here." Nevertheless, Lincoln and Ellis discussed whether to give Johnson an offer to think about, "but it didn't make any sense if he doesn't want to be here. Why go through that charade?"

Yet on the business side of baseball, showbiz sometimes has a place. The Mariners' decision to allow Johnson to play into his walk year without an offer left them open to public criticism that they weren't doing enough to keep a virtually irreplaceable talent. Playing to the crowd is a talent little used among the Mariners execs.

The absence of an offer "was a problem because of the hit we were taking publicly," Pelekoudas said. "But we knew that would happen because we don't comment publicly on negotiations. That's the way we've always operated, even though it might not make sense [to media and fans]. It usually works out for us in the end. "If you're strong enough in your convictions, you shouldn't be worried about those kinds of things."

The theory sounds good. But events have a way of fouling the best intentions. The Mariners' calculated silence on the Johnson talks ended awkwardly. On the same November day that Major League Baseball announced Griffey won unanimously the MVP award, Armstrong blurted to a TV reporter that the club decided not to offer Johnson an extension. The ensuing uproar stole considerable thunder from Griffey's MVP honor, the first in club history, and called into question the club's judgment on two counts–sensitivity and desire to win.

By spring training in '98, Johnson was saying all the right things (good focus, full concentration, etc.) about the season, but his unresolved future ended up betraying his words. His production in the first half of 1998 showed a man with his head elsewhere. He was an eminently hittable 9-10 with a 4.33 earned run average, a shocking fall-off for the game's best pitcher.

Piniella and many players seethed. Johnson went nearly winless in April, and was ejected from a game and suspended for three more for throwing at a hitter. First baseman David Segui tangled with Johnson in the clubhouse. The fight, in which no one was hurt, was said to be over the clubhouse music, but Segui figured to be delivering a message for others too.

Said Woodward, "Lou told me there was a lot of tension among the players."

Street, the *P-I*'s baseball beat writer, in an open letter to Johnson in the newspaper, captured the sentiment:

"There is an impression in the clubhouse that you really don't care how this team does. It shows almost every time you pitch . . . keep that multimillion-dollar arm sound at all costs, even if it means destroying virtually everything you have accomplished this decade, including respect.

"You remain employed by the Mariners and shouldn't be going in the tank, taking 24 teammates and a manager and a coaching staff down with you."

A few days later, Johnson confronted Street in the clubhouse in Anaheim.

"I'm holding myself back," Johnson said, "to keep from smacking you in the face."

"Go ahead," Street said, "if it'll make you feel better."

"Don't you understand that I'm taking medication and seeing a psychiatrist?"

"How would I know that unless you tell me?"

Johnson turned and walked away. Street could not verify Johnson's claim. Trainer Rick Griffin, a close friend of Johnson's, said he had never heard of Johnson undergoing counseling or taking any mood-altering medication. What he was sure about was that Johnson wasn't intentionally quitting on his teammates. But the mental edge—more valuable on the mound to Johnson than his arm or height—was gone.

"Randy had to be 100 percent, and for whatever reason, he wasn't," Griffin said. "But it wasn't because he was dogging it. He's just too competitive. If you'd see him in here after he was hit around, you'd know he wasn't dogging it. He was very upset with himself."

Players tried to reason with him. He withdrew further.

"I felt for Randy more than anything else," Buhner said. "We were real good friends, real close. At the same time, he wouldn't open up. You couldn't get anything out of him. I was more frustrated than anything—I couldn't be there for him.

"I think he's still pissed at me in a roundabout way. It seemed like all of his ties to his friends just slowly went to the back burner. I don't know what was behind it."

⁂

Johnson also had a solid baseball reason for wanting out: the rolling debacle of the Seattle bullpen. Throughout the middle '90s, the Mariners' relief corps was the worst, or nearly the worst, in the league.

Norm Charlton, the hero in '95, was a goat in '97 (11 blown saves and a 3-8 record with a 7.27 ERA). The one most reliable, Mike Jackson, skipped away to free agency after a solid season in '96. The Mariners figured he would be too expensive, but they paid a dear baseball price anyway. In '97, top prospects Jose Cruz Jr., Jason Varitek, and Derek Lowe were traded to acquire relievers

Mike Timlin, Paul Spoljaric, and Healthcliff Slocumb, none of whom was a long-term answer.

It didn't help that Piniella, in his first five years in Seattle, had gone through three pitching coaches, yet inexplicably stuck by pitcher Bobby Ayala, a kid the manager had in Cincinnati whom he grossly overvalued. An urban legend that refused to die was that Ayala had married a member of Piniella's family. It wasn't true, but it was more believable than giving him five seasons of chances based on performance.

"Several times," Buhner said, "Lou would go out to relieve Randy, and Randy would say something like, 'Fuck you, I'm not giving you the ball. If we're going to lose this game, I'm going to lose it. I'm tired of coming out of games and not getting [a win or a loss].' The bullpen problems were big in Randy's mind, without a doubt."

In '97 the Mariners set the single-season major league record with 264 home runs, but all the bashing got them was a single win in the playoffs. Results were worse in '98 because of Johnson's daze. Piniella wanted him gone. The baseball world sensed opportunity: Up to a dozen scouts from other teams were showing up at Mariners games in anticipation of a trade. In late May a deal seemed imminent. A report on MSNBC's Internet news service had Johnson going to the Los Angeles Dodgers in exchange for starting pitchers Ismael Valdes and Hideo Nomo and either outfielder Todd Hollandsworth or Wilton Guerrero.

Sources on both teams later confirmed the primary elements of the trade. But the deal quickly and mysteriously dissolved. On a flight back from a series in Baltimore, Pelekoudas, the assistant GM who had no affection for Johnson, had Griffin summon Johnson to the front of the plane. Johnson sat down next to Pelekoudas and said, "My wife called and said she saw on TV that I've been traded to L.A. When do I go?"

"The trade didn't happen," Pelekoudas said. "Our intent is to keep you."

Stunned, Johnson stood up, returned to his seat, and spoke to no one for the rest of the flight. The Mariners were stunned too, and Piniella was angry. Although it was never explained publicly, the deal was killed indirectly by Hiroshi Yamauchi, the reclusive owner who supposedly had little interest in the club's daily affairs.

It was not that Yamauchi had great affection for Johnson. The owner's interest was in his countryman, Nomo.

He didn't want him.

When Nomo made himself available to U.S. teams after the '94 season in Japan, Yamauchi alerted Howard Lincoln, the Nintendo of America vice president and his representative on the Mariners board of directors, that he was eager to have Nomo join the Mariners. But Lincoln assumed his boss was merely expressing interest, not ordering a signing. The consequences of the misunderstanding would linger for years.

Lincoln may not have wanted to hear a request to hire Nomo. The Mariners were unhappy with their first experiment in Japanese baseball talent. Makato (Mac) Suzuki, a young pitcher who never played professionally in Japan, was proving a bust in the U.S. (Signed for $800,000 out of high school, he eventually washed out with the Mariners by 1999.) Additionally, the industry was coming out of the bitter players' strike. The idea of investing big anywhere, particularly in Japan again, left the Mariners colder than the collective shoulder they were getting back then from baseball fans.

Nor did Nomo's unorthodox corkscrew of a delivery impress Piniella. Nomo worked out for several West Coast teams with some interest in his services, including the Mariners. After Nomo threw in a workout at the Kingdome, Armstrong recalled Piniella waving his arms and saying, "No, no, we don't need that—he can't pitch over here." So the Mariners did not pursue Nomo, oblivious to the dismay it caused Yamauchi.

Three years later, Piniella would be denied the opportunity to see personally if he guessed wrong about Nomo, who to that point had a creditable 45-36 major league record. Yamauchi, showing the stubborn, eccentric character for which he was notorious in his homeland, woke up Lincoln in the middle of the night in an Atlanta hotel room. The Johnson-Nomo trade rumor was all over TV in Japan.

"I thought I told you you can run this damn club," Yamauchi said through his interpreter, "but when it comes to Japanese players, you check with me first."

Lincoln knew nothing of the transaction. After checking around, he reported back to Yamauchi that the trade was a rumor—no deal for Nomo.

"In terms of Nomo," Lincoln said of Yamauchi's policy, "the

Mariners had their opportunity [in '95], lost it, and so wo
never be reconsidered."

However the wires were crossed and uncrossed in the Mariners
office, a slumping Nomo was dealt within a week to the New York
Mets. The Mariners staggered on for two more months with
Johnson in his irredeemable pout. At the trading deadline, July 31,
Woodward hoped for a bidding battle for Johnson between two
contending teams, the Cleveland Indians and the New York
Yankees. The latter were playing the Mariners that night in the
Kingdome. But neither club wanted to give up top players to rent
Johnson only for the remainder of the season, after which he

Minutes before the trading deadline on July 31, 1998, manager Lou Piniella leans
over midgame in the Kingdome dugout to tell Randy Johnson that he's been traded
to Houston. ©1998 SEATTLE POST-INTELLIGENCER/MIKE URBAN

/ould be a free agent. The Indians and Yankees passed.

So Woodward was forced to call up teams that had previously dropped out—San Francisco, Baltimore, and Houston. Minutes before the deadline, he accepted the offer of the Astros. Johnson was off to the National League for young pitchers Freddy Garcia and John Halama and infielder Carlos Guillen, three players Armstrong said later he "wouldn't know if they walked into the room."

For a second time, Woodward traded the franchise's premier pitcher for three virtually anonymous players.

"It was like the [1989] Mark Langston deal all over again," Woodward said. "But people cared this time. That's what winning does."

Indeed, they cared enough to boo. The trade was condemned by fans, media, and especially in the clubhouse. Even among teammates from whom little love was lost for Johnson, trading him for no one who would help the club immediately looked as if the seasonal white flag had been raised.

In fact, it had. The seasons of 1998 and '99 were being sacrificed to the new stadium.

"We were tearing down the team to get ready for the new park," said Piniella, years later. "You couldn't do it at once. It had to be done over a two-year period. We took our lumps, but it was the right thing to do. If we get beat, so be it.

"No question there was a conscious decision. I was asked if I was prepared. I said yes. I couldn't say that to the fans, players, or anybody, but that's exactly what it was. We were putting together a new stadium, and it turned out to be a nice strategy."

At the time, however, Piniella had to quell a small rebellion. The day after the trade, several players asked for a meeting with him in his office to get the deal explained.

"If they had done what they did in 1995, and added players, there wouldn't have been that two-year void," said Buhner, who was in the meeting. "Guys were upset about that. They didn't want to take a step back. Some guys were upset that the organization was throwing in the towel a little bit. You're taking the best pitcher in baseball and you apparently got nothing for him—what the hell is going on?

"But it isn't our job to judge the front office—we just go out and play."

While the Mariners groused, one guy who went out and played was Johnson. For the Astros, he completed the season at 10-1 with a phenomenal 1.28 ERA. Freed from his Seattle demons, real or imagined, he was his old formidable self. Unfortunately for him, he also was his old vulnerable self in the first round of the postseason. He lost both his starts in the Division Series against San Diego, just as he lost both starts a year earlier for Seattle against Baltimore.

It mattered little in the Big Unit's big picture. In the off-season, the free agent was signed by his longtime admirer Jerry Colangelo of the Diamondbacks. In his first year in Arizona (the club's second), Johnson helped the expansion club win an astonishing 100 games. Considering that it took the Mariners fourteen years to get a winning season, Arizona's abrupt arrival as a contender showed how much the economic game had changed in the past twenty years. Liberalized free agency allowed Colangelo to throw huge money at quality veterans, knowing that many of them would enjoy year-round life in the desert. It also showed Colangelo to be a bold risk-taker. Because of the high payroll, the Diamondbacks were said to have lost more than $30 million in cash operations that season.

The gamble paid off in 2001. Johnson teamed with another expensive acquisition, right-hander Curt Schilling, to make one of the best 1-2 pitching combos in baseball history. The D-backs, in just their fourth season, beat the Yankees four games to three to win one of the most riveting World Series in memory.

The run wasn't sustained in 2002, despite winning 98 regular season games. The D-backs were swept out of the playoffs in the first round by St. Louis. Johnson seemed restless again, sharing uneasily with Schilling the team spotlight, just as he had done in Seattle with Griffey and Rodriguez. Johnson would win his fifth Cy Young Award, including four in a row, but somehow felt his accomplishments, much as he did in Seattle, weren't fully appreciated.

"Fans here take that for granted," he told two Phoenix columnists. "And that I find kind of insulting, because at age 38 there are only a few other people my age doing what I'm doing. Roger Clemens is one of them and he's on the disabled list right now. There was much greater appreciation in Seattle."

More appreciation in Seattle? How can it be?

"That was taken wrong," Johnson said during 2003 spring

training. "What I explained to them is that Seattle probably appreciated me from seeing me start in 1989 and progress to what I became as I left. When I came to Phoenix, I was a finished product. I wasn't saying the fans don't appreciate me here.

"They appreciated me more in Seattle because they saw me early on walk 142 batters in 113 innings. Back then, I'd win 12 or 15 games and they thought it was pretty exciting stuff."

Then why leave?

"I don't really like to talk about that . . . opening up old wounds," he said, shrugging. "The team actually performed better in '01 than when me and Edgar, Junior, and A-Rod were there under one Kingdome roof."

True enough. But Johnson has his World Series ring, and with his healthy presence, Arizona is an automatic annual contender. After his departure from Seattle, the Mariners seemed on a much slower boil. Determined as Johnson was to get out, the club's failure to make him an offer left a public impression that the Mariners let him go.

"Edgar once said if Randy had stayed, we'd have won two or three World Series," Griffin said. "He said letting Randy go was the biggest mistake we ever made."

His departure and subsequent payroll reduction did, however, make easier the changes that would help convert the team from an offensive behemoth in the Kingdome to the pattern of most successful teams—emphasizing pitching and defense. Needs were plentiful: The Mariners finished the '98 season 76-85, third behind the Texas Rangers, and would finish the '99 season 79-83, 16 back of Texas.

⁂

The club's teardown-and-rebuild plans did not include demolition of the foundation. The Mariners still had Griffey and Rodriguez and intended to keep both. The biggest tactical problem was the simultaneous expirations of their contracts after the 2000 season. Rival clubs looked at the Mariners' predicament as a blunder: Standard procedure with star players is to stagger the contract expirations to avoid the possibility of losing two simultaneously.

The Mariners thought they were without problems until the terms of the strike settlement emerged after 1995. Because of a new, little-known provision of the settlement, Rodriguez was part of a small class of players in the minor leagues during the strike who were allowed to buy back not only lost major-league service time, but time while in the minors as well. By returning a prorated portion of his 1994 salary (less than $20,000), Rodriguez was able to gain a year of service toward the six-year minimum required to gain free agency. But the Mariners weren't told by major league baseball about the development until five months after Rodriguez signed a four-year extension in July 1996. With service time from 1994 and 1995, that meant Rodriguez would reach his coveted six-year threshold the same year that Griffey's contract expired, instead of after the 2001 season.

Their futures together were complicated by yet another bit of baseball-rules arcana: After ten years of service in the majors, including the last five consecutively with the same club, a player is granted the right to choose the teams where he might be traded. Griffey would qualify for the right after the 1999 season. The development was unusual—few players achieve "10-and-5" status, and if they do, they are usually in their early or middle thirties and have lost market value. But Griffey would hit the mark at twenty-nine, in his absolute prime. If the Mariners attempted to trade him, Griffey would have leverage that would reduce the number of teams the Mariners could play off against one another.

The bottom line with all these Byzantine baseball rules: The Mariners had to get busy. During the final home stand of '98, club execs summoned Griffey and Rodriguez separately to the owners' suite in the Kingdome to receive contract extension proposals:

- ➤ Rodriguez, who was twenty-three, was offered a seven-year deal for $63 million, including a $3 million signing bonus, beginning in 2001.
- ➤ Griffey, twenty-eight, was offered a five-year deal for $64 million, also beginning in 2001. The Griffey deal, with an average annual value of $12.8 million and a peak of $15.5 million, was designed to make him the game's highest-paid player.

Bart Waldman, the Mariners' outside counsel from the Seattle law firm of Perkins Coie, was the primary drafter of the offers.

"The organization made the decision to keep both players, and we wanted to get an early jump," he said. "There was a sense that getting one might help commit the other. We wanted them to know we weren't picking one over the other."

While both players were appreciative and respectful, nothing came of either offer. Rodriguez said he wasn't ready to consider an extension. Griffey likewise was noncommittal. Beyond issues of money and team, looming in the back of each player's mind was another issue—Safeco Field.

The dimensions of the field and the cool air of the most northerly park in baseball made for a pitcher-friendly environment that was, at least in the minds of two of the game's great sluggers, ill-suited for the pursuit of long-term offensive glory. During the season, with the park well on its way to completion, the club asked several players to hype the new yard by taking some batting practice on a makeshift field in front of TV cameras. In the words of one Mariners employee, "It was the worst mistake we ever made."

The incomplete park seemed gigantic. The temporary stadium floor was eight feet below its eventual grade, and the outfield fences weren't installed, so the more distant grandstand concrete appeared to be the final dimension. Afterward, the players said polite things publicly. But their assessments back to teammates were honest: Paul Bunyan couldn't yank one out of Safeco.

Even though the final product was not nearly so forbidding, the first stadium impression lingered. It remains today, complicated by a glare problem during sunny afternoon games that many hitters find not only difficult, but claim to be somewhat dangerous as well because the speed and flight of a pitch are hard to detect.

Since baseball experts had projected both Griffey and Rodriguez to be threats to one of the great records in sports, the 755 home runs of Hank Aaron, as well as other career milestones, the park's hitting difficulties became a liability. After the park opened halfway through '99, the pair routinely lobbied for closure of the roof not only for bright games, but at night, because it made the park seem warmer. Since cool air is heavier, and Seattle almost never has hot, humid days typical of summers most everywhere else in the country, the ball was not going to travel to places Griffey and Rodriguez wanted it to visit. But the bosses rejected the pleas. After a generation in the Kingdome, fans wanted, they said, the complete outdoors experience whenever possible.

Traded to the Mariners in 2002, third baseman Jeff Cirillo, who lived in Seattle in the off-season for ten years, came to understand the hitter' apprehensions.

"What I remember the first time I came to Safeco [with the

Colorado Rockies during interleague play] was how cold it was, a damp feeling," he said. "I don't think Griffey and Rodriguez wanted to spend their careers here. The great hitters want their numbers, and they won't get them here."

Does that mean the Mariners are unlikely to attract a free-agent slugger?

"Bingo."

Beyond Safeco-phobia, the player market ratcheted up again in the off-season, meaning the club had to recalibrate the contract offers that drew no response in '98. The day after Safeco opened in mid-July, the Mariners tried again, having received signals from his agent, Brian Goldberg, that Griffey was open to an improved deal. Awash in their new revenue streams, the Mariners invited Griffey to Armstrong's suite at the yard and displayed the heavy artillery.

The offer: Eight years worth $138 million, starting in 2000, with an average annual value of $17.25 million, plus reopener provisions in case future contracts in baseball exceeded his deal.

"Junior was pleased," Armstrong said. "This was the good Junior. He said, 'You guys really put a lot of work in this. You answered what I was thinking about.' I felt very good about it."

For Rodriguez, who a year earlier underscored his remarkable talents by becoming only the third player to hit 40 home runs and steal 40 bases in the same season, the club delivered a fresh offer in September: Eight years for $117.5 million, starting in 2000, including a $16 million signing bonus, with an average annual value of $14.7 million.

At that time, only the Dodgers, with catcher Mike Piazza and pitcher Kevin Brown, had two players making as much as $10 million apiece, and the Mariners were ready to pay $31 million annually for their dynamic duo. For a franchise that three years earlier let key reliever Mike Jackson go to free agency for fear of a few hundred thousand dollars in extra salary, the leap to bodaciousness was jaw-dropping.

In the company of Scott Boras, one of the most aggressive agents in sports, Rodriguez looked at the offer stone-faced while Boras did most of the talking, said thanks, and left. Nary a yippee or a yahoo, nor even a cocked eyebrow.

"We were disappointed," said Armstrong. "I left there and said, 'What was that all about? We just offered $117 million.' It led us to start believing maybe he didn't really want to be here."

Years later, Rodriguez claimed to have been excited.

"I said this is more money than I can ever fathom, especially a poor kid from Miami," he said. "They offered Griffey a similar deal, so we're talking $250 million.

"I can't sleep, and my mom's about to choke me" for not signing right away.

Somehow, Mom and son patched it up and stayed quiet. So, mysteriously, did Griffey.

⁂

After the All-Star Game break, Griffey's production started to fall, even though he would end up leading the AL in home runs (48) for the third straight year. In August, his wife, Melissa, returned to their Orlando home with the kids; six-year-old Trey was to begin school for the first time. Suddenly, continental geography went from nuisance to heartbreak. Melissa, struggling with the death of her mother, was estranged from her father, and had even less desire to remain in the Northwest.

Griffey's discomfort in Seattle grew with changes in club management. In September, Howard Lincoln, who was retiring from his post at Nintendo, took over as club CEO from the retiring John Ellis. At about the same time, as a second straight losing season was apparent, Woody Woodward, the longest-tenured general manager in the league, quit under pressure after twelve seasons. Woodward, a former Reds player and teammate with Ken Griffey Sr., had known the family for most of Junior's life, and Junior wasn't happy.

Although it was termed a resignation, club insiders knew Lincoln didn't care much for Woodward's work, feeling his close relationship with Piniella allowed the manager to call too many shots. But Woodward, at fifty-six, was ready to depart anyway. He saw big trouble. Already dismayed that ownership hadn't invested a lot in current player payroll while the stadium was going up, he feared that, with no response from Griffey to the huge offer, he would be handed an unthinkable task: trading the most popular figure in Seattle sports history, little more than a year after the firestorm around the Johnson trade.

"I'd been through too much to do that," Woodward said. "Right or wrong, [ownership] knew how I felt."

Earlier in the year, Lincoln, on the verge of takeover, called Griffey out of the blue one morning and asked to come over to his house to talk about the team. The two had known each other from Griffey's endorsement deals of Nintendo games, but Griffey felt awkward answering questions during the visit about the futures of club personnel. He called Goldberg, his agent, who contacted Armstrong.

"I called Chuck and told him Kenny was uncomfortable," Goldberg said. "Chuck later told me he told Howard that he [Howard] was the boss, but he shouldn't put people on the spot like that."

Lincoln was about to put the whole organization on the spot. He had seen enough from Griffey over the years to believe change was about due.

"I was very troubled by the way Junior perceived his role with the Mariners," he said. "Things were happening with Junior where I felt he was out of control. That summer it was apparent he was unhappy. As I looked at it, we had this one superstar who we had no control over. We were not on the same wavelength. He was complaining about this and that. And we'd heard he didn't want to come back."

Griffey had been dropping hints about leaving to teammates and reporters. Strictly from a baseball perspective, it wasn't hard to understand. In addition to the dubious impact of the new ballpark on his numbers, the 79-83 Mariners missed the playoffs a second consecutive year. The club set single-season worsts in six pitching categories: total runs, earned runs, hits, walks, and hit batters, and a 5.24 team ERA. Twenty-eight pitchers saw action, another club record. After chasing down their mistakes in the expanse of Safeco Field, Griffey blurted out during the season: "Where's my pitching?"

In the off-season, the Mariners execs also had a question: "What's wrong with our money?"

Before either question could be answered, the Mariners hired a new baseball leader. Lincoln, aided by No. 2 owner Chris Larson, replaced Woodward with Pat Gillick, one of the most respected executives in the game. Gillick, sixty-two, was the baseball brains behind the Toronto Blue Jays, the Mariners' expansion brethren who blew past them to world championships in 1992 and 1993. Moving to Baltimore, he helped get the Orioles to the American

League Championship Series in 1996 and 1997. A man who knew virtually everyone in baseball, and was blessed with an almost total recall of every prospect he'd ever scouted, Gillick also had the virtue of no emotional involvement with Griffey, making him almost unique in the Mariners organization.

"When Pat talked about the kinds of players he liked to have in the clubhouse, and how important good chemistry was, it really resonated with me," Lincoln said. "That's exactly how I felt. Pat had the same very, very strong feelings. If you have a player not in that group, you have problems."

Gillick jumped into the negotiations, pushing Goldberg for a decision from Griffey, who resented the pressure. He said he had a year left on his contract and was in no hurry. But if push came to shove, he said he wouldn't be coming back. Sensing doom, the Mariners execs in November insisted on a face-to-face meeting. Gillick, Lincoln, and Armstrong flew to Florida to visit the three key principals in the franchise—Piniella in Tampa, Griffey in Orlando, and Rodriguez in Miami.

The club execs planned to talk with Griffey and Goldberg at an Orlando hotel meeting room. "Kenny didn't want to come," Goldberg said. "He said we're friends, and a meeting makes things too formal. I think they knew what his decision was, but since things came out bad with Randy Johnson, they didn't want a repeat."

Griffey finally relented. He met Gillick for the first time, and the five men chatted briefly before Griffey explained the personal and family concerns that had become paramount.

Then came the crossroads moment: He said he no longer wanted to be a Mariner.

Gillick asked: "What if we go to the World Series?"

"No," Griffey said. "It's about my family."

Armstrong, who was club president under former owner George Argyros in 1987 when the Mariners chose Griffey with the No. 1 pick in the amateur draft, asked to speak to Griffey privately. The two and Goldberg left the room and walked down the hall to the lobby for a few minutes. After thirteen years of spectacle, injury, sadness, and breathtaking joy, The Kid who became The Man in Seattle sports and the most popular baseball player on the planet, started to cry. So did Goldberg. So did Armstrong.

"We gave each other a hug, and I told Junior he'd be OK," said Armstrong. "He is a friend. I miss him."

Griffey left the hotel. Goldberg and Armstrong composed themselves, returned to the meeting, and said Griffey was solid in his decision, so let's move on.

After discussing some wording of a joint statement, the meeting quickly broke up. A call was made to the offices in Seattle. Waldman, the attorney who worked on the contracts with Griffey, will never forget the despair in the office that afternoon.

"We were thunderstruck," said Waldman. "This came out of the blue. . . . He didn't want to stay. It was a very tough day."

Said Pelekoudas, "You didn't take him for granted, but he'd been a part of the organization for so long. What we accomplished with and because of him . . . all of a sudden, you say, 'Oh, shit.' "

Similarly profane expressions swept around Puget Sound. Newspapers devoted pages upon pages to the Griffey saga, and how crucial he had been to saving baseball. The radio talk shows were filled with lamentations. There was anger, too, that Griffey would turn his back on Seattle.

But the deed was done. With his ten-and-five rights, Griffey forwarded a list of four teams to which he would accept a trade–Atlanta Braves, New York Mets, Cincinnati Reds, and Houston Astros. All shared a crucial virtue: their spring training sites were an easy distance from Griffey's Florida home. The Braves were scheduled to move to a Disney World sports complex, and Griffey had already figured out he could ride his bike to camp.

One problem: The Braves didn't particularly want Griffey, not at the price he figured to command. They already had a successful, high-payroll team, and didn't want to break the budget, or the clubhouse, given the grapevine word about Griffey's demanding ways in Seattle. Since Griffey's list of acceptable teams was not disclosed, other clubs were hanging back, waiting to see what transpired. The Mariners realized there wasn't much of a market.

"He expressed surprise and dismay through the whole process: 'A lot of people would want me. What are you doing wrong?' " Armstrong said. So the club took calls, with Griffey's OK, from teams not on the list, such as Pittsburgh and Cleveland, in an attempt to create a market. But since those teams were actually offering top players in return, Griffey was asked to reconsider his list of acceptable teams.

"It didn't sit well," Goldberg said. "It became an issue."

As the weeks dragged on, the market was so stale that Goldberg and Armstrong began talking of Griffey's return to Seattle, of doing a two-year bridge deal around Rodriguez's expiring contract. Griffey said he was open to it, but the plot ended at Lincoln's desk.

Goldberg: "Chuck said, 'Howard won't do anything to acknowledge circumstances had changed. We have to stick by the joint statement in November.' "

Finally, an offer came from the Mets during baseball's annual winter meetings that excited the Mariners, despite the fact Griffey had turned down New York once already. Vacationing in Hawaii with Lincoln, Armstrong received the report and immediately called Goldberg, waking him at midnight in Cincinnati, then asking him to call Griffey in Florida.

Then the story went sideways.

Armstrong swore he told Goldberg that if he called back that night, make it in fifteen minutes because they were going to dinner. Otherwise, please call in the morning. Equally adamant, Goldberg swore Armstrong said he had to know in fifteen minutes, or there was no deal. That is what he told Griffey, who was furious that the Mariners wanted him to make such a big decision in so short a time.

"If they had given him forty-eight hours, Kenny might have agreed," said Goldberg, who disagrees with Armstrong to this day about the call's contents. What was certain was that the fateful call provoked Griffey to say no to the Mets—and no to any other team but his hometown of Cincinnati.

Narrowing the field to a single team was a big blow to the Mariners, who already figured the transaction felt like they were walking uphill pulling refrigerators. Reds general manager Jim Bowden suddenly was in a power position. He had been low-balling the Mariners all along, hoping the market would fall away. Even better, Griffey fell to him. Gillick practically had to beg to get an ordinary center fielder, Mike Cameron, an ordinary pitcher, Brett Tomko, and two borderline minor league prospects for the only active player voted to baseball's All Century Team.

The deal depended on the Reds reaching agreement within seventy-two hours with Griffey on a long-term contract extension. That was far easier than the trade itself. Reds owner Carl Lindner offered a nine-year deal, with an option for a tenth, worth $117 million. Despite the fact that the average annual value of the contract, $13 million, was $4.25 million below Seattle's offer of seven months earlier (and with 60 percent deferred annually and spread out to 2025), Griffey readily agreed. Turned out he was a bargain, as well as a steal. Whatever else was said about Griffey, the move wasn't about money.

In Seattle, the deal was condemned as even more lopsided than the Johnson swap eighteen months earlier, although Griffey's leverage in choosing his new team obviously compromised the Mariners' options. But in Cincinnati, February 10, 2000, became an impromptu civic holiday. The Reds, winners of 96 games the previous season, had just added the game's best player. Griffey was hailed as the link to the renaissance of the Big Red Machine days of the 1970s, when his father was an icon.

꧁꧂

Time humbled the hopes of both Griffey and his fans in Cincinnati. His first three years with the team were filled with injuries, conflicts, and controversies. He missed 160 games with physical problems, mostly to torn hamstring muscles. Notorious in the Mariners clubhouse for skipping the weight room and team stretching exercises, Griffey's legs also took a ten-year pounding from the rock-hard surface in the Kingdome.

Although the Reds would be opening a new ballpark in 2003 whose short right-field dimension was designed for Griffey, the nadir of his Midwest tenure was reached in the preceding off-season when the club attempted and failed to trade him to San Diego. In the first week at the new ballpark, Griffey, on another one of his trademark all-out fielding plays, dislocated his shoulder in a fall and missed a big chunk of 2003.

In Seattle, Mike Cameron blossomed into a fine defensive center fielder with frequent big moments at the plate. He was even a late addition to the 2001 All-Star Game roster at Safeco Field. No, he was not a prime-time Griffey. But then, neither was Griffey.

The outcome was a shocker to Griffey's friends in Seattle.

"I don't know if he had in mind to return to Riverfront

Stadium, where his dad played, and it would be Valhalla and everybody lived happily ever after," said Dave Niehaus, the broadcaster. "If that's what he thought, he was dead wrong. It's turned into a nightmare for him. I was sorry to see it."

After the deal, Jay Buhner, for years Griffey's best pal on the team, would have long phone conversations that were more telling than the public rhetoric surrounding one of the most talked-about transactions in baseball's long chronicles.

"I think he wanted to play as strong a hand as he could and—screw it, I'm just going to say it—it backfired on him," Buhner said. "I really think so. He got to a point where he said, 'Oh, shit.'

"He called me and said, 'I fucked up. I overreacted.' I asked him what's wrong with asking for forgiveness?'"

Buhner laughed.

"He said, 'Fuck you, motherfucker.'"

Griffey's ego, as with most high-profile professional athletes, had a hard time finding a reverse gear. Yes, he was troubled by changes in Seattle, disappointed in the baseball results, and uneasy with sharing the clubhouse with Rodriguez. While it was good to be closer to his Florida home, Reds' fans expectations of instant miracles let their disappointments fill Griffey's rabbit ears.

"One of the hardest things in this game is to say, 'Oops, I'm sorry. I fucked up and have to back up,'" Buhner said. "I think everyone knows he made a mistake. If he could have just stepped back and said, 'I tried to play hardball and it didn't work. This is where I want to be . . . greatest place in the world . . . love these fans . . . I started here, want to end here . . . sorry for all the miscommunication.'"

When the Mariners traveled to Cincinnati to play the Reds in June 2002 for the first interleague meeting between the clubs, radio broadcaster Rick Rizzs interviewed Griffey for the pregame show. While endorsing the change for his family's sake, Griffey was wistful, even a little melancholy about his decade in the Northwest.

"It's just that things haven't fell for me here," he said. "A little adversity doesn't hurt anybody, but I've had my share for two, three, four, five people. . . .

"I consider myself raised here, but I grew up [in Seattle]. The thrills I had, my first hit, my first home run, playing with my dad, coming back from 14 down in '95 . . . the fun in Seattle I'll never be able to replace. Those are the memories I'll have for the rest of my life.

"I miss the guys over there. . . . I hope someday I can go back to Seattle with a smile, instead of 55,000 people booing me. . . . I'll tell you what: 98 percent of my time there was good."

However he or others felt about the reasons for his departure, and however his behavior was psychoanalyzed, there was no equivocation about his legacy. Among the key elements in keeping baseball alive in Seattle until it could flourish, Griffey was foremost. To lift the Mariners from their deep ditch, it took the strength of many and the incandescence of one.

⚜

Now that Griffey was gone, the void would require several others to help fill it. With no financial obligations to Griffey, and with thirty sellouts in Safeco's forty-two games of '99, Gillick took a chubby checkbook into the free-agent market.

He finally tapped successfully into the Mariners' connection to the Far East by signing Kazuhiro Sasaki, the best relief pitcher in Japanese baseball. Three days later, Gillick added Arthur Rhodes, one of the game's best setup men, to fix a bullpen with a ghastly 5.94 seasonal ERA. He filled a hole in the starting pitching by signing reliable veteran Aaron Sele, who would join Jamie Moyer and the two pitchers from the Johnson trade, Freddy Garcia and John Halama, in a solid four-man rotation.

First base was upgraded by adding former batting champion John Olerud, a Bellevue native and former star at Washington State University. The bench was bolstered by Mark McLemore, a signing little appreciated until it was discovered over the next three seasons that he could play six positions well, and hit for average.

And at shortstop: Alex Rodriguez, the last baseball superstar standing in Seattle. Even *he* couldn't believe it. "I thought," he said, "Griffey would be here forever."

Over the winter of Griffey's discontent, Rodriguez and his agent, Scott Boras, having watched the Mariners' moves, developed four primary goals for his final contract season in Seattle: Say no to the big Mariners offer, keep from getting traded, play well, then after the season get all the money in the world, even if the world has to borrow from God. It turned out to be a brilliant strategy.

The only commitments he made to the Mariners were to play hard—something Johnson and Griffey did erratically in their walk years—and if a World Series was won, he'd stay.

Boras and Rodriguez got the Mariners to buy off on the plan. In spring training, Lincoln announced the club would allow the shortstop to play out the season with no further negotiations and no attempt to trade him. Then the Mariners would join the rest of baseball in the free-agent frenzy that was destined to produce the most outrageous contract result in sports history.

"I wanted to hear from Alex directly that he wouldn't tail off," said Lincoln, mindful of the fades of Johnson and Griffey. "He gave me the assurance I was looking for—even though I was fairly sure then he wasn't coming back.

"I wanted to give him a leadership role, because I thought our chances of keeping him would be better. He would thrive and be more prone to staying. And I wanted to give him a feeling about why staying in Seattle made sense, and not just from a baseball standpoint."

So began the courtship of A-Rod. Because Boras said Rodriguez had an interest in real business life, not just baseball, Lincoln arranged a tour of Boeing's giant Everett plant, which included time in a jetliner cockpit as well as a visit with the company's commercial-plane chief, Alan Mulally. Lincoln also set up an afternoon of golf with Microsoft chairman Bill Gates. Driving out to the Snoqualmie Ridge course east of Seattle, Rodriguez asked Lincoln if Gates would know who he was. Assured that he did, Rodriguez then remarked on the beauty of the landscape. Lincoln realized that in five years with the club, Rodriguez had never been east of Bellevue.

On the field, Rodriguez was less naive. An All-Star for the fourth consecutive year, he led the offense with 41 home runs and 132 RBIs, with a .316 average, as the Mariners returned to the winning side with a club-record 91 victories, while drawing 3.1 million fans in the first full year at Safeco. But he was anything but a one-man show.

He benefited greatly by hitting a spot ahead of cleanup hitter Edgar Martinez, who had career highs of 37 home runs (including a club-record four grand slams) and 145 RBIs. Mike Cameron, becoming the first regular center fielder in Seattle besides Griffey since 1988, was a popular, pleasant surprise, playing Griffey-like defense while contributing a .267 average with 19 homers and 78 RBIs. In an August game against Boston, his solo homer in the bottom of the 19th inning captured one of the more epic games in club history. Besides the power, the Mariners finished second in the AL in stolen bases and led the majors in walks.

The pitching staff, revitalized by the hiring of a bright young pitching coach, Bryan Price, went from the AL's second-worst ERA (5.24) in '99 to its second best (4.49). Kazuhiro Sasaki, thirty-two, the closer who became AL rookie of the year, saved 37 games in 40 opportunities. Aaron Sele was named to the All-Star team and finished with a 17-10 record.

Despite the 12-game improvement from '99, it wasn't until the last day of the regular season that their postseason fate was known. A 5-2 win over Anaheim slipped them into the wild-card position, one game ahead of Cleveland and a half game behind AL West champion Oakland. For the third time—but the first without Johnson and Griffey—the Mariners were in the playoffs.

Harrowing as was the final week, they made the shortest possible work of the best-of-five Division Series, sweeping Central Division champion Chicago. That set up a rematch of the '95 AL Division Series—the two-time defending world champion New York Yankees were back in Seattle faces, starting with two games in Yankee Stadium (wild-card teams are not allowed the home-field advantage).

The Yanks, who won the East Division with only 87 victories, looked vulnerable. While the Mariners were 22-10 since September 1, New York lost its final seven regular-season games, then in the Division Series was pushed to the full five games before subduing the A's. Unlike the Mariners, whose sweep of the White Sox provided a little respite, the Yanks' starting rotation was messed up.

But the Mariners, who beat the Yanks six times in 10 games during the season, suffered a blow of their own. Starting pitcher Jamie Moyer (13-10), whose left-handed cleverness figured to be most useful against the Yankees lineup, was injured in a morning practice and was lost for the playoffs. Throwing a simulated game of 60 pitches, Moyer asked to throw one more. The pitch was hit back at him, bouncing once before smacking his knee. The freakish moment produced a hairline fracture of the kneecap.

The injury was no problem for Seattle in Game 1. Freddy Garcia

As part of his "recruitment" of impending free agent Alex Rodriguez (left), Mariners CEO Howard Lincoln took the shortstop on a tour of a Boeing plant.

PHOTO COURTESY OF HOWARD LINCOLN

pitched one of the great games of his career, shutting out the Yanks for nearly seven innings. Supplemented by relief from Jose Paniagua, Arthur Rhodes, and Kazu Sasaki, the Yanks were held to six hits in a 2-0 triumph. The win came against the weakest member of the Yankees' rotation, Denny Neagle, a break that did not reappear for a while, owing to three games of hell against veteran aces Orlando Hernandez, Andy Pettitte, and Roger Clemens.

Yet for seven surprising innings of Game 2, Mariners starter John Halama, a native of Brooklyn, actually outpitched Hernandez, one of the great postseason hurlers in Yankees history. Halama's shutout innings, added to Garcia's seven from the night before, made for 14 in a row from the pitchers acquired in 1998 for Randy Johnson. Six outs from a sweep of the two games in New York, no one in Seattle was lamenting the departure of the Big Unit.

Never in their much-lauded postseason history had the Yanks been shut out back-to-back at home. The mark would stay intact.

To start the eighth and leading 1-0, Piniella replaced the tiring Halama with Rhodes, the ace setup man. The game was quickly tied when David Justice doubled and Bernie Williams singled him home. Then came the fateful play that turned the inning, and perhaps the series, denying the Mariners a grand chance at reaching the World Series.

Tino Martinez, the former Mariner traded to New York five years earlier, hit a sinking liner into left field that Al Martin momentarily lost in the lights. Martin, a thirty-two-year-old midseason pickup by GM Pat Gillick who proved to have little pop in his bat and too much pop in his glove, normally was replaced late in the game with a better defender. But he was due up in the ninth, and Piniella wanted his bat in the game.

The decision backfired when Martin staggered and fell attempting to catch the ball. Yankees fans, humbled for most of two nights, exploded in delight. The taut game's momentum had swung. Rattled, Rhodes gave up a single to Jorge Posada for one run, and a sacrifice fly to Paul O'Neill for another run. Piniella replaced Rhodes with Jose Mesa, who was even worse, giving up a single to ex-Mariner Luis Sojo, a double to Jose Vizcaino, a single to Chuck Knoblauch, and, finally, a two-run homer to Derek Jeter. New York scored all its runs in the 7-1 triumph in a single inning, an inning that will haunt Mariners fans for a good long time.

Even though a road split is always considered good in a best-of-seven, the series' arrival for three games in Seattle was worth little. Pettitte and Clemens crushed the Mariners' offense. They managed two hits off Pettitte in Game 3 and one hit off Clemens in Game 4. The 8-2 and 5-0 wins were nearly devastating, particularly the complete game by Clemens, who sent a first-inning message by nearly shaving off the eyebrows of Rodriguez with an inside heater.

Some dignity was preserved in Game 5 by Garcia, who pitched another five strong innings while the Mariners offense had another chance to work over Neagle, the Game 1 loser. The 6-2 win returned the series to New York for Game 6 and a Halama-Hernandez rematch.

This one looked promising for Seattle again, as the Mariners took a 4-3 lead into the seventh. But another bullpen collapse—before the series, the Mariners relievers had a string of 15 consecutive scoreless innings—produced another giant inning and brought down the curtain. Paniagua, Rhodes (a victim of season-long overuse), and Mesa gave up eight hits and six runs in the seventh for a 9-4 lead. Although the Mariners rallied for three in the eighth, star closer Mariano Rivera shut things down in the ninth for a 9-7 triumph and a 4-2 series victory.

The Yankees went on to the World Series against the cross-town Mets. It may have been big in Gotham, especially after the Yanks won 4-1, but in the Northwest the baseball thoughts were about opportunity lost. The Mariners missed out on the World Series—and they also lost the chance to make Rodriguez keep his promise to stay in Seattle if they won.

Rodriguez delivered in the playoffs, hitting .308 against Chicago and .409 against the formidable Yanks staff, including two home runs. Given how beatable the Mets looked in the World Series, Rodriguez almost had to deliver on his promise. Instead, after a few clubhouse tears at Yankee Stadium, he skipped happily into free agency.

The courtship of A-Rod began anew, this time on a much grander stage. Golf with Gates was long forgotten. Boras created a Rodriguez "prospectus" worthy of the most sophisticated corporation, a hardbound, fifty-page book laden with photos, stats, and praise, concluding that he was the greatest player in the game today and would become the greatest of all time. Since Boras contended that joining a long-term winner was a top priority, several teams wooing Rodriguez invited him to their cities and took pains to offer him farm-system analyses proving that quality was in the pipeline. No such stop on A-Rod's world victory tour was accorded the Mariners.

They responded on the home front by re-signing another free agent, Lou Piniella, to a three-year deal. The manager and the shortstop were close, and the club hoped Piniella's return would be influential. They also re-signed Buhner and brought back Jeff Nelson, a member of the Mariners' miracle club in '95 who left the Yankees as a free agent.

Armstrong said the Mariners contemplated offering Rodriguez an eight-year deal for $160 million, a $40 million increase from their previous offer, but were trumped by the market. The Boston Red Sox's identical offer to free-agent slugger Manny Ramirez had been accepted, meaning that Rodriguez, younger and better than Ramirez, would demand and get more.

"The disappointment came when we weren't getting any

favored-son treatment," said Bart Waldman, the club attorney. "We were champing at the bit. In our heart of hearts, we were saying, 'Let us give you an offer first.' "

In early December, Boras agreed to give a Mariners delegation an audience in Miami. Having been led to believe by Boras that Rodriguez wanted a shorter-term deal, the Mariners offered three years for $54 million, with a two-year option for a total of 92 million.

"You are not," Boras told them, "remotely in the market."

He was soon proven to be stupefyingly accurate. At baseball's annual winter business meeting in Dallas, Tom Hicks, the owner of the Texas Rangers and the NHL Dallas Stars, dope-slapped the sports world by offering Rodriguez $252 million over ten years. The original offer was around $240 million, but when Boras realized he was close to doubling the previous greatest contract in sports—the $126 million given Kevin Garnett by the NBA Minnesota Timberwolves—he asked for some spare change. Hicks, a wealthy real estate developer, had no problem, despite the fact that no competing offer was within $100 million of the final tab.

Suddenly, it didn't seem to matter what the Mariners did or did not do, during the season or after the season. It didn't matter what Rodriguez said or didn't say about the Mariners' chances. Nor did anyone give a second thought to the Rangers' farm system, or the big-league club's chances in 2001. The Hicks offer nuked everything. All that was left was the realization that baseball, operating into a third century on the Greater Fool theory, had done it again. A lone ego won the battle over brains.

⁂

Rodriguez and his agent executed their original plan flawlessly and beyond anyone's imagination. The only downsides were his annual returns to Safeco Field, where he was booed mercilessly, and the losing. In his first two seasons, the Rangers finished last in the AL West, winning 73 and 72 games. But $252 million can buy a lot of earplugs, and a lot of get-well cards.

"I told him, 'If you don't take it, I'm going to kick your ass,' " said Buhner of the Texas offer. "I can understand where fans are coming from. The Mariners turned around, and he left, so screw him. But if you think about it, who wouldn't do it?"

The visceral resentment of Rodriguez stemmed from the fact

that he talked one game and played another. That, and the fact that the team's greatest player left and the Mariners received nothing in return. At least the trades of Johnson and Griffey brought talent in return.

"A-Rod was real smooth. It got to the point where even his teammates knew he was usually full of shit," Buhner said, laughing. "I can tell him that and he'll laugh about it—he won't take it the wrong way. He *was* full of shit half the time. But he can play. He's so strong mentally. He's a great teammate, great competitor, and no one—no one!—was more prepared than that guy."

For their part, the Mariners offered no regrets about how they played the Rodriguez deal—or how it played them.

"He fulfilled every part of the deal," Lincoln said. "The Mariners got their money's worth. No question in my mind, it was the right thing to do."

But now, the Seattle marquee was blank. Martinez and Buhner were still around, but the faces most closely identified with Mariners baseball nationally were gone.

Randy Johnson wanted to play in his home of Phoenix. Ken Griffey Jr. wanted to play closer to his home in Florida. Alex Rodriguez wanted to play close to where the money was. None of them wanted to play with each other, or in Seattle. All three had the skills and leverage to make their dreams happen. The stars let themselves out.

But there was a star who wanted in.

While working as a pitching coach for the Orix Blue Wave in Japan's Pacific League in the early '90s, Jim Colborn befriended the club's slender young batting star, Ichiro Suzuki. They talked often about American baseball. After winning his fourth straight batting title in 1997, Ichiro quizzed Colborn, whose major league pitching career ended with the Mariners in 1978, about whether he might be ready to play in the major leagues. He had done about everything he could do in Japan, and was growing weary of the rock-star sensation he created among media and fans.

"He didn't know how good he was," Colborn said. "I reassured him about what he could do."

Colborn, then the Mariners' director of Pacific Rim scouting, earlier helped create a working agreement between Orix and the Mariners. In the spring of '98, before Johnson was traded, Colborn arranged to fly with Ichiro to Seattle to see the

Kingdome and the new ballpark under construction. Then they flew to Phoenix to see the spring training facilities and shake a few hands.

At the airport for the return flight home, the pair stopped in a lounge for a quick bite. As Ichiro downed a hot dog, he said, "*Seguo*," the Japanese word for super.

Colborn looked at him.

"Super? It's an airport hot dog."

"No," he said, shaking his head and explaining what was super. "I'm out in public, and I can be private."

To Ichiro, the most popular—and besieged—pop-culture icon in Japan, America and the Mariners were looking good. Colborn, who had lost out on getting the Mariners a top Japanese pitcher a couple of years earlier, wasn't going to blow this opportunity.

CHAPTER TEN

Ichiro and a Season for the Ages

Flushed in the face and forlorn in the soul, Lou Piniella burst from the clubhouse door into the ground-floor interior concourse at Safeco Field, where he went two-eyes-to-two-hundred with local and national sports media members. Shuffling and kibitzing after watching the Mariners fall upon their lips, losing the first two home games in the 2001 American League Championship Series to the New York Yankees, the press hounds were eager to vacuum the clubhouse for quotes regarding how it was possible to squander one of the great regular seasons in the history of major league baseball.

Barely surviving an opening-round Division Series against Cleveland, the Mariners in the ALCS dropped a second consecutive heart-slasher of a game, and would resume the series in Yankee Stadium against the three-time defending champions. Even for a team that astounded baseball with 116 regular-season victories—an AL record that tied the National League's 1906 Chicago Cubs for the most ever—the Mariners' task was rolling-boulders-up-the-hill formidable in a best-of-seven series.

Six years earlier, the Mariners had a miraculous comeback against the Yankees, winning the final three in a Division Series they also trailed 0-2. Was the Seattle well deep enough for a second helping of serendipity?

If the sheer force of Piniella's will was sufficient, yes. A Yankees hero as a player, manager, and general manager, Piniella was consumed with beating his former club, which also fired him a couple of times. Even if the Yankees' bombastic owner, George Steinbrenner, considers him almost a son, Piniella seethed privately at every loss to the Yankees, particularly in the postseason when his old club is in high swagger.

For Piniella, the Yankees influence doesn't end with the baseball calendar. When he returns every winter to his home in Tampa, Florida, he finds figurative pinstripes everywhere. Yankees teammates Derek Jeter and Jorge Posada live in Piniella's upscale North Tampa neighborhood, where he sees them regularly at the community golf course. Legends Field, the Yankees' spring training park, is a couple of miles from Piniella's favorite restaurant, Malio's, which is not far from the Lou Piniella Softball Field near his childhood home.

The baseball retiree crowd in Tampa is thick with ex-Yanks. Often, the social fulcrum is Steinbrenner, also a Tampa resident, who rarely misses an opportunity to remind Piniella of the old world order in baseball. "I see George at least once a week," he said of his off-season routine. "George has told me many times now, 'You're getting good at what you do, but remember who taught you, and I haven't taught you everything.' "

But Piniella figured that whatever baseball he didn't know, it didn't have to be passed on from Steinbrenner and the Yankees. It was time for the student to school the teacher. This 2001 Mariners team, he thought, would be the team that would end the Yankees' hegemony, which stood at three straight World Series wins and four in the past five seasons.

Even for the baseball cognoscenti who had seen everything, the Mariners' 2001 achievements were hard to comprehend: In first place from opening day, they took the American League West division by 14 games over an Oakland team that won a remarkable 102 games itself; set an American League record with a 59-22 road mark; and became the first team in more than fifty years to lead baseball in the three main statistical categories of batting, pitching and fielding.

To have such feats happen after the departures of Ken Griffey Jr., Alex Rodriguez, and Randy Johnson compounded the astonishment. The marquee figures who first brought the Mariners to baseball prominence all went elsewhere in pursuit of riches and rewards they assumed to be unattainable in baseball's most distant frontier. Yet their exodus, presumed devastating, turned energizing. In 2001, the trio was paid $46 million combined by their new teams, money the Mariners instead spent on lesser stars who created greater success.

"What the Mariners did," said Mike Scioscia, who bore first-hand witness as the manager of the Anaheim Angels, "will be the envy of major league baseball for decades."

By midseason the Mariners were not in a pennant race against other teams but in an imaginary match against history. Area newspapers were filled with daily reports on how the Mariners compared with the 1909 Pittsburgh Pirates, the 1927 and 1998 Yankees, the 1954 Indians, and other legendary teams who also transcended their contemporaries. The season that transfixed baseball also electrified the Puget Sound market. The Mariners led both leagues in attendance, drawing more than 3.5 million fans at Safeco Field from a fan base across four Northwest states, Alaska, and western Canada. But at the moment, the seasonal achievement was in jeopardy, because as Yankees fans would soon remind them, by handmade ballpark sign and bellicose bleat, "It don't mean a thing without the ring."

The Mariners were not the same team in the playoffs. After scratching by Cleveland three games to two in the opening round, they managed just 10 hits and four runs in the first two games against New York. The Mariners were on the edge of cratering the World Series expectations that built in Seattle, which had last seen a pro sports championship in 1979, when the SuperSonics won the NBA title. Since then, with one exception, every other U.S. market that had three or more pro sports teams would experience the joy of a title. Only Cleveland, whose Browns won the 1964 NFL (pre–Super Bowl) championship, had been a loser longer.

Desperation was upon Piniella, because in the 2-3-2 format of a best-of-seven series, the two home losses meant a return to Seattle for the sixth and seventh games was in serious jeopardy. He was searching for something that would make even a small difference for a team that was sagging under the pressure as well as the Yankees' great pitching. Seeing the media horde that was ready to pounce on his team and unintentionally but inevitably make things worse, Piniella's legendary passion once again seized his better judgment and beat the hell out of it.

On his way to a room where TV cameras were set up for the standard postgame interview session, Piniella abruptly stopped to address the reporters who were about to enter the clubhouse.

"I want to say it so you all can hear it," Piniella bellowed, stilling the murmur and freezing movement. "We're going to be back here for Game 6. Just print it. You don't have to ask any questions. Just print it."

He marched off to the interview room, leaving a rising gaggle of voices that sounded as astonished as they were delighted. Several writers abandoned the cattle-call rush into the clubhouse and sprinted to the press-box elevator, knowing there was no better story awaiting them in the clubhouse than what Piniella had just handed them—on a tight deadline, no less. As they passed Piniella on the concourse, one yelled, "Thanks, Lou!" But Piniella kept his head down, striding purposefully to the room, where he repeated himself.

"Before we get to the questions, I want to say something," he said as he settled into a chair at a table with a microphone, facing a room with perhaps sixty chairs that were half filled, while a dozen TV cameras on tripods lined the back of the room. He began slapping the table rhythmically, which the mike amplified into a startling drumbeat.

"We're going to be back here for Game 6, OK? I told the people outside the same thing. Now you can ask any question you want."

Silence. For a moment, Piniella stunned the yelping hordes, taking over the situation by changing the subject from how the Mariners reached 0-2 to how they intend to get to 2-3, or even 3-2, which would return the series to Seattle. It was a clever deployment of an unusual but not unprecedented sports maneuver in which the manager or coach absorbs media and public curiosity, deflecting it away from the team.

Piniella instantly made himself the coast-to-coast baseball buzz. Instead of being peppered with questions about why they were suddenly playing so poorly, Mariners players were mostly asked, "Whadja thinka Lou?"

Piniella explained himself: "I've got confidence in my baseball team. We've gone to New York and beat this baseball team five out of six times [in the regular season], and we're going to do it again." Not only did the tactic put the media onto a fresh trail away from the clubhouse, it told his players the boss believed they were still the same team that hammered the record books.

Desperate as was the tactic, it was not necessarily a reach. In Piniella's nine years, the players and the franchise demonstrated a repetitive knack for returning from the obituary pages to the sports pages. Absurdity had become an old pal of baseball in Seattle, never more intimate than in this season, when the Mariners without Johnson, Griffey, and Rodriguez improved 25 games over the 2000 season of 91 wins.

His players endorsed Piniella's move without reservation.

"I think the fans are ready, and they would love to get a World Series in Seattle," Edgar Martinez said. "They deserve it. It's been a long wait. We also have a good team that we believe can make it there, so I do share the same thought as Lou."

Said center fielder Mike Cameron, "I really don't think he would have said something if he had a very young team. Obviously, Lou knows what type of team he has, and what type of response he can get. Three or four years ago, I would have went into a panic, but playing with some of the best guys in baseball, we obviously know how to handle this situation."

⁂

Up to this point, Piniella had not needed feints. He had a team of professional grinders that operated at close to maximum efficiency for six months, as lucky as a towel boy in a cheerleaders' locker room and as resilient as Styrofoam gum. The Mariners had only one player on the roster, Martinez, who had hit as many as 30 home runs in a season. Patience and opportunism were the key offensive virtues. Whether it was two strikes on the batter or two outs in the inning, the Mariners figured a way to string together small links that made a strong, if unobtrusive, chain.

"Tighteners" is what Piniella called the high number of close games the Mariners played. A game in early August against the Toronto Blue Jays was a vivid demonstration of the club's style of wearing opponents down instead of blowing them up.

Arriving in Seattle from a road trip at four in the morning after giving up 26 runs in the previous three games (but still winning two), the Mariners' bullpen was worn out. The starter for the series opener against the Jays, rookie Joel Pineiro, needed to stay in the game for a while. He was brilliant, striking out 11 in seven innings, leaving the game with a 3-1 lead. But tired relievers Arthur Rhodes and Jeff Nelson faltered, and the Mariners trailed 4-3 in the bottom of the ninth.

With one out, Cameron scratched out an infield single. He went to second on a passed ball and scored the game-tying run on Carlos Guillen's bloop single. The game went into extra innings. John Halama, who had been replaced in the rotation by Pineiro a few weeks earlier, came out of the bullpen to pitch five scoreless innings.

With one out in the bottom of the fourteenth, reserve outfielder Stan Javier had an infield single and fired up his thirty-seven-year-old legs to steal second base, then took third on the Toronto catcher's throwing error. After a strikeout, John Olerud was intentionally walked, and took second on fielder's indifference. Bret Boone, after working the count to 3-0, was intentionally walked to load the bases and create a force play at any base. Against reliever Matt DeWitt, Cameron worked the count full while fouling off several pitches. Finally, DeWitt gave in, throwing ball four about two feet above the strike zone to force in the winning run.

The 14-inning game would be the Mariners' longest of the year (4 hours, 37 minutes) and easily could have been a fatigue-induced defeat that no one would have noticed, not with an 81-31 record entering the contest and a 19-game lead in the division. Instead, deploying walks, bloops, dribblers, and opponent goofs, they threw marshmallows at the Blue Jays until they couldn't stand it anymore.

"We always," said Boone, "have a chance."

The players weren't ashamed to acknowledge good fortune as well as good ball.

"We were great, but you had to get breaks, and we got all of them," said Boone, who had the greatest offensive year of a second baseman in AL history. "In baseball, on any given day, a world champion can get its butt kicked by the worst team. I think if you assembled an all-star team and put them in our division, they couldn't win 116 games.

"I don't care how good you are, you got to get breaks."

The chief blessing was health. The club had almost no major injuries; only seven players were put on the disabled list, a low in the eighteen-year tenure of trainer Rick Griffin. The one main casualty was Jay Buhner. A foot problem limited him to 19 regular-season games, and in the postseason, just nine at-bats. At age thirty-eight, after fourteen seasons as a Mariner, Buhner's abused body finally had enough baseball and in the off-season would demand, successfully, that he retire.

Over Buhner's final four years, a variety of ailments and injuries limited him to just 290 games. In his medical honor, Griffin modified a full-size anatomical chart in the clubhouse to show, with push pins holding up notes of description, more than seventy physical problems Buhner had during their time together. Amazingly, none required major surgery, but several took extensive rehabilitation time in the training room. No one was certain over the past five years whether Buhner had spent more time with his wife, Leah, or Griffin.

"He rehabbed the same way he played," said Griffin, "with reckless abandon."

Replacing Buhner's contribution figured to be daunting. But his successor in right field became a symbol of the sort of karma that hung around this '01 team, as thick as the smell of garlic fries at the ballpark: a rookie who became the league's most valuable player. The story of how it happened is almost as compelling as the season he helped create.

◦⟡◦

At 5-foot-9 and 160 pounds, with wispy sideburns and a deferential personality, Ichiro Suzuki, twenty-seven, was without a doubt the most unimposing desperado who ever tore up a baseball league. The first Japanese position player to make it in the major leagues, Ichiro—owing to the ubiquitousness of his last name in Japan, he was known by his first—shared with baseball immortal Jackie Robinson something besides a barrier-breaking cultural achievement. They were the only players in the last half century to lead the majors in batting average and stolen bases in the same season.

After Kingdome patrons thrilled to years of home runs, Ichiro made the Safeco Field legions admire the overlooked virtue of the 100-foot base hit. He was so fast out of the left-side batter's box that almost any grounder had a chance to be a single, creating some deep-nerve twitching among defenders. When he lofted the ball, it was apt to drop anywhere on the outfield green. His hand-eye coordination created bat control so precise it allowed him to drive a pitch in any direction that seemed easiest.

"He doesn't hit," said Piniella. "He serves like a tennis player."

Equally dynamic in the outfield, Ichiro flashed his gun once early in the season and made foes tiptoe the rest of the year. Attempting to go from first to third on a single, the Oakland A's Terrence Long found himself cut down by a throw from Ichiro that arrived sizzling in third baseman David Bell's glove at the bag with no weave or hump in its flight pattern. Ichiro could have blown the smoke from his figurative gun barrel, but self-aggrandizement was never part of his show.

Ichiro became a fascinating study for teammates and fans. In his batting stance, Ichiro goes through a ritual before each pitch that includes extending the bat in a counterclockwise circle, followed by a tug of his right sleeve with his left hand. The routine helps him achieve what he calls his "normal mental state" that keeps his concentration focused on the moment with the pitcher. In the on-deck circle, his routine of squats and stretches never varies. After the game, Ichiro sits at his locker for several minutes working the soles of his feet with a small wood dowel. Just as carefully, he works over his handmade fielding glove, cleaning it and oiling the leather.

Teammates teased him a little about his habits, but they saw the results and never pressed the issue. For his part, Ichiro, whose English is better than he publicly lets on, was frequently engaged in the clubhouse banter. With a love for American pop culture, especially hip-hop, he quickly picked up on the nonsense vernacular of the street, greeting teammates with "Wassup dawg?" and "Chillin' like Bob Dylan," even though he was clueless about the American rocker. He even took to swearing at Piniella in Spanish, which delighted the manager. Buhner nicknamed him "Ichi-balls," while teammates preferring names easier on polite company called him "Wizard."

His seamless transition to American ball dumbfounded every expert. They were certain that the better pitching, longer schedule, and harder travel he faced in the U.S. would keep him ordinary. Maybe in a few years, they said, he might be all right. At least, that was the opinion of every American but one.

Jim Colborn, the Mariners' director of Pacific Rim scouting, was so certain of Ichiro's success that before the Mariners decided to sign him, Colborn presented a list to general manager Pat Gillick of what he expected to see on Ichiro's résumé after five years in the United States: an All-Star selection, a batting title, two or three Gold Glove awards, and single-season high marks of 15 outfield assists, 80 RBIs, 200 hits, 14 home runs, and an on-base percentage of more than .400.

After the 2001 results, even Colborn was amazed. "I didn't expect them to be all in the first year," he said.

It wasn't quite: Entering 2003, Ichiro had yet to reach Colborn's goals in home runs, RBIs, and on-base percentage, and the outfield assists may never happen because no base runner dares take the chance. But never mind the quibbles. What Ichiro brought to the Mariners was larger than any number. He delivered a big part of the answer to the question of how the dazzle-free Mariners would reload without rebuilding.

His arrival after the door closed on a big chapter in club history completed the conversion to a style dictated by a bigger ballpark,

Ichiro Suzuki was ready for the Mariners long before they were ready for him.

©2002 SEATTLE POST-INTELLIGENCER/PAUL JOSEPH BROWN

and glitzed up a roster lacking charisma. For the industry, his presence also opened a market for American baseball only lightly tapped before. Because of Ichiro's popularity, Japanese network NHK televised most Mariners home games live to his homeland. And his exotic, edgy demeanor charmed his new countrymen.

"I love the guy," San Francisco Giants manager Dusty Baker told *Baseball Weekly*. "He's cool. He's got a cool hairstyle. Cool clothes. Cool car. Anybody that just goes by one name has got to be cool."

Ichiro's help in the transformation of the Mariners wasn't planned that way: The club signed Ichiro three weeks before free agent Alex Rodriguez left for the Texas Rangers, hoping it might be influential in keeping the shortstop. Nor was it purely luck that made Ichiro a Mariner; he had been courted slyly.

But his arrival was consistent with all the developments that transformed the franchise—it hung by a thread. In this case, Ichiro became a Mariner through an improbable, long-running friendship with Colborn.

"He looked at me with fair and honest eyes," Ichiro said through the team's translator, Hide Sueyoshi. "He knows baseball on both sides [of the Pacific] and has a wide range of knowledge. He never said whether or not I could play in the major leagues. He just always made me realize how tough it is. He said I would have to be very aggressive in the majors, always take the extra base when the opponent makes a mistake.

"Jim is a good friend."

When the two met in Kobe in the early '90s, Colborn was the pitching coach for Orix and Ichiro was a teenager shuttling between the big club and the minors.

"It was hard to gain confidence for me then," Ichiro said. "One day he threw me batting practice, I don't remember where, and he came up to me and compared me to [former Kansas City great] George Brett. He said I was better than George at the same age. Maybe that was just lip service, but it gave me a lot of confidence."

In 1994, Ichiro won the first of seven consecutive batting titles and was named the Pacific League's Most Valuable Player. But his American mentor was not there to watch. Orix wanted a new pitching coach and Colborn had grown weary of Japan, calling his four years there "the most difficult thing I've done in my life."

Married with three kids, Colborn lied to his family in 1990 to get them to try Japan, telling them he had signed a one-year deal when it was two years. But by 1993, when he said he was done, they resisted mightily a return to the U.S.

"I had to drag them back," he said. "We might have stayed if it weren't cost prohibitive. Mostly for me, the work life was extreme anxiety—real tough," because of differences in language and culture.

In the U.S., Colborn's eleven-year career as a major league pitcher with four teams peaked in 1973 in Milwaukee, when he was named to the All-Star team. He finished the season with a 20-12 record. But the end was near in 1978 when, as a member of the Kansas City Royals, he was traded to Seattle for outfielder Steve Braun while the Mariners played in Kansas City.

"On Saturday, I took the stadium elevator down and went right, to the home clubhouse," he said. "On Sunday, I took the elevator down and went left, to the visitors' clubhouse. It was extremely humiliating.

"In a sense, the elevator took me to the basement. The Mariners were the doormats of the league."

He started 19 games, finishing 3-10 with a 5.35 earned run average, which made for career marks of 83-88 with a 3.80 ERA. What he remembers as a Mariners player was the club's place on the local sports ladder.

"To get fans to come, they'd show Sonics games on the big screen," he said, referring to the NBA team's first deep run into the playoffs in '78 that reached the NBA finals against the Washington Bullets. "I'd be down in the bullpen getting ready to start, and they'd tell me to stop because everyone was watching the Sonics game. When it was over, they'd say OK, you finish your warm-ups."

Depressing at it was, Colborn never lost his sense of whimsy that was more of a legacy than anything he did on the mound. Once in Milwaukee, where the grounds crew dressed in lederhosen, Colborn popped out of the dugout in yellow leather shorts in the seventh inning of the season's final game, working over the dirt around first base with a rake.

For another season-ending contest, he dressed as an umpire for the pregame meeting at home plate. Some of his teammates were in on the gag and began yelling obscenities at him. They had their cars packed for the drives to off-season homes, and were hoping for an ejection so they could get an early start.

"I threw a couple of 'em out," he said, smiling. "Hey, I even threw me out, hoping it would take and I could leave early too."

For what would prove to be the final game of his career, he had to come up with something to maintain his little tradition. He had sales experience—during the off-seasons in Milwaukee he sold tickets for the club—so he told a peanut vendor near the Kingdome's home bullpen that he'd like to help him. Vaulting the fence, Colborn took the man's tray and spent an inning in his baseball uniform hawking goobers to startled patrons.

Sensing a potential sales career, Colborn left baseball and sold real estate, which proved not nearly as much fun as peanuts. He rejoined baseball as a minor league pitching instructor with the Cubs, then moved to Japan after being sought there by one of his former managers. Upon his return to the U.S., he took a job in the Oakland A's minor league system for three seasons before he heard the Mariners were looking for a Pacific Rim director. He interviewed with Roger Jongewaard, the vice president for scouting.

"At the time, no other clubs were talking about Japan," he said. "Roger was very alert. He was a visionary, no question. I thought any team looking over in Japan would have an advantage. I thought there were two dozen pitchers and maybe fifteen position players who could be in the majors."

Hired in October 1996, Colborn thought he snagged a good one for his new old club when Japanese free-agent pitcher Shigetoshi Hasegawa, who was staying in Colborn's house while he worked out and looked for a U.S. team, was ready to sign with the Mariners. But in the infamous interregnum when the club was up for sale in a dispute over stadium construction, Hasegawa was lost to the Angels.

If that wasn't a sufficiently strange rebeginning, weirdness found a higher gear in October 1997 when Colborn was embroiled in the pursuit of Tomoya Kawaguchi, a name no Mariners fan has ever heard, for what will be seen here as good, if peculiar, reasons.

The Mariners' majority owner, Hiroshi Yamauchi, who publicly professed little interest in either baseball or television, nevertheless become enraptured with a high school pitcher who was dominating the national prep tournament in 1997. Watching the Koshien tourney one day on TV—the event is likened to the NCAA men's basketball tournament in popularity—Yamauchi saw Tomoya Kawaguchi, a 6-foot-2 left-hander from a high school in Yamauchi's hometown of Kyoto, pitch a shutout in a semifinal game.

Yamauchi would soon order Howard Lincoln, his representative among the Mariners owners, to sign him, saying, "I knew that day Kawaguchi was destined to become a Mariner."

A small panic ensued, because the Mariners had not scouted the kid. They later learned that others who had, figured Kawaguchi for a marginal major leaguer at best. But Lincoln didn't want to offend Yamauchi. His judgment, after all, made Nintendo the most successful video game company in the world. So he dispatched Colborn, Jongewaard, and club president Chuck Armstrong to Kyoto to sign the kid. Armstrong, who hadn't met Yamauchi, knew some who had, and didn't want any part of the brusque, demanding video game titan. He thought Lincoln should go.

"Are you crazy?" Lincoln said. "If I got over there and we fail, I might get fired."

"I might get fired?" Armstrong asked, his booming voice squeaking up to falsetto, as it often did in moments of excitement.

Said Lincoln, smiling just a little, "Well, better you than me."

Already aware that Yamauchi was upset with Lincoln for failing to sign Hideo Nomo in 1995, Armstrong found his task made more difficult when he was told to make sure news of the meeting didn't leak into the Japanese media. He became further exercised when marching orders came from Yamauchi:

Do not fail.

Do not leave Japan until you have succeeded.

Do not contact me until you have succeeded.

And Armstrong thought his days under former owner George Argyros were hard.

The cover for the visit was legitimate: The Mariners trio stopped first in Kobe to sign a working agreement with the Orix Blue Wave, Ichiro's club, which would provide a written framework for what was hoped to be a prosperous business relationship. The meeting had its own surprise: Orix was going to draft Kawaguchi with its No. 1 draft pick. But the Orix baseball people were willing to accommodate the Mariners' desire, presumably for favors down the road.

Orix even helped arrange the clandestine meeting, in a Chinese restaurant in the windowless basement of a nearby hotel, with Kawaguchi's coach, English teacher, and representatives. The key question of money came up quickly. When Armstrong offered a $1 million signing bonus, eyes lit up, although they didn't know Lincoln had authorized up to $1.5 million. They agreed to set up a meeting with Kawaguchi and his parents for the next evening.

Even though he wasn't supposed to call Yamauchi, Armstrong decided he needed advice. He arranged for the party to meet Yamauchi the next day at Nintendo's world headquarters building. That night, Armstrong put the finishing touches on a speech he prepared for his first meeting with the big cheese, a speech he practiced repeatedly on Colborn and Jongewaard, to their bemused dismay.

Shortly after the three were ushered into a spartan, wood-paneled room with thirty-foot ceilings, Yamauchi burst through double doors with Yasuhiro Minigawa, Nintendo's vice president of communications and Yamauchi's primary translator. After brief handshakes and bows, all sat and Minigawa said, "You asked for this meeting."

Armstrong started in on his speech, offering thanks and gratitude from the Mariners and the people of Seattle and the state of Washington for his purchase of the ballclub. He went on to talk about the great deed by Yamauchi, and how successful the team had been, and what gifts he had brought—or in the words of Jerry Seinfeld, yada, yada, yada.

Yamauchi suddenly sliced the air horizontally with both hands, a universal signal to stop. He launched angrily into what seemed to the Americans like a five-minute tirade. Colborn spoke some Japanese, and Armstrong glanced over to see him sweating. Finally, Yamauchi paused for the translation.

"Mr. Yamauchi," Minigawa said, "is not pleased."

That was it. No elaboration. What air remained in the room hung stale as a library archive. It occurred to Armstrong, a Stanford-trained lawyer used to the local public-speaking circuit, that he must have given the worst speech of his life.

He felt the dead air getting heavier. He couldn't think of anything else, so he jumped back into his stem-winder speech. Again and more quickly, Yamauchi slashed at the air, then pounded on the table.

This time, Minigawa elaborated, saying that Yamauchi blamed Lincoln for failing to sign Nomo. He also explained why he liked Kawaguchi, and why he was disappointed he had not been signed. When Armstrong suggested the kid might not be ready for the major leagues, Yamauchi said, "I don't care. You will make him good."

Armstrong said the Mariners would try. As matters calmed, Colborn thought he might impress Yamauchi with another angle. He said the Mariners signed a working agreement with the Orix Blue Wave that would pave the way for other Japanese players to come to the U.S.

Yamauchi sneered.

"Orix? There is only one team in Japan—the Yomiuri Giants," he said.

Colborn countered that there was one good Orix player who was interested in coming to the U.S. someday. Had Mr. Yamauchi heard of Ichiro Suzuki?

"Of course."

Colborn worked up the courage to drop the big one: "Even if we don't sign Kawaguchi, our long-term plan is to sign Ichiro."

Again, another sneer.

"You cannot," said Yamauchi disparagingly, "get Ichiro."

Yamauchi knew many things. He did not know everything.

The tense meeting broke up, and the next night the Americans met Kawaguchi and his parents. He looked and sounded impressive, but at eighteen, his discomfort with leaving home and country for America was obvious. Besides, he said, he didn't want to make a decision until after final exams, even after the Mariners upped the offer to $1.5 million.

Great, thought Armstrong. He called his wife, Susan.

"I hope I'm home for Thanksgiving."

"You're joking," she said.

"I'm not joking."

Informed of the temporary stalemate, Yamauchi surprisingly relented on his order to stay in Japan, provided the Mariners made daily contact with Kawaguchi's family and reported on the negotiations. Ten days later, back in Seattle, Armstrong received the bad news, and reported to Lincoln: Kawaguchi was too scared to come to America.

"We are," said Lincoln, "in trouble."

They transmitted the news to Yamauchi, again fearing the worst. But as he had done throughout his business career, Yamauchi confounded the expectations.

"If he is too stupid to take this wonderful offer," came the reply, "then he's too stupid to be a Mariner." His baseball executives were off the hook.

"Howard doesn't show much emotion, but he said, 'Wow!' " Armstrong said. "I think he thought I was going to be toast.

"I did too."

⁂

Jim Colborn, done with duty on the Kawaguchi episode, recalled a conversation from his Orix days with Ichiro's father, Nobuyuki Suzuki, who attended every one of Ichiro's games in Japan, pushing his son relentlessly to baseball success.

"Will you please take care of my son?" the elder Suzuki said.

"I'm not his coach. I'm the pitching coach."

"I don't care. Please take care of my son."

Colborn said he knew enough of the culture to understand such a request was not casual. It was meant sincerely.

"If I say yes to him, it's a charge I have for my life," Colborn said. He agreed, "and I still have that charge."

Colborn did his best, which is why the Mariners were fortunate to have Colborn in their employ. By '97, Colborn knew Ichiro was serious about coming to the United States, not only because of the challenge but because his overwhelming popularity began to smother him. Japan's best player by miles, Ichiro was fascinating to fans and media. His consistent success, clutch play, edgy looks, and independent manner inspired endless coverage and persistent paparazzi, who hectored him in almost every public outing, and a few private ones. When Ichiro married TV personality Yumiko Fukushima, the ceremony was held in Los Angeles to escape the hordes.

"He could not go anywhere to enjoy his life," Hiro Ichioka, a producer for Japan's Fuji television, told the *P-I*'s Dave Andriesen. "When he went into the rest room, people would follow him. It was not happy for him."

The media lionized Ichiro in a country, and in a sport, that values the group over the individual.

"As players, most of us want some of the spotlight," Ichiro said. "But the media tend to overrate an individual player. In Japan, I got overrated. Other players were doing good jobs, but the focus was on me."

To help prepare for Ichiro's escape, Colborn, on the stop in Kobe before meeting Yamauchi, quietly introduced Armstrong and Jongewaard to Ichiro. Ichiro told them he would like to become a Mariner someday. Colborn knew he wasn't kidding: When he thought no one would see him, Ichiro would sometimes wear a Griffey-replica Mariners jersey.

But as a club employee, Colborn in subsequent visits had to be careful about being seen with Ichiro in public, lest rumors begin about the covetous eyes of an American team. He would go to Orix games and pretend to watch pitchers in the bullpen, when Ichiro would wander over from right field, finding a place away from photographers.

"We couldn't talk long, or someone would wonder what's going on," Colborn said. Sometimes after games they would adjourn to a private restaurant, one specializing in an Ichiro favorite, beef tongue, and talk ball.

"I always mentioned playing with intensity," Colborn said. "Don't ever sag and go through the motions. A player at his level can never do that."

Ichiro became a master of intensity and focus. He was also a goal setter and a goal achiever like Colborn had never seen.

"Reggie Jackson could focus in the postseason, but Ichiro is much broader," he said. "He can focus for a whole season. He can do season-long goals. Every year in Japan he did something different that was remarkable. He had 200 hits in a 130-game schedule. He had a record of consecutive games without striking out. I told him once [in 1995] he could hit for power, and he hit 25 home runs."

After Colborn in '98 took Ichiro on a preseason visit to Seattle and Phoenix, Ichiro came back the next spring with two Orix pitchers and worked out with the Mariners. The club hired one of Ichiro's friends from the Orix organization, Hide Sueyoshi, who had a law degree in Japan and a degree in history from the University of Oregon, to be a liaison with Japanese players. He later would become Ichiro's interpreter, but first served to signal the

Mariners' interest. Although Ichiro's trip was cut short by a bout of food poisoning, the American baseball experience was crucial.

"Unless I was missing something, I realized I could play at this level," Ichiro said. "I realized I had to be a complete player."

Besides the challenge of the game, Ichiro was motivated by a weariness with his rock-star celebrity: "He told me he came to the U.S. because it wasn't fun anymore in Japan," Colborn said.

After the 2000 season, Ichiro was "posted," the new mechanism by which qualified Japanese players declare their eligibility for U.S. teams. A blind-bid system was set up in which any one of the thirty major league teams could make an offer to Ichiro's team for the right to negotiate a contract. Major league baseball kept the bids secret, but the Mariners' offer had a complication: Colborn was about to become pitching coach for the Los Angeles Dodgers. The man who had done the most to make Ichiro a Mariner couldn't be trusted with the final step.

"He was sort of part of the competition; we thought the Dodgers would be there," Mariners general manager Pat Gillick told the *Post-Intelligencer*'s John Hickey. "I like Colborn, but he could have been a double agent."

Gillick laughed. But the money wasn't funny. The Mariners won the auction with an offer of $13.1 million. Within a week, the club reached an agreement with Ichiro on a three-year contract worth a minimum of $14 million, which included a $5 million signing bonus and base salaries of $4 million in 2001, $2 million in 2002, and $3 million in 2003. Additionally, he would earn a $2 million bonus in 2001 and 2003 if he made a minimum of 450 plate appearances, as well as smaller bonuses for awards such as MVP, rookie of the year, and Gold Glove. Reaching all incentives would be worth $5 million over the term of contract, meaning that including salary and the bid fee paid to Orix, Ichiro could cost the Mariners more than $32 million over three years. The amount was considerably less than what they planned to pay Griffey or Rodriguez, but a heady sum for a player from a nation that had never before supplied the major leagues with a position player.

Mariners executives flew to Kyoto to join Yamauchi at Ichiro's press conference. Afterward, Armstrong was surprised by a summons to see Yamauchi in private.

"Mr. Armstrong, when you came over in 1997, I treated you badly," Yamauchi said. "I was not happy. You told me then of your plan to sign Ichiro. I criticized you and said it would never happen. I want to apologize to you and tell you the signing of Ichiro is one of the happiest days of my life. Thank you. I am amazed you pulled it off."

Nearly dumbstruck, Armstrong expressed his appreciation. Then he told Lincoln, who had been dealing with Yamauchi's demands for more than fifteen years without hearing such words. His response again was "Wow!"

Yamauchi, a reserved, distant man with few interests beyond work, did another extraordinary thing. He went to lunch with his new star player. Yamauchi's daughter Yoko, married to Nintendo of America president Minoru Arakawa, was startled.

"That was very unusual," she said. "My mother said she couldn't believe it. He wouldn't say anything about why. I think Ichiro really has a charisma."

Ichiro also was surprised.

"I didn't know then that he wasn't a baseball fan," he said. "Looking back, I was surprised he knew me. I wouldn't think he would know my value as a player.

"Then he said, 'Thank you very much.' I should have been the one thanking him."

Colborn, who accepted the Dodgers' job offer, had fulfilled his obligation and taken care of Nobu Suzuki's boy. Now it was time for the boy to take care of the American League.

⁂

Defying expectations for a slow start, Ichiro hit .336 in April and was selected rookie of the month. His offensive style was unprecedented in Mariners history, and rarely seen anymore in a sport addicted to home-run power. Ichiro used superlative bat control and eye-blink speed to disrupt pitchers and defenses. He was a master of the worm-burner, a scorching roller just beyond the reach of infielders. In ways different from previous Mariners stars, he nevertheless brought electricity to each at-bat, which was as entertaining for his teammates as for fans.

"Personally, I think he's very exciting," catcher Dan Wilson said. "He's similar to Junior Griffey in that way—every game, it's something. It's such a different style and approach, almost unique. He hits a ground ball and it's not an ordinary play. The defense knows he could beat out anything less than a perfect play."

A small but significant virtue was Ichiro's ability to adjust in a single at-bat to pitchers he was facing for the first time. During a game in mid-May against Toronto, Ichiro, fooled on a slider that was so low and inside it nearly bounced at his feet, took a loopy, off-balance swing that may have been the worst in his infant major league career. The count fell to 0-2 and the next pitch was in the same spot. This time, he lifted the ball nearly from his shoe tops into deep right center for a triple that had the power and parabola of a Tiger Woods two-iron shot. The one-pitch adjustment was computer-like, the execution perfect.

What might have been: The Mariners hoped that the signing of Ichiro would help induce shortstop Alex Rodriguez to stay with the Mariners.

©2001 SEATTLE POST-INTELLIGENCER/PAUL KITAGAKI JR.

"He kept his head down and stepped into the ball when he swung, and hit into center field," said Piniella. "Normally on a down-and-in pitch like that, a batter pulls his head slightly and pulls the ball. He put it into center. He's a very intelligent young man."

The ignition from the leadoff spot helped the Mariners become the first team in history to win 20 games in April. At the end of June, they had a 20-game lead in the AL West. Ichiro was on the cover of every major American sports magazine.

By the arrival of the All-Star Game, whose rotation fortuitously stopped in '01 at Safeco Field, the Mariners (63-24), bludgeoned any prospect of a pennant race and were off to chase records set in the Roosevelt presidency—Theodore's, not Franklin's. Leading the fan balloting with 3.4 million votes, Ichiro was one of eight Mariners selected to play in the hometown All-Star Game, including Bret Boone, Mike Cameron, John Olerud, Edgar Martinez, Freddy Garcia, Jeff Nelson, and Kazuhiro Sasaki. The selections, and the season, made for a renaissance celebration of baseball in Seattle that was unimaginable a few years earlier.

The Mariners' pace defied conventional limits.

"Baseball has the toughest schedule in pro sports, and to win 70 percent of the time, it's almost never been done," said Kevin Kennedy, an analyst for ESPN and a former major league manager. "Especially with Seattle's travel schedule, which is baseball's longest. In baseball, your nine best players aren't out there, because of the five-man pitching rotations. That's not the case in football or basketball, where you typically put out your best players for each game, except for injuries. The Mariners were having as close to a perfect season as you can expect.

"I've managed for thirteen years in the majors and minors, and I know this: To maintain excellence and interest every day is amazing, because the competition didn't provide it. The race was over by the All-Star break."

Important as was Ichiro to the Mariners' success, a more subtle change that fixed a long-running problem was significant. A year earlier, the organization finally found a pitching coach who could keep manager Lou Piniella from chewing up his mound staff.

"I'd heard the same thing for years: Pitchers come up and aren't given a chance to struggle," said Bryan Price. "But Lou told me something important. He said, 'I'm aware I'm creating some intimidation, and an uncomfortable environment. My gut feeling is the pitchers would be better off dealing with the pitching coach than the manager.'"

With that, Piniella did something rare for most successful fifty-eight-year-old men, especially in baseball: He admitted a shortcoming and did something about it. Appointed in 2000, Price, the fifth pitching coach under Piniella, was finally the right guy with whom to trust the keys to the organization's future. A career minor league pitcher who washed out because of an arm injury, Price spent ten seasons coaching in the Mariners system. He saw some of his pitchers come up, only to be cut down by Piniella or traded away when he lost patience. GM Pat Gillick was well aware of the pitching casualties when he interviewed Price for the job.

What would you do, Gillick asked, if Lou wanted to use a pitcher who was tired and needed a day off?

"Lou would know before the game," Price said. "He'd know the pitcher was unavailable."

What if Lou pressed you?

"The problem isn't with your pitching coach, it's your manager," Price said. "I don't need this position. I'm not going to sell my soul to be a major league pitching coach. I'd love the job, but I've heard what the relationships have been like with Lou and the pitching coaches in Seattle. I'm not afraid of that. But if you're looking to find somebody to get beat up on, find somebody else."

Price, just thirty-eight, was nobody's patsy. Hardworking, self-assured, and controlled, he was the perfect antidote for the impetuous Piniella.

"In spring training of 2000, Lou said, 'Bryan, the pitching staff is yours—set it up however you want,' " Price said. "That was a great show of faith.

"With Lou, you had to understand that, most of the time, all he was doing was venting. You have to let him be competitive. During a spring game, Ryan Franklin gave up a ground-ball single to the first hitter, and Lou says, 'He can't pitch up here.' But you can't take those kinds of things seriously.

"With veteran pitchers, those kinds of criticisms would slip off. But younger guys would misunderstand who Lou is. It was my job to take care of that."

Pitcher Jamie Moyer flourished under Piniella, owning the best winning percentage in the majors from 1996 through 2002 (105-49, .682). But when he arrived in Seattle via trade in '96, he was thirty-three and on his sixth major league team, so his baseball hide was thick.

"I came here at the right time in my career, because I probably would have been intimidated too," he said. "There would be days when Lou would be screaming, 'What the fuck is going on?' and the young pitcher would be sunk. You'd lose the kid for a couple of weeks. They'd be out there pitching with one eye on Lou and one on the batter. When they screwed up they wanted to crawl under the carpet to get to the dugout.

"I don't want to say Bryan has answers for everything, but he has answers. He thrives on helping. It's a very positive breath of fresh air. I've been on teams where the pitching coach doesn't want to talk to you during a bad spell. If you don't have somebody to lean on, you feel like you're going through it yourself.

"Bryan is right there with you. If you need a kick in the butt, he can do it. If you need coddling, he can do it."

Price helped lead a transformation from the second-worst team earned-run average in '99 (5.24) to the best in '01 (3.54). The Mariners had four pitchers (Moyer, Garcia, Paul Abbott, and Aaron Sele) with at least 12 wins, led by Moyer's first 20-win season of his career. At age thirty-eight, he was the oldest ever in baseball to win 20 for the first time.

With the starters and bullpen humming, the defense nearly flawless, and the offense discovering every available gap, the Mariners did little wrong as they pressed on through the summer—without Johnson, Griffey, and Rodriguez—toward the greatest single-season mark in baseball history. The Mariners never lost more than two in a row until September, a remarkable feat considering the huge division lead could have prompted a release on the throttle. Reserve catcher Tom Lampkin thought that single-mindedness was the most impressive club characteristic: "To maintain the intensity we've had in front of [crowds of] ten thousand people as well in Yankee Stadium is pretty impressive," he said.

There was, however, something wrong elsewhere.

After a five-game winning streak, the Mariners were 104-40 on September 10 and in position to clinch the division title the next night in Anaheim, should they win and Oakland lose. But the climactic moment was put off when the players awoke to a changed world.

The terrorist attacks in New York and Washington that savaged the American soul froze everyone where they were, including the half of major league baseball that was on the road. Stuck in their Anaheim hotel, the Mariners were immersed in the national shudder—watching the horror unfold on TV, calling home to check on loved ones, and groping with sorrow, rage, and helplessness. In the lobby, Price spotted Kevin Cremin, the club's radio producer, walk by in search of a newspaper.

"I'll never forget the expression on his face—it was so expressive it was haunting, an expression I'd never seen on a guy who was mostly upbeat and funny," he said. "Then I realized that's how all of our faces looked."

Baseball was in lockstep with the rest of American life—shut down until further notice. Among the Mariners, anxiety manifested in odd ways. In Edgar Martinez's room, an express-mail letter slid under his door with his name on it—a name he never uses in hotels. It was hand-printed, vaguely in the fashion of the anthrax letters that were prominent in the news. He called security, which picked up the letter.

"I never found out what it was," he said. "I didn't think it was a threat, but I never use my real name and I don't ever remember getting something under the door like that."

After several days of such anxiety, President George W. Bush gave the OK for sports to resume. But with civil aviation still restricted and rental cars sold out, the Mariners first had to get home. The club chartered a pair of buses for the tedious twenty-four-hour drive from Los Angeles. Martinez hired a bellman to buy him an air mattress so he could sleep on the bus floor, but the kid came up empty. Just as they were about to board for the long drive, they caught a break: Word came that their air charter had received security clearance to return to Seattle.

As all anticipated when games resumed September 18, things were not nearly the same. Security and tension at stadiums were high, as was patriotism.

"The last time I remember hearing 'U-S-A' chants was with the 1980 U.S. Olympic hockey team," said catcher Dan Wilson. "It was powerful stuff. You'd get chills before the game."

❀

The Mariners began the restart with two wins in Seattle, 4-0 and 5-0 over the Angels, the second one clinching the division after Oakland lost earlier in the evening. Given the national and local mood, the traditional celebratory hijinks on the field seemed out of place.

At the end of the game, the team gathered near the mound and knelt for a minute of prayer, hushing the 45,000 fans. As the players broke and stood, a large American flag on a pole was brought out. For the next several minutes, the Mariners walked the flag and themselves around the infield, waving and applauding to the sellout crowd, which gave it right back to them. The moment was remarkable. They found a way to honor their achievements, fans, and country without histrionics, triteness, or bad taste. A season of greatness found a seminal expression apart from the game.

"It was just one of those things that happened," utilityman Mark McLemore said. "No one planned it. We knew we were going to bring the flag out on the field, and that was all. Everything else was off the cuff. It was totally spontaneous."

Said Boone, "It was cool. It was fitting."

As with the rest of life, the moment was different: a celebration without celebrating. The baseball was different, too. The record betrayed no clues—after the tragedy, they won 12 of the final 18 games to finish with an almost inconceivable 116-46 record—but something had been lost. Since every team was dealing with the same set of external events, the impact figured to be the same on the Mariners—except almost no one in a century had played with such a crisp edge.

"The toughest thing was taking a week off," Wilson said. "We were reaching a crescendo, ready to clinch the division, and then it happened."

So much of baseball psychology is built on momentum that players typically loathe any disruption when a positive roll is under way.

"When baseball players get a streak going, they don't want time off," said Kennedy, the ESPN analyst. "You have to ride whatever it is you've got going for as long as possible. It's a game of streaks, and you want to avoid any abrupt end."

With the pennant race long resolved, the Mariners pushed themselves by pursuing the AL record for wins in a season (114) and then went after the 116 wins of the '06 Cubs.

"For the last month and a half, the chase was for the record," said Boone. "The worldwide media coverage was intense in the countdown. Once we [tied the MLB mark], it was a kind of a relief: 'Oh, it's over—no, wait a minute, next is the playoffs.' Not to use that as an excuse, but the grind and the scrutiny kind of beat us down."

With typical jock resolve, no one accepted any rationalizations for what was to come in the postseason.

"I don't think you can say we shouldn't have gone for the record," Boone said. "If you can do something in a sport that's never been done, you gotta go for it. That's greatness. Lou did the right thing. Take your chances. No matter how bittersweet the end result, everyone on that team and in that organization will be a footnote in history.

"When I'm seventy, I'll be able to say I played on the team that won the most games in history."

Still, with the terrorist attacks and pressure to reach the outer limits of the record book, the Mariners' September was something less than raindrops on roses and whiskers on kittens.

"The record chase," said Griffin, the trainer, "put more pressure on Lou than anything he's ever done."

The pressure seemed to tighten everyone in the first game of the Division Series. Cleveland, the opponent from the 1995 AL Championship Series, was back again as Central Division champs with a 91-71 record (in the other Division Series, the AL East–winning Yankees met the Oakland A's, the wild-card entry). Although the Indians lost five of seven regular-season games to the Mariners and were decided underdogs, they changed the seasonal perspective in a single game.

Behind starter Bartolo Colon, a young right-handed ace with a 97 mph fastball, the Indians stunned the Safeco sellout by winning easily, 5-0. He struck out 10 and allowed six hits. Not only had the Mariners lost the home-field advantage, they were in a place they had never been all season—behind. Suddenly the World Series expectations created by the regular season looked fragile. The number 116 sounded as if it was police-radio code for baseball fraud. In the postseason, baseball panic forms quickly.

Fortunately for the Mariners, the rest of the Indians' starting pitching was less formidable. After getting four first-inning runs off Cleveland's fading thirty-seven-year-old starter, Chuck Finley, in Game 2, the Mariners' 5-1 win behind Moyer permitted regional exhalation.

But diaphragms were back in full spasm after the series moved to Ohio for the next two games. The Mariners picked Game 3 for their worst of the year, a 17-2 debacle. Starter Aaron Sele, a notorious postseason flop, didn't make it to the third inning. His first reliever, Paul Abbott—a 17-game winner as a starter—allowed nine hits, five walks, and eight runs. The Mariners made three errors and Boone struck out four times.

From the baseball pinnacle a week earlier, the Mariners were back to the cliff—a do-or-die Game 4 against a pitcher who shut them out three days earlier. For six innings, the worst seemed inevitable—another string of zeroes from Colon. The Indians were up 1-0. But in the seventh, the Mariners mustered a rally that was the paradigm of their post-Kingdome offense—walk, single, walk, sacrifice fly, single, single. There was even a hit-and-run play that had first baseman John Olerud, slower than a tax refund, going from first to third. The 3-1 lead chased Colon and wound up a 6-2 victory that saved the series, and much dignity.

Back at home for Game 5, Moyer dominated the Indians as he had in all three previous meetings that season, including the first in the series. Combined with a second consecutive evening of shutout relief from Jeff Nelson, Arthur Rhodes, and Kazu Sasaki, Moyer rang up seasonal win No. 4 over Cleveland. The Mariners prevailed 3-1, taking the series three games to two. McLemore, whose two-run single in the second inning was the decisive blow, summed up the excruciating escape from the first round: "What you call tension, we call excitement."

The excitement grew again when on the same day in the other Division Series, New York beat Oakland, also in five games. That set up the AL Championship Series as a rematch of the 2000 disputants. Against the A's, the Yankees crawled back from an 0-2 hole with three straight wins, just as the Mariners had done to them in 1995. Mariners-Yanks III was the rubber match in what was becoming a tidy little postseason sports rivalry.

But the good karma the Mariners packed almost all season began to fade. Shortstop Carlos Guillen missed the Indians series with a mild case of tuberculosis, which was presumed to have been contracted in his native Venezuela, where the disease remains largely uncontrolled. He would play in only three ALCS games. Against the Indians, designated hitter Martinez pulled a groin muscle, which would render him almost inert against the Yanks.

Beyond the physical, there was the emotional. As good a story as the Mariners had been, they were usurped in the national sporting consciousness by the Yankees because of what their success would mean to the spirit of a metropolis beleaguered after September 11. Perhaps for the first time in their storied run as America's premier sports franchise, the domineering Yanks were looked upon nationally as sympathetic figures.

The Mariners understood it, and were apprehensive about the emotional undertow that might compromise their approach that was locked into beating the Yankees, not New York and its people.

"You could feel it at the ballpark," said Price, the pitching coach. "You knew everyone was pulling for the city of New York. That was just another battle for us."

※

Energized by their comeback against the A's, the Yanks in the first two ALCS games in Seattle were crisply efficient, winning 4-2 in the opener behind Andy Pettitte's three-hitter over eight innings, and 3-2 in the second game with six innings of four-hit ball from Mike Mussina.

Again, the sincerity of the 116-victory season was in play, although a championship-series loss to the Yanks would hardly be considered shameful. Still, the AL victory record the Mariners beat belonged to the '98 Yankees, who won 114—and they backed it up by winning the World Series.

Piniella knew the '01 Yankees weren't as formidable as the '98 group, and he had to make sure his team knew. So when they arrived in New York for Game 3, they saw headlines proclaiming Piniella's faith in them—his guarantee the series would return to Seattle for Game 6.

His players also saw something else in New York—Ground Zero. Piniella was worried about the distractions in what became a morbid, irresistible ritual for sports teams as well as most visitors to New York. But once in Manhattan, interest was high in the traveling party. Despite misgivings, Piniella agreed to go along on the off day before Game 3 to visit a fire station near the World Trade Center site. What he didn't know, as he and about thirty other coaches, players, executives, and spouses boarded buses for the drive from their midtown hotel to the fire station, was what a symbol he was for many of those doing the work in the WTC tombs.

"Sweet Lou" was an icon for 1970s fans of the Yankees, when they made four World Series appearances in six years. An outfielder sometimes derided for having little power, speed, or arm, Piniella nevertheless was enormously popular in New York for his fiery demeanor and ability to make things happen. Not a bling-bling sort of guy, Piniella's one item of ostentatious jewelry was his championship ring from the '77 Yanks.

When Piniella walked into the fire station, gloom vanished for a few cherished moments. The exhausted firefighters, mostly men in their thirties and forties, were little boys at Yankee Stadium when Piniella, Reggie Jackson, and Billy Martin were lighting up the Big Apple. "They remembered him," said Price. "When you win a World Series here, you get remembered for life. Lou being there had a real impact on them."

Piniella was hardly oblivious to his New York popularity—every time he pops from the visitors' dugout, long-tenured fans serenade him with "Lou . . . Lou!"—but the enthusiastic reception from the firefighters surprised him. The Seattle tourists shook hands, posed for pictures, offered souvenirs, and were given some in return. Particularly important to Piniella was an FDNY ball cap. "I got mine signed by all of them," he said wistfully. "It's a keeper. They took a lot of pictures too. . . . They were kids here when I played. I'm glad I went. They were happy to see us."

If the once-dreaded visit had turned into a heart-warmer for Piniella, it was an unexpected energizer for his team. The next night in the Bronx, the Mariners clobbered starting pitcher Orlando "El Duque" Hernandez for five runs and routed the Yankees 14-3. Whether it was the always-charged atmosphere of New York baseball in October, the inspiration of the firehouse, Piniella's guarantee, or finally rising to their regular-season level for the first time in the postseason, they looked flawless and the Yankees appeared inept. Unintimidated by the hostiles—improved security over 1995 made field life tolerable the last two Octobers—Piniella's forecasted return to Seattle, much mocked in New York media, suddenly looked prescient.

Lou as the new Nostradamus lasted all of twenty-four hours.

Needing only to win one of the next two to force the series back to Seattle, the Mariners in Game 4 faced four-time Cy Young Award winner Roger Clemens, who had dominated them like no other opponent in club history, including the 2000 ALCS. The Mariners answered with Paul Abbott, the oft-injured journeyman who was drilled in relief by Cleveland in Game 3. Yet through five innings, the Mariners could have asked for no better from him. Even though Clemens shut down the Mariners on just a single hit, Abbott did him one better, no-hitting the Yankees in their own house. Only problem was, he gave up eight walks. But backed by the club's trademark superlative defense, Abbott had an answer for each jam.

Despite the scoreless count, in the sixth inning Piniella and his Yankees counterpart, Joe Torre, went to their bullpens, the two best relief units in the AL. Clemens (four walks) and Abbott had exhausted themselves, as well as all observers. The game's 15 walks broke a twenty-six-year-old ALCS record—by the end of the sixth inning. In the eighth, the tension broke in favor of the Mariners. Boone, recovering from a wretched series against Cleveland (2-for-21), connected on a solo home run off setup reliever Ramiro Mendoza, who retired eight of the previous nine batters.

That 1-0 lead in Game 4 turned out to be the apex of an other-worldly season. The nadir came swiftly.

In the bottom of the inning, Seattle reliever Arthur Rhodes, coming off a spectacular season but with a dyspeptic history against the Yanks, tried to blow a one-out, 3-2 fastball on the inside past center fielder Bernie Williams. But the pitch sailed over a chubby part of the plate, and on a night when a favorable wind was drifting toward the right-field stands, Williams lofted what looked like a playable fly. But having seen many a mysterious parabola in his home park, he suspected otherwise. "At Yankee Stadium, you never know," he said. "With our short porch out there in right field, you hit a ball in the air and there's always a good chance it might go out."

Ichiro drifted back steadily, looking to settle under the ball, but its arc kept extending. When the pop fly landed four rows up in the seats, the shock in the Northwest might have awakened Richter. "I've always had a history with the Yankees," Rhodes would say later in a surprisingly nonchalant manner. "Sometimes you get 'em, and sometimes you don't."

Mariners fans couldn't remember when Rhodes got 'em. Williams's jolt sent memories rewinding back to the 2000 ALCS, when Rhodes pitched a total of two innings over four games, but gave up seven runs on eight hits and four walks. His 31.50 ERA in that series was not lost on the Yankees, against whom he had a 6.62 lifetime ERA over ten big-league seasons. Any time Rhodes wants in a big game against New York, the Yankees will happily supply full cavalry escort to the mound.

Williams's solo shot tied the game, leaving the outcome to a ninth-inning showdown between baseball's best closers, the Yankees' Mariano Rivera and the Mariners' Kazu Sasaki. But there was a crucial difference between the well-matched stars. Rivera had pitched in two of the series' three games, while Sasaki, a workhorse, had not pitched in six days. Rivera could not have been sharper. He threw three pitches to get three outs. John Olerud, Stan Javier, and Mike Cameron discovered the hitters' rule against Rivera—swing early—was as useful as entering the batter's box with chopsticks.

Sasaki lacked Rivera's edge. In his most recent appearance in New York, on August 18, he had given up three singles in the bottom of the ninth, then forced in a run with a hit batter. But he wound up getting the save—his club-record 38th—in a dramatic 7-6 win when he induced Alfonso Soriano to pop out weakly to left field for the final out of the game. In the same matchup this night, Sasaki would not be as fortunate.

With one out, Scott Brosius nicked him for an infield single, which brought to the plate the No. 9 hitter, Soriano. A twenty-three-year-old rookie second baseman who had been the brightest position prospect in the Yankees farm system, Soriano was 4-for-12 in the series and oblivious to pressure. The Sasaki specialty pitch of a well-placed forkball, with its snap drop as it reaches the batter, might have induced a grounder for an inning-ending double play. Instead, the choice was a fastball and the location a dagger into the heart of an otherwise epic Mariners season. Soriano lifted the pitch into right center field as Suzuki and Cameron converged at the wall. Having seen so much that was inexplicable the last six months, each was hoping the other would become fifteen feet tall.

Instead, the walk-off homer catapulted New York into a frenzy and the Mariners into the abyss. The series was all but over.

Game 5 quickly became anticlimactic when the Yankees blew up pitcher Aaron Sele with a four-run fourth inning on the way to a 12-3 rout. Shocked after the wrenching Game 4 result, the

Mariners for the first time had no rally, no gumption, no cash for the check Piniella wrote with his mouth at Safeco Field. The series ended without the promised return to Seattle.

"It wasn't supposed to be like this," said Boone, a little-boy-lost look on his face. "It wasn't supposed to end here."

A .211 team batting average against superb Yankees pitching rendered inert the glories of the preceding six months.

"You don't play to set records," said McLemore. "You play to win the World Series. "When you don't, it's very disappointing."

The Yankees' Torre acknowledged there was more at work in the series than baseball.

"Our responsibility was to more than just fans," he said. "It was to the city, to represent it and to bring a smile to everyone's face. Maybe it was an unfair advantage."

Whether the reasons were cosmic or tangible, the Yankees fans indeed had a good, derisive laugh. As Piniella changed pitchers midgame and stood on the mound, he was bombarded with the chant, "No Game 6! No Game 6!" They loved Piniella in Gotham, and they loved to beat him too.

Considering the fifteen-year sweep of the Mariners renaissance, Piniella's prediction was almost unique: For the first time since the finessing of the Griffey draft in 1987, a bold Mariners move to return from the precipice didn't work out.

The discovery of Hiroshi Yamauchi and his approval as owner, the unlikely hiring of Piniella, the stadium campaign wrapped around the unfathomable rally of 1995, the for-sale sign in '96, and the departure of three marquee players followed by the arrival of Ichiro—all were pivotal points that could have seriously damaged or doomed the franchise in the Northwest. But each time, the fateful episodes turned the Mariners' way.

Piniella's tactic didn't carry the same significance as the others, because it wasn't the reason the Mariners would have lost or won. But the events loomed large for him. The stellar season and its disappointing denouement turned out to be his last, best shot at a championship. After leading a decade-long legacy of rallies from the edge, soon it would soon be Piniella who wasn't coming back to Seattle.

CHAPTER ELEVEN

A Final Thunderclap and a New Day

Bending under the weight of what was done, and not done, in 2001, the Mariners in 2002 creaked and moaned almost from the start of spring training. By the time interleague play arrived in mid-June, the casualty list was larger than it had been the entire previous season.

Edgar Martinez was down with a hamstring injury and pitchers Paul Abbott, Jeff Nelson, and Norm Charlton had various arm problems. A new acquisition, Jeff Cirillo, couldn't get over the impatience of Lou Piniella and the fact that he was brought to Seattle to improve a team that won 116 games. He was floundering at third base as much as newcomer James Baldwin was flailing in the starting rotation. Second baseman Bret Boone, third in the Most Valuable Player voting a year ago, was staggering. Center fielder Mike Cameron was worse. Names of farm-system youngsters unheard of by most fans—Chris Snelling, Ron Wright, Julio Mateo, Brian Fitzgerald, Rafael Soriano, Justin Kaye, Eugene Kingsale, Mark Watson—began dotting the daily lineups as replacements for the wounded and slumping. The Mariners hadn't won more than two in a row in a month and looked less and less like the team that began the season 17-4. As the season ground on, the unspoken truth was that duplicating a once-a-century phenomenon not only was impossible, it was aggravating too.

"The expectations around 116 wins put a tremendous amount of pressure on the organization," CEO Howard Lincoln said.

"The pressure to a large extent got transferred to Lou. He's the guy out there living and dying every night."

The manager knew things weren't right, but a glance at the standings suggested little was wrong. When the Mariners began a nine-game interleague trip in mid-June to three cities the club had never visited—San Diego, Cincinnati, and Houston—they were 41-25 and in first place by a game over Anaheim. But the beachhead of '01 made most baseball standards moot. As irrelevant as baseball logic insisted the comparisons were, the emotional link was irresistible and inevitable.

After losing two of three to the Padres, the club reunited in Cincinnati with the former franchise icon, Ken Griffey Jr. Three years gone from the Mariners, whose roster had seen considerable churn, there were still several longtimers glad to see him. Nor was there doubt about his feelings.

"You could see how happy he was to see somebody in a Mariners uniform," said broadcaster Dave Niehaus. "He was just elated to chat with people. I gave him a big hug and talked with him around the batting cage."

Griffey had just recovered from yet another leg injury, one of a series that compromised his return to the team of his childhood. He played in the three Mariners games, getting three singles in seven at-bats and preventing a run with a fine sprinting catch at the center-field wall. But the chance to renew acquaintances was the only highlight for him. The Mariners swept the weekend series from the first-place Reds.

⁕

Although no one knew it as the road trip moved to Houston, the Seattle fate of another longtime Mariner was about to take a sharp turn. Lou Piniella was sought out by a Houston writer who wanted the manager's thoughts on the trade four years earlier that brought another marquee name from the Mariners past, Randy Johnson, from Seattle to the Astros for a half-season run at the National League pennant. What Piniella said wasn't startling. But it did help spell the end of his time in Seattle—and, as is usually the case with Piniella departures, in tumultuous fashion.

"They were trying to win the World Series, and they thought Randy would be a major factor," Piniella was quoted as saying. "I think if you have a team that's one piece short, you owe it to your fans to give it a go—and to your players. How many teams get in position that way? But you have to make darn sure that's the piece. You can decimate your farm system real quick."

Larry Stone, *The Seattle Times'* national baseball reporter, had the remarks in his Sunday notebook column. Piniella's thoughts seemed such standard thinking—the trade-deadline axiom he expressed was accepted baseball wisdom in many circles—that they didn't appear until the fourteenth paragraph of a story headlined "Hunsicker doesn't regret Unit trade," referring to the Houston general manager who made the deal, Gerry Hunsicker. The Astros, behind Johnson's 10-1 record after the trade, made the playoffs, but flamed out in the first round, Johnson losing twice. In the off-season, he became a free agent and was signed by the team of his dreams—the hometown Arizona Diamondbacks, an expansion team that began play in 1998. The Astros gave up Freddy Garcia, Carlos Guillen, and John Halama for less than three months of work from Johnson, then lost him for no return—baseball's classic rent-a-player story.

But Hunsicker said in hindsight, he would do it again, agreeing with Piniella that opportunities are rare and must be seized.

In Seattle, Howard Lincoln read Piniella's comments and did a slow burn. Although the Mariners' current situation wasn't referenced by Piniella, Lincoln read between the lines and took the remarks as a veiled shot at his own club's lack of success in improving the roster. Lincoln had heard Piniella's not-so-subtle campaign for more offensive firepower since spring training, especially after the club decided to carry on the bench not one but two defensive specialist/pinch-runner types—holdover Charles Gipson and newcomer Luis Ugueto, neither of whom could hit much.

Piniella became so repetitive in spring that Kevin Cremin, the longtime producer-engineer for the team's radio broadcasts, began editing out of the audio reports the "we need another bat" quotes from Piniella's daily media briefings. Even though similar points had been made by general manager Pat Gillick, he was designated by Lincoln as the club's voice on personnel matters. The season's results would prove Gillick and Piniella correct. By season's end, the Mariners would lead all of baseball in runners left on base; only three AL clubs had fewer home runs; and the team did not have a pinch hit for extra bases until the last weekend of the season. The absence of clutch and bench hitting was galling to

Piniella, particularly because the year before, the Mariners were habitual heroes of the big moment. His irritation worsened as other AL teams began picking up roster help via trades.

Lincoln saw it differently. He knew how much effort the baseball execs–Gillick, Lee Pelekoudas, and Roger Jongewaard–put into finding a deal. He also knew that the likeliest resource for a trade, the organization's minor league pitching, had been crushed by injuries. Prospects Soriano, Ryan Anderson, Gil Meche, Ken Cloude, and Jeff Heaverlo went down for all or parts of the season. One young position player who might have drawn interest, Australian outfielder Chris Snelling, was called up to the big club and blew out his knee rounding third base eight games into his major league career.

More important to Lincoln, he gave instructions before the 2001 season that trade-deadline needs and options were not to be discussed specifically in the media. Whatever was said would be done with one voice, primarily Gillick.

Upon the team's return from the road trip, Lincoln sent a memo to Gillick, with instructions to share it with Piniella. Lincoln wrote that he was disappointed to read Piniella's remarks because they weren't consistent with the understanding Lincoln thought he had with the baseball staff about public discussion of potential moves. He was concerned there was a communications breakdown, and wanted no recurrences.

Angered with Lincoln's take on his remarks, Piniella, according to a Mariners source, said of the memo, "I don't read any chicken-shit memos from Lincoln. Tell him if he has the balls, he can talk to me."

Piniella later would say his words weren't quite that strong, "but along the same lines.... I wasn't pleased. I really wasn't."

Regardless of precise language, there was no disputing the sentiment. Steaming, Piniella left his ground-floor office at Safeco Field and went to see Lincoln upstairs in his office, where, according to Lincoln, Piniella "exploded."

Unfortunately for a public that had come to revel in Piniella's eruptions, there were no TV cameras to add the episode to a legacy of tantrums that made him second only to basketball coach Bobby Knight in sports-show anthologies of low-light moments by high-profile people. In his first year as Reds manager in 1990, he loosened first base from its moorings and heaved the bag into the outfield—his answer to a bad umpiring call. No one recalled seeing such a maneuver before, but Piniella was nothing if not original in his tempestuousness. Offended by a remark from Reds relief pitcher Rob Dibble questioning his honesty, Piniella burst into the clubhouse and tackled Dibble into his locker before the two were separated. Two months into his time as Mariners manager, Piniella was thrown out after his club brawled for twenty minutes during a game in Baltimore. Orioles pitcher Mike Mussina hit a Mariners batter, which began the hostilities. Piniella was irate that Mussina was not among the seven players ejected, and kicked dirt on home plate before he was thrown out too.

CEO Howard Lincoln was upset that Lou Piniella had gone against club policy, which prompted a June confrontation with the manager.

PHOTO COURTESY OF THE SEATTLE MARINERS

In May 1994, his first Kingdome tantrum featured sixteen kicks and four scoops by hand to cover home plate with dirt. His most intense period of rage was in late 1996, when the Mariners were in a tense pennant race. He was ejected three times in a span of ten games. Two years later in Cleveland, Piniella was enraged when one of his base runners was called out for leaving the base path.

After being ejected for protesting, Piniella refired his engines, throwing his cap down and kicking it at least a half-dozen times before throwing it into the stands, whereupon it was promptly thrown back. In '99, after failing to dislocate third base during another storm, he threw bats onto the field. Just a few weeks before his encounter with Lincoln, Piniella, at Tampa Bay's Tropicana Field, in front of his parents seated just a few yards away, erupted against umpire John Shulock over the dimensions of his strike zone. After his ejection, Piniella again buried the plate in dirt. This time, Shulock refused to clean the manager's mess, forcing catcher Dan Wilson to borrow the umpire's whisk broom to clean the plate.

Piniella's rages usually had a point, although targets varied from the umpiring crew to the opponents to his own players. But sometimes they were just Piniella being the same uncontrollable desperado he was thirty-five years earlier in the outfield in Portland, where the then–minor leaguer kicked the wooden fence so hard that it fell upon him, requiring a rescue by the grounds crew.

On this June day in 2002, there was no fence, or base, or bat, or hat. Lincoln's office had no dirt, but it did have an executive unused to verbal abuse by an employee. Unlike the inanimate objects that suffered Piniella's distemper, Lincoln spoke back, telling Piniella to shut up.

In the tumultuous baseball career of Louis Victor Piniella, that might have been a first.

"He was strong in what he said; I was strong in what I said," Lincoln recalled. "I wouldn't allow him to back me down. It was not a pleasant meeting, but it was the kind of thing that happens in organizations all the time with a very high-strung, emotional guy who lives and dies the game. I appreciated that; I appreciated how strongly he felt about things."

⁂

Six months after the confrontation with Lincoln, Piniella, as the new manager of the Tampa Bay Devil Rays, reflected on the collision between the Mariners' two most powerful figures. Cigarette in one hand, glass of wine in the other, Piniella was at Malio's, his longtime steak-house hangout on Tampa's Dale Mabry Boulevard. In his favorite booth in the back, in the corner, in the dark, illuminated by a single lamp above the table, Piniella was relaxed and candid. A Tampa native, he grew up with the restaurant's owner, Mario Iavarone, who provided Piniella and fellow Tampa resident George Streinbrenner with their own tables and rooms whenever they called. Piniella seemed to know everyone who passed by the table, all of whom drew a wink, a wave, a handshake, or a kiss.

A few weeks earlier, Piniella had surprised the baseball world by leaving Seattle and accepting the job with the Devil Rays, the most misbegotten franchise in baseball. His family's need for him at home was paramount, but there was a baseball subtext to his Seattle departure.

He spoke fondly of his decade with the Mariners. But he was bothered by the fact that in June he had been misunderstood by Lincoln, and was disappointed about the perception that he went against club policy.

"I've been an organization guy for ten years," he said. "You never once saw me complain about something the ballclub did or did not do. When we traded Randy, I was supportive. When Junior was traded, I was supportive. When Alex went on the free-agent market, I was supportive.

"What surprised me was, when I said something in Houston, which didn't pertain to our situation in Seattle, how I was admonished and chastised for it. It was surprising, that's all."

Considering the arc of Piniella's career, the conflict was not surprising. His previous managerial jobs ended in disputes with the club owners, George Steinbrenner and Marge Schott. The blowup with Lincoln was similar to a conflict he had with Steinbrenner in 1987, when Piniella was manager and failed to be in his hotel room as ordered by The Boss, who planned to lecture him over the phone about roster moves.

The subsequent dispute was splattered all over the back pages of New York's tabloids. After the season, Steinbrenner fired Piniella. A letter of reprimand, citing insubordination, that Steinbrenner placed in his file is one of the few souvenirs Piniella kept from that time. As with Lincoln's interpretation of Piniella's thoughts on the Johnson trade, the hotel-room episode in New York was a small thing that opened the door to a closet full of conflicted emotions.

Of his ten Seattle years, which doubled his previous managerial tenures combined, Piniella said earlier in the summer that he endured so long in the Northwest because he came to the realization that his bosses were assets that helped him do his job better. It was up to him, not them, to make the relationships work.

When reminded of his earlier observation, he said, "You're right. I said that, and then I went against the grain."

But contradiction and impulse have been Piniella's companions throughout his uproarious career in baseball. A sports life lived on the edge has taught him many lessons, but none so strong that his fiery Spanish heritage and his competitive passion ever ended up second.

"You know what I should have done with the memo?" he said of Lincoln's note via Gillick. "I should have ignored it and said nothing about it. That's what I should have done. But you know what? That's not my disposition. I fought for what I thought was right—nothing more, nothing less."

Lincoln, whose reputation for confrontation in the video game industry was only slightly less formidable than Piniella's in baseball, also was dug in.

"This was one of the few times in Lou's life where somebody was pissing him off and didn't back down," Lincoln said. "His point was his remarks [in Houston] had nothing to do with the Mariners. My point was 'Please.'

"We had a difference of opinion. It had to do with a strong view of following the rules. If you read what we [as an organization] agreed to say and not say, and if you go out and completely disregard that, I have an obligation as CEO to say, 'Now, wait a second. That's not right.' If I don't do that, then I'm not doing my job.

"Lou wasn't used to having somebody take him on. But I wasn't taking him on on a baseball issue; I was taking him on on an organizational issue. My strong feeling was that nobody was bigger than the organization. Everybody needs to follow the rules. That's the way of any successful business. He had a hard time with it because he felt my criticism was not correct, that I misinterpreted what he said. He was upset because I was upset and had no reason to be upset.

"You have to have an organization that works. You have to follow the rules."

Above all, Howard Lincoln is an organization man. From law school to military duty to business, Lincoln has a passion for order and accountability, and little tolerance for deviation from group goals and tactics.

An Oakland native, Lincoln as a boy was sufficiently clean-cut to have appeared in a group for a Norman Rockwell painting that appeared in a 1956 Boy Scouts calendar, for which he received a modeling fee of $50. Guessing that wasn't going to be a steady line of work, Lincoln successfully pursued a law degree at the University of California–Berkeley. Although the Bay Area was awash in free-speech and antiwar movements, Lincoln chose to sign up with the Navy as a seaman recruit during the Vietnam War draft.

Lincoln eventually earned a commission as a judge advocate (military attorney) and was stationed at Seattle's Sand Point Naval Air Station on Lake Washington, where he met his future wife, Grace. After leaving the Navy in 1970, he joined a Seattle law firm. His practice was primarily banking and corporate law, and clients included the fledgling Nintendo of America. After persuasion by NOA's president, Minoru Arakawa, Lincoln joined Nintendo in 1983 as senior vice president and general counsel.

In their nearly seventeen years together—Lincoln moved above Arakawa to CEO in 1994—the tandem led Nintendo to the pinnacle of the video game world and, for a time, the entire U.S. toy industry. Their personal relationship became close, which seemed a little unusual given the good-cop, bad-cop contradiction in their business styles.

"Arakawa is a very low-key individual," said former Senator Slade Gorton, who became acquainted with both during the pressurized days of early 1992 when the Nintendo-led purchase of the club was engineered. "He doesn't have sharp elbows, and was always accommodating and graceful. If there was anything tough to be said by Nintendo, it was by Howard."

Nor was Lincoln shy about such expression. In 1994, when Nintendo was facing stiff competition from rising powerhouse Sega, the rival suffered a business setback that Lincoln found irresistible. He penned a ditty to the Sega chairman that read:

"Roses are red,

Violets are blue.

So you had a bad day,

Boo-hoo, boo-hoo."

"I begged him not to put that out on the wires," said Perrin Kaplan, a Nintendo marketing vice president, of her old boss, laughing at the recall. "But he did, and it ended up in *The Wall Street Journal*."

One of the Mariners' minority owners from the McCaw Cellular group, Wayne Perry, saw a competitive toughness in Lincoln and Arakawa that belied the benign facade.

"Arakawa comes across as some kind of smiley happy guy, but that is one smart dude," he said. "You look inside Nintendo and see how they ran it, and you see those guys know how to play hardball. They're tough, hard-nosed guys, even though they have this sort of deferential attitude.

"I also had the impression they were honorable guys—straight shooters."

As employers, they ran NOA in a way different from many American companies. A Japanese-style belief in the group nature of the endeavor that emphasized team results over individual glory permeated Nintendo. The hierarchy was muted, and largely absent were the trappings of the typical U.S. executive class. When Arakawa and Lincoln ran Nintendo, their side-by-side offices were ordinary spaces of about eighteen by twenty-four feet on the ground floor. The office windows opened onto the Redmond company's parking lot, which contained no reserved stalls for them.

"Arakawa had a strong influence on me as far as how a company should be managed," Lincoln said. "He and I were very much alike on the idea that we should have people who worked together, follow the rules, and treat and compensate them properly. I remember visiting the [onetime business rival] Atari Corp. headquarters, where they had a private dining room for executives and all of that elaborate crap. Neither of us were comfortable with that."

The egalitarian approach extended to the ultimate perks: the company-built homes side-by-side on the beach on the Big Island of Hawaii, south of Kona. Aside from a few holiday weeks for the bosses, the homes are available the rest of the year to employees, whose names are drawn by lottery.

The management style proved popular. When Arakawa, at the age of fifty-five, retired as president of NOA in January 2002—some industry speculation had it that his father-in-law, Hiroshi Yamauchi, asked him to step aside—he wanted no announcement until he was out the door. But word spread quickly in the company offices. By 4 P.M. that Friday, when he stepped out of his office, a crowd in the hundreds broke into applause and cheers. An impromptu line stretched out of the building, and a misty-eyed Arakawa greeted each of his well-wishers.

But there also were plenty of tense, hostile moments for both men in defending Nintendo's interests, testy exercises that offered plenty of practice for Lincoln's encounter with Piniella.

"There's always some department in a particular organization that will challenge you," Lincoln said, "whether it's the marketing department at Nintendo or someone in baseball. There's always one department that feels dominant. Mino and I talked over the years how we felt that sort of thing was poison in the organization."

Lincoln didn't regard Piniella as poison, but he did see him as increasingly hard to handle, especially that afternoon in June.

"He didn't have to get that upset and use the kind of language in front of me he did," Lincoln said. "But he chose to do that. If he thought I was going to back down, he was wrong. When we parted, I wouldn't say we were bosom buddies or anything like that, but we parted with an understanding of where things were. Subsequent to that, he cooled off a little."

Lincoln's own anger was tempered by his awareness of the pressure building around Piniella and the club.

"I think he lost it, but I think he lost it because he was under a lot of stress, here and in Florida. I think he was embarrassed by the fact he'd gotten upset. He apologized later."

⁂

Piniella was edgy because so many things were slipping away. The bullpen was hurt, the starting pitching inconsistent, and offense frequently punchless. The Angels and the Oakland A's were recovering from slow starts, and a pennant race was on, something the Mariners didn't experience throughout 2001. For Piniella, the personal pressure had increased as well.

Each season in Seattle, he had grown wearier of the distance between his Tampa home and his job. His wife of thirty-five years, Anita, used to make frequent visits to Seattle, to the residence they rented in suburban Medina, but that happened less lately because of the "sandwich generation" demands of caring for elderly parents as well as kids and now grandkids.

Anita's father died in 2001. Piniella's own father was hospitalized in March in such serious condition that the manager flew home from spring training for a few days. Lou Sr. eventually recovered. But daughter Kristi, a single mother, had moved back home, where Piniella's presence, however infrequent, was a great comfort.

"I can't be away from home that much," Piniella said. "When I come home, so many things have happened over nine months that I can't keep up.

"It's probably a fault of mine, but I get so damn engrossed in the baseball team that it's hard for me to concentrate on too many things at once. Some can do that. I'm not one of them. I take pride and a tremendous amount of responsibility for the team to do well."

Divided attention couldn't have come at a worse time. The Mariners made blunders on the field that were nowhere to be seen a year ago. After the All-Star Game break, in which they were still in first place by three games with a 55-33 mark, No. 1 starter Freddy Garcia began a mysterious fade. He finished the second half of the season with a 5.66 ERA. Left fielder Ruben Sierra, a reliable performer in the first half of the year, contributed almost nothing in the second half. Ichiro, having been scouted by opponents for a full season, was beginning to be corralled. He also was walked intentionally 27 times, a club record that led the AL, because the hitters behind him were easier outs. He missed a few games in April after banging his knee against an outfield wall, and wasn't nearly the base-stealing threat of a year earlier, dropping from 56 steals to 31. He would hit .248 in September, perhaps a sign that the greater demands of the American schedule and travel had caught up to him after two seasons.

Even though Martinez and Nelson had returned from their injuries, they weren't making the Mariners sufficiently better than their rivals. That was apparent in mid-July when the Angels swept a three-game series in Anaheim by scores of 15-3, 7-6, and 7-5. Less than a week later at Safeco, results were similar between the teams: Anaheim won 8-0 and 1-0, and only a brilliant game by young starter Joel Pineiro in a 3-1 triumph avoided a second straight sweep. The Angels were demonstrating then what the baseball world would come to find out in three months—that they had quietly assembled a formidable lineup and a solid pitching staff that would make them world champions. In many ways, the Angels were mirroring in style and accomplishment the Mariners' season of '01.

"They're on a good streak right now, kind of like we had last year," Pineiro said. "Everything's falling for them, the ground balls are getting through, their pitching, everything."

Meantime, the only management response was to claim relief pitcher Doug Creek off waivers after he was of no further use to baseball's worst team, Tampa Bay. The July 31 trade deadline came and went without any other acquisitions by the Mariners for the stretch run.

Besides the injury problems that continued to compromise the organization's quality minor league pitchers, the major league roster was loaded with veterans too valuable, too old, or too expensive to be attractive in trade to clubs in a pennant race. Additionally, an external threat complicated potential deals—another possible labor disaster in baseball. The prospect of a ninth work stoppage over the last three decades was particularly loathsome in Seattle, where the immense popularity of the Mariners kept the club highly profitable. At around $90 million,

Leading the American League in strikeouts, Mike Cameron was one of several Mariners in 2002 who found the feats of 2001 difficult to replicate.

the Mariners already had the eighth-highest payroll in baseball, and the bosses were unwilling to add a large salary with so much uncertainty about revenues.

Nevertheless, other contending teams added payroll despite the threat of a strike, a development not lost on Piniella.

"A lot of good players exchanged a lot of uniforms," he said. "When you get close, and if it's within reason—you don't deplete your farm system—you take your best shot. That's what we did in '95. That turned out well."

To the surprise of baseball cynics, which included just about every follower of sports, the work stoppage was averted when owners and players reached agreement on a four-year contract. Although both sides attempted to hail the deal as a sign of real progress, the driving force in the settlement was the country's low tolerance for nonsense following the September 11 terrorist attacks. Already faced with declining attendance and TV ratings, both sides recognized how foolish they would have appeared if they stopped play with a national tragedy still fresh.

After the threat passed, the Mariners did claim two players unwanted by their clubs—utility man Jose Offerman from the Boston Red Sox and pitcher Ismael Valdes from the Texas Rangers. In 41 games for the Mariners, Offerman wound up hitting .235. In eight starts, Valdes was 2-3 with a 4.93 ERA. Creek, the reliever picked up earlier, had a 5.84 ERA in 25 relief appearances. The three cost the Mariners little, and gave about the same in return.

After the confrontation with Lincoln, Piniella attempted to keep quiet publicly about his perception that the Mariners weren't moving in ways he thought contenders should. While he betrayed no public hints that the frustration was forcing him to consider whether to stay on in Seattle, his restlessness began to seep out. When asked about his future, he would tell reporters blandly, "I have another year on my contract, and I intend to be here."

Piniella's chastisement by Lincoln, which was not disclosed publicly, took on some irony in July. The manager had to quiet down a clubhouse disturbed over remarks attributed to Lincoln in a column by Blaine Newnham of *The Seattle Times*. In explaining the reluctance of the club to make bold trade-deadline moves, Newnham wrote, "The goal of the Mariners is not to win the World Series," bracketed by quotes from Lincoln saying, "If you don't operate as a business, all sorts of bad things happen," and "People want us to do something exceptional, but what we want to do is have the discipline to stick with our plan." Several players assumed that meant Lincoln was happy merely with a full house and a contending team, and that the World Series wasn't a goal. But Piniella refused to lay off the team's troubles to Lincoln's remarks.

"I had to address it a few times individually," Piniella said. "My job is to handle situations. I addressed it and it was over with. That's not why we didn't win. It was over in two days."

Indeed, the seasonal fade was on well before the in-house politics were known. The Mariners gamely hung on to their division lead until late August, when, on a gloomy night in Cleveland, they surrendered the top—as it turned out, for good—in forlorn fashion.

Scoreless through six innings, the game against the Indians was delayed two hours by rain. When play resumed, the Mariners scored twice in the seventh, and the Indians countered with two in their half of the inning. By the ninth, Piniella's only real relief option was erstwhile starter Baldwin, who had pitched himself out of the rotation. With one out, Baldwin walked the first batter, then gave up a first in baseball history—a game-winning, walk-off home run by a rookie. Catcher Josh Bard, who had his first major league hit a few innings earlier, took Baldwin deep and the Mariners deeper. The 4-2 defeat, which helped put the A's in first place, became the breaking point of the season.

"I don't know what's going on right now," said a crushed Baldwin, who was better at summarizing the clubhouse's feelings than he was at retiring a batter. The next night held a similar ghastly defeat. This time the ninth-inning pitcher was Creek, and the Indians' hitting hero was Karim Garcia, who hit a walk-off, two-run homer just as Bard had, in a 5-3 win. Afterward, reliever Jeff Nelson said, "We're playing almost like a team that's looking forward to going home in September. Right now, I can't say I have a good feeling about this team."

The feeling was never quite right all season. After the twin heartbreaks in Cleveland, the Mariners played the season's final 32 games at 16-16, which included another shocker in early September—a four-game sweep by the lowly Rangers in Texas. By then, utility man Mark McLemore and closer Kazuhiro Sasaki had joined the long list of the injured and the lost.

Meanwhile, Oakland in August and September set an AL record with 20 consecutive wins. As the A's cooled, the Angels won 16 times in a stretch of 17 games. After owning the division the previous season and having led it for much of 2002, the Mariners at season's end were dust-covered spectators behind the California rivals. The Mariners' 93 wins were the second-best win total in their history, which this season was good enough only for third in a division in which Oakland won 103 and the Angels 99. For the first time in three years, there would be no playoffs for the Mariners.

In the postseason, the baseball results grew more astonishing. The Angels, who had not been to the playoffs since 1986, stunned the Yankees 3-1 in the Division Series. In the American League Championship Series, the Angels beat the Minnesota Twins 4-1, then bested the San Francisco Giants 4-3 for the club's first World Series triumph. A year earlier, the Angels finished 41 games behind the Mariners. Now they were champions. Disneyland, just a few blocks from Anaheim's stadium, had never concocted a ride so preposterous.

The Mariners were left to convince themselves they still had had a good season, despite the chapped skin from the Angels' blow-by. The consolation prizes included the best division record, 34-24, of any team against the AL West, and an average of 100 wins over three seasons (91, 116, and 93)—one of only sixteen teams in history to have reached such a threshold of sustained excellence. But another way to look at that history was that the Mariners were the only one of those sixteen teams that failed to advance to at least one World Series.

The absence of a Series appearance for Seattle ate at Piniella.

"For me there is always urgency," he said. "Sometimes it causes a little friction. Sometimes you put a little too much urgency into it. That's the way I am. I knew my time was short in Seattle, and I wanted to get a team to the Series as much as I've wanted to do anything.

"They hired a manager to get a job done. I don't like losing—I really don't. You need to get things done."

In mid-September his discontent boiled over in an outburst at Safeco that went to the top of Piniella's legacy of managerial eruptions, not to mention the top of the nation's TV sportscasts that night. On the play that provoked him, replays showed that Ben Davis beat out a hit at first base, but umpire C. B. Bucknor had no technological assistance, calling the Mariners hitter out and sending the game against Texas into extra innings tied at 2. Piniella burst from the dugout to confront Bucknor, who ejected him within seconds, then made the mistake of smirking. Piniella was in the umpire's face deep as nostril hair.

Fuming, Piniella slammed his cap to the dirt, then stomped and kicked it. When first-base coach Johnny Moses tried to pull him away, he ordered Moses, "Get my fuckin' hat!" Moses obliged, and Piniella pitched it to the dirt and kicked it again. From twelve years earlier in Cincinnati, he reached back for an epic gesture: He unhitched first base from its moorings, chucking the bag into right field. He followed it out, then threw the bag again, adding to his major league record of bases thrown, career.

"I didn't want it to happen," Piniella said afterward, smiling. "But it just happened."

The Safeco crowd cheered long and loud. Over the years Piniella had endeared himself to Mariners followers with his unbridled, unambiguous passion for winning. He was never afraid to look the fool for caring. In an increasingly cynical, transient sports world, there were no doubts about Piniella's agendas and priorities. His judgments, strategies, and pitcher-handling could be called into question. But it was not possible to cast aspersions upon his dedication to triumph. In a fading season, in a game of little consequence in the standings, Piniella offered Seattle what turned out to be a farewell glimpse into the fire.

Yet Piniella's passion on and off the field has, over the years, proven radioactive, to others as well as himself. In 2002, the radiation made Lincoln glow.

"You can't," the Mariners boss said, "have prima donnas."

In Lincoln's mind, it wasn't so much the field tantrums that were troubling. It was Piniella's bellicose, impulsive baseball personnel judgments that became unreliable. That was true even in the Kingdome days, when the manager had in-game access to some of the execs who were watching games from the field-level "bunker" directly behind home plate. After a serious miscue on the field, Piniella sometimes would glare into the bunker. Occasionally between innings, he would stroll over to offer a profane demand that the miscreant player be sent to the minors, traded, or otherwise dispatched from his sight.

"Quite frankly, Lou's views of what we should do was so ever-changing, and so wrapped around emotion that I didn't pay that much attention to them," Lincoln said. "I paid a lot more attention to the views of Pat, Chuck, and Lee Pelekoudas."

A line had been drawn between Piniella and Lincoln in June. The franchise for ten years had been dominated by one personality, but it was about to be succeeded by another. Piniella knew it, and knew his time in Seattle was near an end.

"I like Howard personally," Piniella said. "I enjoyed working with him. He's a bright guy, a charming guy. But I'll tell you this—he's bottom line. Howard likes total, total control.

"Pat wants to win. Howard just doesn't know how."

Lincoln believed the achievements of 2001, done without the marquee players that rescued Seattle baseball, showed what could be done without superstars. Yet there was no tangible reward for the deed of 116 wins. But that provocative baseball debate was never engaged, because by the season's end, Piniella and the demands of his family changed the parameters. Besides the fading health of his parents, daughter Kristi and granddaughter Kassidy were involved in a car accident in Tampa during the final week of the regular season. Anita was in Seattle at the time, and her cross-country travel home took more than eleven hours.

Piniella's guilt over his long absences to the Northwest was weighing heavily.

"The accident really affected my wife, but we both panicked," he said. "It wasn't as serious as we thought it was. But it reminded me again that the distance was too far. Truthfully, it was getting to the point where I can't be away from home that much." Another reminder of values beyond baseball came with the unexpected death October 7 of Gary Mack, a close friend who was for a time in charge of the club's employee assistance program, and who occasionally counseled Piniella.

As had Rodriguez, Griffey, and Johnson before him, Piniella decided that it was time to move on. Whether baseball or family became primary for Piniella was debatable. Anita later would tell The Seattle Times' Bob Finnigan that when they learned the house they rented in Seattle for several years had been put up for sale by its owners, the couple took it as an omen that change was at hand.

Whether the thinking amounted to a rationalization or cover for avoiding a public showdown, Piniella knew it was over in Seattle.

.ﷺ.

Piniella had a year remaining on his contract. But custom in baseball and all major sports dictates that it is not wise to keep an unhappy manager or head coach in position if the desire no longer remains. That understanding didn't mean the departure would go down easily.

In Anaheim, on the next to last day of the season, Piniella told Gillick he was seriously considering retiring. Piniella knew Lincoln was flying down from Seattle the next day to address the team, and he wanted Gillick to know first. When Lincoln was informed, he wasn't shocked. In fact, he may well have been relieved. Annoying as it was to have to undergo the upheaval of a managerial change, the tension between the two had grown to the point where it seemed as unlikely that Lincoln would offer Piniella a new deal after the 2003 season as it was that Piniella would seek one.

Piniella was asked by his bosses to go home and think about the decision. By the next day, however, outside forces complicated the decision. Retirement was not going to be a likely option.

Two managerial jobs opened up that couldn't have been better if Piniella wrote the script. The New York Mets fired Bobby Valentine, and the Tampa Bay Devil Rays fired Hal McRae. Both moves had been anticipated in baseball, but neither the teams nor the public knew Piniella was about to put himself in play. Although there was some muffled speculation in the Seattle media that the restless Piniella might be ready to leave, nothing was known until after Lincoln, Armstrong, and Gillick flew to Tampa on October 12 to meet their departing skipper.

Piniella not only told them he wanted out of his final year in Seattle, he wanted out bad enough to consider Tampa, a five-year-old franchise that set a new low even by its own wretched standards with a 55-106 season, baseball's worst.

"When I told Howard, he said, 'Are you crazy?' " Piniella said, smiling.

Ten years earlier, Piniella heard the same sentiment regarding his last move. Baseball's wise guys said then the Seattle post was a dead man's job. But while there were parallels between the current

Devil Rays and the '92 Mariners—underfunded ownership, poor attendance, bad indoor stadium—the Devil Rays had no one who played like Ken Griffey or Randy Johnson or Edgar Martinez.

Piniella was different, too.

"I'm older; I don't have all that much time anymore," he said, staring into his drink at Malio's. "We'll have the smallest payroll in baseball. My modest goal here is to win 70 games next year.

"If it were anyplace but Tampa, the decision to come here would have been very difficult."

It was so difficult that no one who had been around Piniella believed he preferred Tampa to the Mets. Since the franchise began in his hometown in 1998, Piniella had repeatedly denied any desire to go down that dead end. But a return to New York—now that would be some grand baseball theater. Although he was long over his desire to go back to the Yankees, a return to New York with the Mets was something else. The chance to steal the back pages of the Gotham tabloids from George Steinbrenner's crew would be a source of delight. And his Tampa home would be just a two-hour nonstop flight away.

But the seeming inevitability of his choice created a hubris that worked against the Mets, and ultimately Piniella.

Once the Mariners executives were convinced Piniella truly wanted out, they shook hands—Lincoln and Piniella even had a hug—and flew back to Seattle to reveal the surprise publicly and to work on compensation. Because he was under contract, an interested team not only had to have the Mariners' permission to talk to him, but they also had to offer up something, presumably players, should he be signed.

The New York sports media went into a frenzy over the prospect of the beloved Piniella's return. Mets owner Fred Wilpon was so certain of Piniella's intentions that he offered the Mariners three prospects, none of whom appeared to the Mariners to be a major league certainty. Meanwhile, Devil Rays managing general partner Vince Naimoli—who ten years earlier thought he had the Mariners franchise lured to Tampa under Jeff Smulyan's ownership—was on vacation in a remote part of Mexico when he spotted a copy of the *The New York Times* that had news of Piniella's availability. He scrambled desperately to find a pay phone, attempting more than fifty calls before finally reaching the Mariners, pleading with them not to do anything until he could fly home and deal.

Even though Naimoli and Piniella lived in the same golf-course community in North Tampa, they didn't know each other except for some courtesy hellos. But Naimoli knew that Piniella would bring the same instant credibility to his club that he brought to the Mariners. Six days after Piniella told his Seattle bosses goodbye, the Devil Rays privately agreed to give the Mariners a quality young veteran entering his prime: twenty-eight-year-old outfielder Randy Winn, Tampa's representative in the All-Star Game, who hit .298 with 14 home runs and 27 stolen bases. The Mariners also agreed to give Tampa a shortstop prospect, Antonio Perez, who was acquired from Cincinnati in the trade for Griffey.

Since Piniella and the Devil Rays hadn't negotiated yet, the compensation issue stayed quiet. The Mets chafed. Several New York media outlets harpooned the Mariners for being unreasonable. The *New York Daily News* ran an illustration depicting a screaming Piniella juxtaposed opposite photos of Lincoln, Armstrong, and Gillick, all smiling. Above the graphic was the headline: "Axis of Evil."

The Mets assumed the Mariners had an agenda to screw them or Piniella or both. But the simple fact was Tampa was so desperate they surrendered an All Star–quality player who could play a position, left field, the Mariners had been unable to fill adequately for fifteen years.

"Wilpon shot himself in the foot," Lincoln said. "He thought he was the only one bidding for Lou."

Piniella quickly discovered the Devil Rays were as serious about him as they were with the Mariners, offering a four-year contract for more than $13 million, plus $3 million in incentives (he earned $2.5 million in his final Seattle year). Exasperated, the Mets gave up four days later and signed Art Howe, who had just managed Oakland to a 102-win season. Surprised at the money, and disappointed that the Mets didn't compete seriously, Piniella accepted the Tampa offer.

"I see why Seattle didn't let me talk to anyone else, when they had a chance to get Winn," Piniella told the *Seattle P-I's* John Hickey. "Everybody assumed I was going to New York. And I would have liked to talk to them. I just wasn't sure Tampa would make the financial commitment. You never know if an organization is just interested in a little publicity. But after our first meeting, it was obvious."

He was comfortable enough with the deal to find amusement, telling *The Seattle Times,* "In ten years in Seattle, the Mariners never got a left fielder for me. Now they get a left fielder *for* me."

At a crowded press conference October 28 at Tropicana Field in St. Petersburg, swarming with well-wishers and family, including Anita and Lou Jr., Piniella pulled on a Tampa Bay jersey. He made an odd bit of baseball history: He became the first manager to walk away twice from teams that won 90 or more games (his last team in Cincinnati in 1992 was 90-72). Even odder, he chose to go from near the pinnacle to a sub-basement in the valley. Managers in their prime just don't do that. But Piniella's career never did follow the sheet music. It was pure jazz, a John Coltrane CD over forty years.

For observers from the Northwest, Piniella's return to Tampa was rich. Ten years earlier and twenty minutes away in downtown Tampa, John Ellis, then the newly appointed leader of a group trying to purchase the Mariners, had arrived from Seattle to meet with a committee of highly skeptical baseball owners. Before the meeting, the utility company executive stopped at the hotel's gift shop and was stunned to discover his own bit of Gulf Coast baseball fashion: a table of T-shirts that read, "Tampa Bay Mariners." He had to buy one to let the folks back home see the eagerness in Florida that awaited their failure. Denied the team then, Tampa now celebrated the return of its prodigal son from Seattle to fix the chaotic expansion outfit they received in 1998.

Piniella's decade with the Mariners gave the Northwest and baseball time to hook up in a raucous relationship loaded with compelling sports theater. In his time, the short, fat kid of baseball grew muscles, added height, and picked up attitude. The route was beyond-absurd difficult, mined with as much hardball politics as hardball play, leaving bruises along with the brilliance. Piniella's passion was the juice for success. But now it was gone, and Lincoln was eager to establish that the Mariners could run on alternative fuels.

Lou Piniella shocked baseball by returning to manage the Devil Rays in his hometown of Tampa, which 10 years earlier . . . ASSOCIATED PRESS PHOTO BY CHRIS O'MEARA

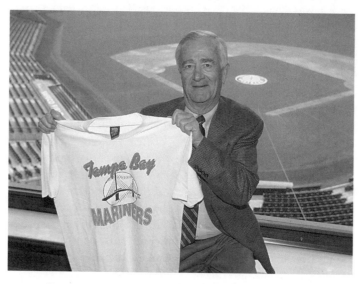

. . . was all set to shock Seattle by taking the franchise out of the Northwest. Retired CEO John Ellis bought this expression of Gulf Coast optimism in a Tampa hotel when in 1992 he attended a meeting of baseball's owners.

PHOTO BY BEN VAN HOUTEN

It would not be possible in Seattle to replace a man of Piniella's stature and popularity. However, it would be possible to marry the organization to something less than a volcano. So general manager Pat Gillick was given the charge to find a good baseball man who could work well with the baseball men already assembled. Baseball pedigree, it turned out, wasn't as important as personality.

Over the next three weeks, Gillick interviewed in Seattle a dozen candidates who generally could be described as low in profile and maintenance and high in potential and smoothness. Four came from within the organization: Piniella's right-hand man on the Mariners' bench, John McLaren; the pitching coach, Bryan Price; Lee Elia, part-time hitting instructor; and minor league manager Dan Rohn. Another four had previous big-league managerial experience: Buddy Bell, Jim Riggleman, Tony Muser, and Terry Francona. Four were coaches who had never managed in the majors: Sam Perlozzo, Willie Randolph, Ron Roenicke, and Bob Melvin.

The Mariners played no media games with the candidates—all were announced to the public. Conspicuous by his absence from the list was Dusty Baker, who had just led the San Francisco Giants to the World Series against Anaheim, and was known to be sufficiently at odds with club ownership to want a new job. Because he was a manager under contract, the Mariners had a built-in excuse for not talking to him. But when he was not offered a new deal by the Giants, making him a free agent before the Mariners made a decision, Baker's candidacy, by far the most popular with fans and media, was tersely dismissed by Gillick: "He's not a fit."

Despite being a West Coast guy with an expressed affinity for Seattle, Baker didn't fit for two reasons: His considerable track record as a major league manager made him the most expensive candidate, and, more important, he would be too much like Piniella. Though different in personality, Baker was a flamboyant character who ran a loose clubhouse and had more than a few run-ins over the years with ownership and management. He was definitely not a Howard Lincoln kind of guy. Baker would eventually be hired by the Chicago Cubs.

The Mariners cut their list to four. Bell, Riggleman, Perlozzo, and Melvin came in for a second round of interviews, while McLaren and Elia decided to join Piniella's staff in Florida. On

Bob Melvin was one of the twelve candidates interviewed by general manager Pat Gillick (left), who was impressed with Melvin's baseball brains as well as demeanor, which was the opposite of the predecessor, Lou Piniella.

©2003 SEATTLE POST-INTELLIGENCER/SCOTT EKLUND

November 15, president Chuck Armstrong announced the club had selected "the absolute perfect person to lead us at this time," even though almost no one outside some very small circles in baseball would have predicted Bob Melvin, the youngest and least experienced man in the field, would be the successor to Piniella in Seattle.

Not only had he never managed in the majors or minors, and had no history with the franchise, but Melvin at forty-one was barely older than a couple of his players, Jamie Moyer and Edgar Martinez. A tall, thin native of the Bay Area not far removed from his ten-year major league career, Melvin did possess the trendiest characteristic in major league managing: He was a former catcher.

The 2002 champion Angels were managed by Mike Scioscia, an ex-catcher. The 2001 champion Arizona Diamondbacks, where Melvin had spent the previous two years as bench coach, were managed by an ex-catcher, Bob Brenly. And the champions of four of the five previous seasons before that, the New York Yankees, were led by another ex-catcher, Joe Torre. Since catchers are in the unique position of participating in all aspects of the game—pitching, fielding, hitting, and strategizing—they must know nearly everything a manager knows. And Melvin, more than any other candidate, got across what he knew in interviews with club executives.

"The thing that came through is that he's so smart," Gillick said. "He's a very perceptive guy with a lot of ideas. He picks up on things very quickly.

"We think we got a real gem."

Melvin came well recommended throughout baseball, but what stood out in crisp relief was how different he seemed to be from Piniella. His rookieness, eagerness, and appreciation for the job meant that any power struggles with his bosses were as likely as choices in a Cuban election.

Lincoln would say later that Melvin's seeming pliancy was a misimpression.

"I wouldn't use the word pliant," he said. "That implies he's going to fall over and do what Pat and Lee [Pelekoudas] tell him. I don't perceive Bob that way. In my mind, it's extremely helpful that Pat and Lee and the baseball people communicate on a non-emotional basis with the field manager, and he with them.

"I'm not discounting the fact that Bob may have a helluva tough time. I don't think there will be misunderstandings. There's already been a free flow of ideas. He will assert himself strongly, but on a less emotional basis. We could have communication with no success; then the argument will be if you had more screaming and yelling, you'd have more success. But no one knows that."

From across the country, Piniella said he saw coming a selection such as Melvin.

"Invariably, when you get an aggressive, urgent manager, you're going to go the other way with the next hire," he said as the afternoon wore on at Malio's. "They can say, 'Lou did his job, but let's get somebody in here a little less aggressive.' Somebody that allows them to make the decisions. If they had a passive manager for ten years, they'd probably go with a guy who's more aggressive. That's the way it is.

"I hope the young man does well. I'm very impressed with him."

Lincoln didn't see a bad-cop, good-cop analogy, only that Melvin would be different than Piniella.

"I don't think it's fair to say that Lou was wrong or right, or we were wrong or right," he said. "There's no 'right' way. It's more luck. Lou's ten-year tenure was remarkable. It's a tribute to Lou, and to the others in the organization, that we all worked together.

"But life moves on."

Despite the friction generated by Piniella, Lincoln was right. The manager, players, and executives of the past ten seasons had worked well together, producing spectacular results in 1995 and 2001 and transforming a frail franchise into a robust success.

Sometimes it was done with stars, sometimes with bit players. Some years, winning required home runs in record number; other years, precision pitching lead the league. Whether in a gray barn or green cathedral, it was done against all odds and in spite of the past. There was luck, too, loads of it, as well as the love of a region's fans from whom all financial blessings came.

Now players and fans would be asked in 2003 to accept yet another abrupt change, this one in leadership style, a makeover akin to going from Bette Midler to Carly Simon, from waterfall to sponge bath, from brass knuckles to velvet gloves. As much as baseball has been hailed as an enduring cultural legacy, its yearly churn is constant and the Mariners its poster children for convulsion. Life does indeed move on especially fast in sports, with fading concern for what was done last season and insistence on a fresh set of thrills. Success is acutely ephemeral, as fragile as porcelain. In Seattle, the Sonics once seemed to own the town; so, once, did the Seahawks. But there is no such thing as a mortgage on the hearts of sports fans. The Mariners simply have the current lease. It is never long-term.

Melvin knew he was handed a rare burden, difficult to master for the inexperienced: stewarding quality.

"When you get your first job as a manager, it's usually when a team is not doing very well," he said during his introductory press conference. "For me to come in as a first-year manager to a situation like this . . . it's too good to be true."

Too good to be true.

Whether Melvin's sentiment was accurate for him would await the 2003 season and beyond, but the expression also might be applied by many witnesses to the renaissance of major league baseball in Seattle. Even after a decade of steady developments that nearly always worked out for the Mariners, it remains a reach to grasp the transformation. Somehow, upon entry to Safeco

Field, there is still a small dread that compels the longtime fan to check for trapdoors, or for anvils poised overhead.

But with each season, the dread eases. During a 2003 spring training stop in the press box at Peoria Stadium, commissioner Bud Selig, the onetime purloiner of the Seattle Pilots and longtime member of the chorus of Seattle bashers, pulled aside a writer.

Speaking in a hushed tone, in the manner of delivering a scoop, he said, "You know, the Mariners really are a model franchise."

Maybe the remark was just another ill-considered Selig exaggeration, but given all that baseball had done to the region and to itself to deny the franchise success, even an insincere plaudit coming from the lord mayor of baseball made for the mother of all thigh-slapping horselaughs.

The Seattle Mariners, model franchise. Can you believe it, Mario Mendoza, George Argyros, Steve Trout, Jeff Smulyan, and Bill Plummer?

Maybe not yet, at least until the arrival of a World Series. Until then, a decade of thrills and a future of stability rests easily on the baseball souls of those who knew a day when the Kingdome was quiet enough to hear fans snore, opponents snicker, and pitchers sigh.

Epilogue

Since baseball seems to have created statistical categories for everything down to flatulence per extra inning (day games versus left-handers), it was surprising to discover there was no record for fastest ownership growth from snot-nosed to gray eminence. So in the absence of contradictory evidence, the declaration here is that the Baseball Club of Seattle, born in 1992, leads the major leagues in the category.

The basis for the contention is that only seven other franchises have had longer continuous ownership tenures—the Milwaukee Brewers (the old Seattle Pilots, 1970), New York Yankees (1973), Atlanta Braves (1976), Chicago White Sox (1981), Chicago Cubs (1981), Minnesota Twins (1984), and New York Mets (1986). Ownership turnover in baseball has become rapid because profit is less frequently made in annual cash operations than in equity appreciation. So the wealth and stability of the Hiroshi Yamauchi–led group has become a large franchise asset that has precluded the management upheavals that plagued many franchises. The only change in the sixteen-member Seattle ownership was in 2001, when an original minority investor, John McCaw, sold his small percentage to another former McCaw Cellular executive, John Stanton.

In less than a decade, the baseball refugees became landed gentry in a new castle.

The franchise is also part of another small group, this one of more dubious membership. Since the Mariners' inaugural year of 1977, Major League Baseball has seen twenty-two of its thirty franchises reach the World Series, including Florida and Arizona, two expansion teams of the 1990s. The Mariners are among the eight that remain tardy to the party, which includes the Chicago White Sox, Texas Rangers, and Tampa Bay Devil Rays in the American

League, and the Cubs, Houston Astros, Montreal Expos, and Colorado Rockies in the National League.

The juxtaposition of the developments raises the questions of when and how the Mariners will exploit prosperity and stability to match the baseball expectations that were created with financial success. In other words, is the club willing to fight, and not merely run with, the big dogs?

For longtime watchers outside the market, even asking the question of Seattle baseball has been almost unthinkable.

Veteran sports broadcaster Bob Costas did NBC's *Game of the Week* with Tony Kubek from 1983 to 1989. He recalled the telecast of two Mariners games during the period.

"One was at Fenway Park, the other at Yankee Stadium," he said. "Believe me, the Mariners weren't the draw."

But for reasons explained in the previous pages, the Mariners changed all that. Rooted in one of the game's premier retro-style ballparks, the club led the major leagues in attendance in 2001 and 2002, while pulling baseball's largest regional cable-TV audience. Their radio contract in Seattle is the sport's most lucrative. The club reported to the Public Facilities District, the state agency that regulates the stadium, a net income of $10.7 million for a 2002 season that didn't include the cash machine of home playoff games. Income was up from the previous season, reported at $7.5 million. In 2002, the 23,600 season tickets sold were more than the club's first seven seasons combined. The 2002 *Forbes* magazine survey put the value of the franchise at $385 million, sixth highest in baseball.

Besides their popularity in the Northwest, the owner and players from Japan helped raise the club's profile in a nation with the world's second-largest population of baseball fans, not to mention playing talent. The Mariners are so successful that the former small-market waifs are paying $28 million in 2003 into baseball's revenue-sharing plan that is supposed to help the ne'er-do-wells that they once were.

"The Mariners' success clearly showed a way for teams in trouble," Costas said. "They found ways to get new revenues that can change the faces of franchises. Other teams start to look at them as new models."

Costas, who wrote the best-selling baseball book *Fair Ball: A Fan's Case for Baseball,* which offered numerous progressive suggestions for industry reform, also pointed out that being a financially successful team is a reward that usually means little to those in the seats whose purchase of expensive tickets pays the bills.

Fans have little interest in a logical virtue to an emotional investment.

"If George Steinbrenner truly wanted to run a good business, he would take all his revenues and cut his payroll in half and hire Billy Beane," he said, referring to the Oakland general manager often hailed for his shrewd moves that have kept the A's in contention despite a limited payroll. "If you can spend big, you do. And if you also have competent business management, you have a substantial advantage."

It's clear Steinbrenner doesn't care about running a good business. Denied what he considers the franchise birthright of a championship in 2001 and 2002, and targeted in the new collective bargaining agreement with penalties for overspending, the Yankees owner said to hell with everyone. His club began the 2003 season with a mind-numbing player payroll of nearly $160 million, $35 million more than the previous season and about $70 million more than the Mariners'. Taxes? Penalties? Mere spitwads against Battleship Steinbrenner.

The Yankees remain the gold standard of baseball, and they remain in the Mariners' way. Steinbrenner doesn't necessarily buy himself a championship with profligate spending, as the last two seasons proved, but he does purchase room to get away with more personnel mistakes that won't end up hurting the club's chances. In baseball's hyperinflated, minimally regulated system of player salaries, that is the key long-term advantage. If a well-paid Yankee proves a bust, there will be plenty more where he came from.

It is an advantage that rivals can no longer negate by the financial blessings of a new stadium. Since 1991 the Mariners and thirteen other teams opened new ballparks, sold in part to a public with the claim that their tax dollars would help assure perennial contention. In most instances, that has not proven to be the case. In fact, the preponderance of new parks has merely raised the minimum threshold for competitiveness while failing to close the gap with the Yankees, who do not have a new-generation stadium.

"At the time that the new stadiums in Baltimore [1992] and Cleveland [1994] were opened, and when Seattle's stadium was approved, the revenues from the stadiums could make up for a lot of the difference with the big-revenue teams," Costas said. "But that was before the big cable revenues made a huge difference for the biggest-market teams like the Yankees. A stadium can do nothing about that disparity.

"If teams such as Kansas City or Tampa want a new stadium, they can't sell the notion anymore that the park alone will make them automatically better and more competitive. You can sell the idea that they will be less bad, but they still won't be close to big money. The fan will ask, 'How does this stadium assure competitiveness?'

"The gaps perpetuate themselves to the point where it feeds the monster. If every team has a new stadium, how does that change the income disparities?"

Short of Donald Rumsfeld entering the Bronx with tanks to effect regime change, the Mariners and the rest of the industry, ever resistant to true reform in competitive balance, are left annually to wait for the giant to stumble. While Arizona and Anaheim proved it was possible for the strategy to be rewarded, both clubs were losers of serious money despite the championships. In fact, the Angels' owner, the Disney Company, sold the club in 2003, mere months after the franchise's first title. The price of approximately $180 million was far less than the $300 million Disney sought three years earlier, in part due to steady annual losses.

The Mariners, operating debt-free with annual operating profits in a regional monopoly containing a broad fan base, are as well managed as any team in baseball and in as strong a position as any for annual challenges to the Yankees.

But is there the will to risk seizing the day?

That's the question former manager Lou Piniella posed to his bosses over his final three seasons in Seattle, which included two American League Championship Series confrontations with the Gotham goliaths. He wanted to know whether the club would take the chance on adding veterans' salaries and sacrificing minor league prospects, as well as some profit, for a shot at real and rare baseball history—beating the Yankees and winning it all.

Or is being good enough, good enough?

Piniella never heard the answer he wanted. But he also never heard them say that if he hadn't been so famously impatient with some young players, they still would be in Seattle helping the Mariners to a second or third title. The unspoken criticism was that urgency in baseball can cut both ways. If you're not the Yankees, a mistake here or there can be devastating. Yet fear of risk is equally crippling.

The ultimate arbiters of the decision-making are baseball fans, and as the 2003 season began, Mariners season ticket sales, attendance, and TV ratings were down from the previous year. For some fans, good enough is not good enough.

In a sport where the pinstriped gold standard distorts all, competitive decisions are not easy. But it's not as if making tough calls is unfamiliar. The future of the franchise remains in the hands of nearly the same people who seemed to make almost permanent camp on the edge, showing no fear. But the Mariners would not be the first enterprise to which prosperity became an impediment to ultimate success.

Back from the precipice and secure, the franchise is destined to be for years upon another turning point—choosing the safety of being good, or the risk of being great.

Appendix 1

THE MARINERS, YEAR BY YEAR

Year	Record	Finish	Games Back	Attendance	Manager	General Manager/ VP Operations	Principal Owner	CEO	President
1977	64-98	6th	38	1,338,511	Darrell Johnson	Lou Gorman	Danny Kaye/Lester Smith	------	Danny Kaye/Lester Smith
1978	56-104	7th	35	877,440	Darrell Johnson	Lou Gorman	Danny Kaye/Lester Smith	------	Danny Kaye/Lester Smith
1979	67-95	6th	21	844,455	Darrell Johnson	Lou Gorman	Danny Kaye/Lester Smith	------	Danny Kaye/Lester Smith
1980	59-103	7th	38	836,204	Darrell Johnson Maury Wills	Lou Gorman Dan O'Brien	Danny Kaye/Lester Smith	------	Danny Kaye/Lester Smith Dan O'Brien
1981	21-36	6th	14.5	636,276	Maury Wills	Dan O'Brien	George Argyros	------	Dan O'Brien
	23-39	5th	6.5		Rene Lachemann				
1982	76-86	4th	17	1,070,404	Rene Lachemann	Dan O'Brien	George Argyros	------	Dan O'Brien
1983	60-102	7th	39	813,537	Rene Lachemann Del Crandall	Dan O'Brien Hal Keller	George Argyros	------	Chuck Armstrong
1984	74-88	5th	10	870,372	Del Crandall Chuck Cottier	Hal Keller	George Argyros	------	Chuck Armstrong
1985	74-88	6th	17	1,128,696	Chuck Cottier	Hal Keller Dick Balderson	George Argyros	------	Chuck Armstrong
1986	67-95	6th	25	1,029,045	Chuck Cottier Dick Williams	Dick Balderson	George Argyros	------	Chuck Armstrong
1987	78-84	4th	7	1,134,255	Dick Williams	Dick Balderson	George Argyros	------	Chuck Armstrong
1988	68-93	7th	35.5	1,022,398	Dick Williams Jim Snyder	Dick Balderson Woody Woodward	George Argyros	------	Chuck Armstrong
1989	73-89	6th	26	1,298,443	Jim Lefebvre	Woody Woodward	George Argyros	------	Chuck Armstrong
1990	77-85	5th	26	1,509,727	Jim Lefebvre	Woody Woodward	Jeff Smulyan	Jeff Smulyan	Jeff Smulyan
1991	83-79	5th	12	2,147,905	Jim Lefebvre	Woody Woodward	Jeff Smulyan	Jeff Smulyan	Jeff Smulyan
1992	64-98	7th	32	1,651,398	Bill Plummer	Woody Woodward	Jeff Smulyan Hiroshi Yamuchi	John Ellis	Chuck Armstrong

Appendix 1 • *The Mariners, Year by Year.* cont.

Year	Record	Finish	Games Back	Attendance	Manager	General Manager/ VP Operations	Principal Owner	CEO	President
1993	82-80	4th	12	2,051,853	Lou Piniella	Woody Woodward	Hiroshi Yamauchi	John Ellis	Chuck Armstrong
1994	49-63	3rd	2	1,104,206	Lou Piniella	Woody Woodward	Hiroshi Yamauchi	John Ellis	Chuck Armstrong
1995	79-66	1st	+1	1,643,107	Lou Piniella	Woody Woodward	Hiroshi Yamauchi	John Ellis	Chuck Armstrong
1996	85-76	2nd	4.5	2,723,850	Lou Piniella	Woody Woodward	Hiroshi Yamauchi	John Ellis	Chuck Armstrong
1997	90-72	1st	+6	3,192,237	Lou Piniella	Woody Woodward	Hiroshi Yamauchi	John Ellis	Chuck Armstrong
1998	76-85	3rd	11.5	2,644,305	Lou Piniella	Woody Woodward	Hiroshi Yamauchi	John Ellis	Chuck Armstrong
1999	79-83	3rd	16	2,916,346	Lou Piniella	Woody Woodward	Hiroshi Yamauchi	Howard Lincoln	Chuck Armstrong
2000	91-71	2nd	0.5	3,150,034	Lou Piniella	Pat Gillick	Hiroshi Yamauchi	Howard Lincoln	Chuck Armstrong
2001	116-46	1st	+14	3,507,975	Lou Piniella	Pat Gillick	Hiroshi Yamauchi	Howard Lincoln	Chuck Armstrong
2002	93-67	3rd	10	3,540,658	Lou Piniella	Pat Gillick	Hiroshi Yamauchi	Howard Lincoln	Chuck Armstrong

Appendix 2

THE MIRACLE RALLY OF 1995

Entering a strike-shortened 1995 season, the Mariners struggled until August, when an improbable string of late-game rallies, coupled with a collapse by the division-leading California Angels, produced the first post-season appearance in franchise history. The run was doubly crucial because it helped produce the political momentum for a new stadium after a ballot measure September 19 in King County failed by less than a thousand votes.

Following is a chronicle of the late-season 1995 games and events that helped save baseball in Seattle.

August 1995

SEATTLE: Following the July 31 trading-deadline acquisition of pitcher Andy Benes from San Diego for pitcher Ron Villone and outfielder Marc Newfield, the Mariners entered the month with a 43-44 record (third in the AL West) and trailed the Angels by 11 games. The M's lost their first two in August to fall 13 games out of first, then proceeded to tie a franchise record for wins in any month with 16. The Mariners scored 182 runs in August, topping their previous monthly record of 152 set in June 1986.

CALIFORNIA: The Angels entered August in first place in the AL West with a 54-33 record and holding an 11-game lead over second-place Texas. But after scoring 201 runs in July, the most in any month since the Yankees scored 202 in July 1958, the Angels fell to 141 runs scored and finished the month with a 13-17 record.

September 1995

SEATTLE: Seattle began the month 7 games behind California but erased the deficit in 20 days. Due to a 16-6 start, the Mariners blew past Kansas City, Texas, and the New York Yankees to take the wild-card lead. Between September 13 and 26, the M's picked up nine games in the standings. By the time the regular season ended, the Mariners had posted the third-greatest comeback in the standings in ML history by wiping out a 13-game deficit on August 2. The Mariners won 19 games in September, the most in any month in their history. They set a record for most consecutive home wins with nine between September 12 and 26. They also set a club record by hitting 46 homers in September. The 160 runs scored by the M's in September were the second most in club history behind the 182 they scored in August.

CALIFORNIA: After a 13-17 August, the Angels collapsed, going 11-16 for the month and days. On August 25, California was 8½ games ahead 24-33 for August and September combined. On August 25, California was 8½ games ahead in the AL West. On September 23, California was two games behind—a loss of 10 games in the standings in slightly less than a month. The only collapse greater than that of the Angels was by the New York Giants in 1914 (14 games), which gave rise to the so-called "Miracle" Boston Braves.

Date	Result	Record (Sea/Cal)	Games Back or Ahead (Sea/Cal)	Notes
8/24	@Sea 9, NYY 7	55-55	−11	Joey Cora drives in tying run, Ken Griffey Jr. 2-run HR off John Wetteland with 2 out in 9th to win it.
	@Cal 6, Balt 4	67-44	+7	J.T. Snow 4 hits, 4 RBIs as Angels put damper on Cal Ripken's 35th birthday.
8/25	@Sea 7, NYY 4	56-55	−10	Down 2-0 in 2nd, M's tie it on Dan Wilson 2-run single, win it on Edgar Martinez 3-run HR.
	Balt 11, @Cal 2	67-45	+8	Scott Erickson tosses 6-hitter; Rafael Palmeiro blasts 3-run HR in 5-run 3rd.
8/26	@Sea 7, NYY 0	57-55	−9	Randy Johnson 15th career shutout, limits Yanks to 3 hits, his third 3-hit shutout of year.
	Balt 5, @Cal 2	67-46	+7	Kevin Brown wins for first time in 5 weeks; Palmeiro blasts 30th HR of season.
8/27	NYY 5, @Sea 2	57-56	−9	Wade Boggs, Bernie Williams, Paul O'Neill go 8-15 off Tim Belcher, who yields 11 total hits.
	Balt 4, @Cal 0	67-47	+7	Mussina tosses complete-game 4-hitter with 11 strikeouts; Palmeiro 3-for-5, 31st home run.
8/28	Off day			
8/29	Sea 6, @Bos 4	58-56	−8	Trailing 3-4 in 6th, Jay Buhner RBI single in 6th ties it, Griffey wins it with sac fly in 7th.
	@NYY 12, Cal 4	67-48	+7	Williams 3-for-3, 3 RBIs, Yanks pound Finley for 10 hits, 8 runs.
8/30	@Bos 7, Sea 6	58-57	−8	Edgar and Tino Martinez homer in 4th, Seattle leads 5-2, loses by giving up 5 in 7th, 4 off Jeff Nelson.
	@NYY 4, Cal 1	67-49	+7	Andy Pettitte tosses 5-hitter; Sierra 3-for-4, 2 RBIs; Jim Abbott yields 11 hits.
8/31	Sea 11, @Bos 2	59-57	−7	Rookie Bob Wolcott makes emergency start (Johnson can't get loose in pen) and wins.
	@NYY 11, Cal 6	67-50	+7	O'Neill 4-for-5, 8 RBIs; Mariner Sterling Hitchcock wins 7th of season.
9/1	Sea 4, @Balt 3	60-57	−6	Joey Cora, Dan Wilson solo HRs off Mike Mussina; Tim Belcher 9th win, Norm Charlton 4th save.
	@Bos 11, Cal 3	67-51	+6	Shawn Boskie meltdown: 11 hits, 6 earned runs in 5 innings; Tim Naehring 3 RBIs for Sox.
9/2	@Bal 3, Sea 2	60-58	−6	Edgar Martinez hits 26th HR but Jeff Huson drives in 2 key hits for Orioles.
	@Bos 5, Cal 4	67-52	+6	Zane Smith (7-7) and Rick Aguilera combine for win, save.
9/3	Sea 9, @Bal 6	61-58	−5	Rich Amaral, subbing for sore-wristed Ken Griffey Jr., hits 3-run HR to key comeback win.
	@Bos 8, Cal 1	67-53	+5	Tim Wakefield 4-hitter over 8 innings pitched; Naehring 2-for-4, 3 RBIs off Chuck Finley.
9/4	@NYY 13, Sea 3	61-59	−6	Salomon Torres yields 4 ERs in 1st, Bobby Ayala 3 in 2nd; Bernie Williams 3-for-6, 4 RBIs.
	Cal 5, @Bal 3	68-53	+6	Tony Phillips, Chili Davis HRs off Jamie Moyer; Cal Ripken 2 RBIs for Orioles.
9/5	Sea 6, @NYY 5	62-59	−5	Jay Buhner belts 3-run HR to win for rookie Bob Wolcott.
	@Bal 8, Cal 0	68-54	+5	Scott Erickson hurls complete game for O's; Ripken ties Lou Gehrig's 2,130 consecutive games.

Appendix 2 • The Miracle Rally of 1995—August 1995 cont.

Date	Result	Record (Sea/Cal)	Games Back or Ahead (Sea/Cal)	Notes
9/6	@NYY 4, Sea 3	62-60	-5	Yankees score 4 in 6th; Randy Velarde 2-run double off Belcher.
	@Bal 4, Cal 2	68-55	+5	Ripken plays in 2,131st straight, homers off Boskie in 8th to spark O's win.
9/7	@Cle 4, Sea 1	62-61	-6	Carlos Baerga, Jim Thome drive in 2 runs each off Chris Bosio, who loses 8th of season.
	Off Day, Cal	68-55	+6	Angels have outscored opponents 704-590 to this point of season.
9/8	@Sea 4, KC 1	63-61	-6	Randy Johnson wins 14th as M's move into tie for wild card with Kansas City.
	@Cal 9, Minn 3	69-55	+6	Tony Phillips and J. T. Snow homer, ex-Mariner Mark Langston-fans 7 in 7 innings.
9/9	@Sea 6, KC 2	64-61	-6	Andy Benes retires 19 in a row at one point en route to win.
	@Cal 6, Minn 5	70-55	+6	Phillips homers; ex-Mariner Rich Monteleone picks up win in relief of Finley.
9/10	@Sea 5, KC 4	65-61	-5	Cora RBI double in 8th is game winner as M's complete sweep of Royals.
	Minn 9, @Cal 8	70-56	+5	Kirby Puckett goes 2-for-6, hits 34th homer, drives in 3 runs.
9/11	Minn 12, @ Sea 10	65-62	-6	Belcher (3), Bill Risley (4), Bobby Ayala (2) meltdown; Rich Becker 4-for-5, 4 RBIs for Twins.
	@Cal 4, Chi 1	71-56	+6	Boskie throws complete-game 5-hitter, Snow 2 RBIs.
9/12	@Sea 14, Minn 3	66-62	-6	Buhner hits 2 homers (32nd, 33rd), Mike Blowers cracks 20th; only 12,102 in Kingdome.
	@Cal 3, Chi 1	72-56	+ 6	Garrett Anderson hits homer in support of Langston, who allows 1 ER in 7 innings pitched.
9/13	@Sea 7, Minn 4	67-62	-5	Trailing 4-0, M's score 7 in last 2 at-bats, including Buhner 3-run homer.
	Chi 6, @Cal 1	72-57	+5	Frank Thomas 3-for-5 with 2 homers; Troy Percival allows 4 ER in 2/3 of an inning
9/14	Off day			
9/15	Sea 3, @Chi 2	68-62	-4	Vince Coleman 4-for-4, 2 runs scored; Benes allows 2 over 7 for 5th win as Mariner.
	KC 5, @Cal 0	72-58	+4	Kevin Appier complete-game 3-hitter for Royals; Jim Abbott allows 5 runs on 10 hits for Cal.
9/16	Sea 5, @ Chi 3	69-62	-3	Belcher hurls 8 innings for 10th win; Wilson 9th-inning solo HR breaks 3-3 tie.
	KC 7, @ Cal 6	72-59	+3	Keith Lockhart 2-for-3, 3 RBIs; Boskie shelled: 6 runs allowed in 2/3 of an inning.
9/17	@Chi 2, Sea 1	69-63	-3	Eric Mouton game-winning homer off Wolcott in 7th.
	KC 10, @Cal 8	72-60	+3	Joe Vitiello 2-for-3, 5 RBIs; Langston surrenders 7 earned runs in 4 innings.
9/18	@Sea 8, Tex 1	70-63	-2	Johnson wins 15th as M's begin 8-game Dome stand vs. AL West.
	@Oak 4, Cal 0	72-61	+2	Future Mariner Stan Javier drives in two for A's, swipes 2 bases; Doug Johns complete-game 2-hitter.

Date	Result	Record (Sea/Cal)	Games Back or Ahead (Sea/Cal)	Notes
9/19	@Sea 5, Tex 4	71-63	−1	Doug Strange pinch 2-run HR in 9th ties it, Griffey's single in 11th scores Strange to win.
	@Oak 3, Cal 2	72-62	+1	Terry Steinbach 3-for-5, 2 RBIs; Percival tagged for two runs in eighth.
9/20	@Sea 11, Tex 3	72-63	Tie	Benes wins for 6th time since joining Mariners July 31.
	@Oak 9, Cal 6	72-63	Tie	Mark McGwire 3-run homer; ex-Mariner Danny Tartabull 2-for-4, RBI; Javier RBI, run scored.
9/21	Off day			
9/22	@Sea 10, Oak 7	73-63	+1	Coleman grand slam off Todd Van Poppel to tie it; Alex Diaz pinch 3-run HR, off (former Mariner) Rick Honeycutt to win it.
	@Tex 8, Cal 3	72-64	−1	Juan Gonzalez 2-for-4, 3 RBIs; Langston allows 7 earned runs in 6 innings.
9/23	@Sea 7, Oak 0	74-63	+2	Buhner 36th, 37th homers, 4 RBIs; Johnson whiffs 15 in 7 innings.
	@Tex 5, Cal 1	72-65	−2	Gonzalez 3-run homer; Finley allows 5 in first inning.
9/24	@Sea 9, Oak 8	75-63	+2	Tino Martinez 2-run HR in 9th off Dennis Eckersley to win game.
	Cal 5, @Tex 0	73-65	−2	Abbott complete-game 3-hitter; Tim Salmon 3-for-4, 2 RBIs.
9/25	Off day			
9/26	@Sea 10, Cal 2	76-63	+3	Benes wins No. 7 as a Mariner as club takes 3-game lead over Angels.
		73-66	−3	Griffey 2-for-4, 3 RBIs with 7th homer; Boskie can't get out of 2nd inning.
9/27	Cal 2, @Sea 0	76-64	+2	Salmon, Snow run-scoring hits in 1st off Belcher.
		74-66	−2	Finley, Percival, Lee Smith hold M's to 3 hits.
9/28	Sea 6, @Tex 2	77-64	+2	Johnson wins 17th as Griffey snaps 8th-inning tie with mammoth grand slam.
	Cal 4, Oak 1	75-66	−2	Langston holds A's to 6 hits, 1 run in 6+ innings.
9/29	Sea 5, @Tex 4	78-64	+2	Sac flies by Edgar, Tino erase 3-2 deficit as M's post 43rd come-from-behind win.
	@Cal 9, Oak 6	76-66	−2	Cal survives 6-run meltdown by Abbott; Javier 3-for-5, 3 RBIs.
9/30	@Tex 9, Sea 3	78-65	+1	Despite loss, M's clinch at least a tie for AL West title.
	@Cal 9, Oak 3	77-66	−1	Mike Harkey gets win in relief of Boskie; Davis, Snow combine for 6 RBIs.
10/1	@Tex 9, Sea 3	78-66	Tie	Buhner smacks 40th, Blowers 23rd, but Kenny Rogers outduels Belcher.
	@Cal 8, Oak 2	78-66	Tie	Finley wins 15th of season; Jim Edmonds 4-for-5, 3 RBIs.
10/2	@Sea 9, Cal 1	79-66	+1	Johnson allows 3 hits, fans 12 as M's reach postseason for first time in 19 years.
		78-67	−1	Langston throwing error on Sojo's bases-loaded double in 7th results in 4-run play.

Appendix 3

MAJOR LEAGUE BASEBALL FRANCHISE VALUES

In 1991, *Financial World* magazine (now defunct) estimated the value of the Seattle Mariners at $71 million. In late 2001, *Forbes* magazine valued the Mariners at $373 million, an appreciation of 425.3 percent over ten years—a rate of increase second only to Atlanta in Major League Baseball.

The teams in new-generation ballparks (built since 1991) occupy the first six places on this list and ten of the top eleven places.

Estimated values are based on gate receipts, radio and TV revenues, operating income, player salaries, debt service, and other expenses. The estimates are not confirmed or endorsed by MLB or the clubs.

Team	1991 Est. Value	2001 Est. Value	Increase
Atlanta Braves*	$74 million	$424 million	473.0%
Seattle Mariners*	$71 million	$373 million	425.3%
Cleveland Indians*	$75 million	$360 million	380.0%
Houston Astros*	$92 million	$337 million	266.3%
Texas Rangers*	$101 million	$356 million	252.4%
San Francisco Giants*	$105 million	$355 million	238.1%
New York Yankees	$225 million	$730 million	224.4%
Colorado Rockies*	$110 million	$347 million	215.4%**
Detroit Tigers*	$84 million	$262 million	211.9%
Pittsburgh Pirates*	$82 million	$242 million	195.1%
Milwaukee Brewers*	$81 million	$238 million	193.8%
New York Mets	$200 million	$482 million	141.1%
Boston Red Sox	$180 million	$426 million	136.7%
Chicago Cubs	$125 million	$287 million	129.6%
Los Angeles Dodgers	$200 million	$435 million	117.5%
Arizona Diamondbacks*	$130 million	$280 million	115.3%***
St. Louis Cardinals	$128 million	$271 million	111.7%
San Diego Padres	$99 million	$207 million	109.0%
Cincinnati Reds	$102 million	$204 million	100.0%
Anaheim Angels	$102 million	$195 million	91.2%
Chicago White Sox*	$125 million	$223 million	78.4%
Philadelphia Phillies	$130 million	$231 million	77.7%
Florida Marlins	$81 million	$137 million	69.1%**
Baltimore Orioles*	$200 million	$319 million	59.5%
Minnesota Twins	$81 million	$127 million	56.8%

Team	1991 Est. Value	2001 Est. Value	Increase
Montreal Expos	$75 million	$108 million	44.0%
Oakland Athletics	$116 million	$157 million	35.3%
Kansas City Royals	$122 million	$152 million	24.6%
Tampa Bay Devil Rays	$130 million	$142 million	9.2%***
Toronto Blue Jays	$178 million	$182 million	2.24%

Sources: 1991 estimated values, *Financial World;* 2001 estimated values, *Forbes.*

 * New-generation ballpark

 ** Since 1993

*** Since 1998

Bibliography

Corr, O. Casey. *Money from Thin Air.* New York: Crown Publishers, 2000.

Costas, Bob. *Fair Ball: A Fan's Case for Baseball.* New York: Random House, 2000.

Danielson, Michael N. *Home Team: Professional Sports and the American Metropolis.* New Jersey: Princeton University Press, 1997.

Dewey, Donald, and Nicholas Acocella. *The New Biographical History of Baseball.* Chicago: Triumph Books, 2002.

Madden, Bill. *Pride of October: What It Was to Be Young and a Yankee.* New York: Warner Books, 2003.

Sheff, David. *Game Over: How Nintendo Zapped an American Industry, Captured Your Dollars, and Enslaved Your Children.* New York: Random House, 1993.

Vincent, Fay. *The Last Commissioner: A Baseball Valentine.* New York: Simon & Schuster, 2002.

Wallace, James. *Overdrive: Bill Gates and the Race to Control Cyberspace.* John Wiley & Sons, 1997.

Wallace, James, and Jim Erickson. *Hard Drive: Bill Gates and the Making of the Microsoft Empire.* John Wiley & Sons, 1992.

Zimbalist, Andrew. *May the Best Team Win: Baseball Economics and Public Policy.* Washington, D.C.: Brookings Institution Press, 2003.

Index

About the Author

Art Thiel has been around the Puget Sound area sports scene for more than 30 years. He was in the stands for the opening game of the Pilots in 1969 and the Mariners in 1977. He began reporting for the *Seattle Post-Intelligencer* in 1980 and was named columnist in 1987. He has covered local teams such as the Mariners, Sonics, Seahawks, and University of Washington teams. He has also covered five Olympic Games and many national events such as the World Series, NBA Finals, Super Bowl, and major golf championships.

Thiel has won numerous newspaper writing awards, and was named one of the nation's top 20 sportswriters by *Men's Journal*.

He lives with his wife, Julia, on Vashon Island, Washington.